SENSORY DECEPTION

A scientific analysis of hallucination

The Johns Hopkins Series in Contemporary Medicine and Public Health

Also of interest in this series

SENSORY DECEPTION

A scientific analysis of hallucination

Peter D. Slade and Richard P. Bentall

Sub-department of Clinical Psychology
University of Liverpool

THE JOHNS HOPKINS UNIVERSITY PRESS
Baltimore & London

To Sally and Rhiannon

© 1988 Peter D. Slade and Richard P. Bentall

Published in the United States of America by
The Johns Hopkins University Press
701 West 40th Street
Baltimore, Maryland 21211

Library of Congress Cataloging-in-Publication Data

Slade, Peter D.
    Sensory Deception.
    (The Johns Hopkins series in contemporary
    medicine and public health)
    Bibliography: p.
    Includes index.
    1. Hallucinations and illusions. I. Bentall,
    Richard. II. Title. III. Series. [DNLM: 1.
    Hallucinations. WM 204 S631s]
    RC553.H3S57 1988 154.3   88–45398
    ISBN 0–8018–3760–X

Printed and bound in Great Britain

Contents

Preface

The main reason for writing this book is a simple one. There is currently no authored, academic text which provides a comprehensive review of both facts and theories about the nature of hallucination. The only contemporary books on the subject are either edited proceedings or more specific accounts of the hallucinatory process, which are usually derived from a single theoretical perspective.

Surprisingly, not only are there no contemporary reviews of the area but, as far as we have been able to establish, no book has ever been written which addresses itself to a broad coverage of the medical and scientific literature on hallucinations. It is possible that we should have learned an important lesson from this observation! Nevertheless, we have tried to fill the vacuum that we have identified.

The subject matter of hallucinations should be of considerable interest to both fundamental and applied students of human behaviour. The former, who include experimental, developmental and social psychologists, sociologists, social anthropologists and others will be concerned with the processes that influence the accuracy and content of normal human perception. As with all areas of scientific enquiry, a study of errors, deviations and exceptions has a lot to teach us about normal functioning.

By similar token, clinicians, including psychiatrists, clinical psychologists, behavioural pharmacologists, general practitioners and others, will be interested in the light that a study of hallucinations has to throw on the understanding and treatment of psychological disorder. Hallucinations represent one of the most common symptoms of major psychiatric illness, yet they are poorly understood in clinical practice even today.

The book is divided into eight chapters. In the first we consider the historical background to the study of hallucinatory experiences, attempts to specify the unique characteristics of hallucinations, and essential defining criteria. The second chapter is concerned with the kinds of pathological conditions, both physical and mental, that have been associated with hallucinatory experiences. The third chapter concentrates particularly on the very real and largely unrecognised phenomenon of hallucinations in 'normal', healthy individuals.

Chapter 4 is concerned with the major psychological variables, both external to the individual and internal, which have been found to affect the probability of a given individual hallucinating. This chapter represents an update of the earlier functional account given by the first author (Slade, 1976b). In Chapter 5, the evidence for a range of psychological theories of pathological hallucination is reviewed and evaluated, and in Chapter 6 major biological theories of hallucination are briefly outlined.

The seventh chapter focuses entirely on treatment. The first part is concerned with drug therapy and the major pharmacological compounds which have been evaluated for the treatment of hallucinating persons. The second part of the chapter is concerned with the various kinds of psychological intervention which have been tried with drug-resistant hallucinating patients. Eight distinctive methods have been evaluated, but we argue that these are probably reducible to three specific processes. In Chapter 7, we also review the limited evidence available on the methods that patients themselves find useful when attempting to cope with their disturbing experiences. Chapter 8 then presents an integrative account of hallucinations that calls on the data reviewed in Chapters 4, 5 and 6 and also tries to explain some of the treatment effects described in Chapter 7. Responsibility for the individual chapters has been roughly as follows: Richard Bentall wrote Chapters 3, 5, 6 and 8, and Peter Slade wrote Chapters 1, 2 and 7; both authors contributed to Chapter 4.

The book represents our best attempt at the present time to review existing data and current theorising on the subject of hallucinations. We have attempted to be reasonably thorough. However, we readily admit that, because we are concerned to promote a particular theoretical viewpoint, we may be guilty of some bias in our perceptions of particular data and theories. In this respect the psychopathologist may be not all that different from the subjects of his or her investigations.

Peter Slade and Richard Bentall

1

The Concept of Hallucination

Information about the world comes to us through our senses. But the process of perceiving the world about us owes as much to our attempts to construe and make sense of our sensory input (i.e. judgement and interpretation) as it does to the input itself. Perceptual inaccuracy or sensory deception is as much the norm as perceptual accuracy. If this were not the case, magicians who ply their trade through the production of simple but effective examples of sensory deception would have been out of work centuries ago. What is clearly of great importance to all of us is the extent and nature of such perceptual inaccuracy and in particular the personal and social consequences involved.

Consider the following two examples. First, an undergraduate psychology student taking part in a practical class on the Muller–Lyer illusion (see Figure 1.1) overestimates the length of the line with the arrowheads pointing outwards by 15 per cent in comparison with the line with inward-facing arrowheads. This represents an error of perception. Given that this kind of error is the norm for able and mentally alert students, with good eyesight (corrected if necessary), the student in question is likely to be strongly rewarded for her perceptual inaccuracy providing she writes up her experimental results clearly and accurately and hands them in on time.

Compare the above example with that of a patient in a secure unit, recently seen by the second author:

Brian was aged 36 when interviewed, and had been admitted to the secure unit following an attempted assault against his father. Although

1

Figure 1.1: The Muller–Lyer illusion. The vertical line in the figure to the left is typically perceived as longer than that in the figure to the right, although both are of the same length. See Gregory (1970)

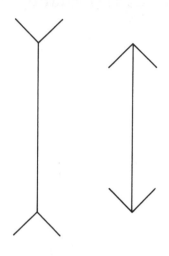

he had a long history of mental illness and had been diagnosed as schizophrenic, there was no known history of mental illness in the family. His mother had died of cancer two years previously and his younger brother and sister were both pursuing successful careers in accountancy and advertising.

Brian's first breakdown had occurred following his unsuccessful attempt at 'A' levels (High School Certificate). He had hoped to study medicine at university but instead drifted on to a biochemistry course at a local college. While studying there, he had become lonely and isolated and he dropped out during the second year. He became depressed and began to express the conviction that a secret organisation was plotting against him. It was at this stage that he was first admitted to hospital.

Over the following years, Brian lived for the most part on his own in the community, drifting from menial job to menial job or surviving on social security. He inhabited a succession of unsatisfactory lodgings in various parts of the country and was occasionally admitted to psychiatric hospitals for brief periods when his symptoms returned or when he failed to look after himself adequately. On three occasions he made serious attempts to end his life. On one occasion he had thrown himself from a twelve-storey window and had been seriously crippled as a consequence; afterwards he was forced to walk with a limp and movement was often painful. He was involved in a number of inadequate sexual relationships. Throughout this period he kept in touch with his mother, to whom he felt especially close, but his relationship with his father was strained.

When his mother died he became extremely depressed. He became involved with a young Jewish woman who had a similarly unsuccessful life history. She wanted to have a child by him but their sexual relationship never really got off the ground, partly because his injuries made intercourse difficult. After eighteen months they split up. Because of his lack of care for himself and his belongings, he was thrown out of his lodgings shortly afterwards. On the day of his attempted assault he had gone to visit his father to ask for help.

When interviewed, Brian had been on phenothiazine medication for two months. He reported that he was a victim of a 'thought-control' experiment being carried out by a team of parapsychologists who were probably known to the second author. The parapsychologists were implanting voices in Brian's head and he asked the author to make sure that this intrusion was brought to an end. The voices had a limited repertoire, telling him that there was a Jewish plot to put Gentiles in concentration camps and repeating the phrase, 'Give cancer to the crippled bastard.' He felt that the 'crippled bastard' was himself. It was the taunting of the voices which had finally made him snap and attack his father. When asked whether there might be any other explanation for his voices, Brian, who could reason about the issue quite lucidly, conceded that they could be products of his imagination but argued that this was unlikely because of their vividness and their content.

Over the following few months, Brian was required to monitor the voices more closely and record them in writing (see Chapter 7). Also, an attempt was made to explore the meaning of the voices in the context of regular psychotherapy sessions. Exploration of his own and his family's history revealed a number of events that appeared to relate to what the voices were saying. His mother was of German extraction and had left Germany before the Second World War. For much of her life she had been preoccupied by thoughts about the concentration camps. Brian's girlfriend, who had been born after the war, came from a family that had lost relatives in Germany, and she also spoke frequently about the Holocaust. (It may have been this similarity to his mother that attracted him to her.) The voices seemed to relate in some way to this constellation of ideas about cancer and Nazi Germany. Gradually (no doubt helped by the medication), Brian's voices became less and less frequent and he came to accept that they represented a part of his mind that he had repressed and denied as being part of himself.

These examples represent two extremes of sensory deception. The former involves the almost universal tendency for an individual to misjudge the length of vertical or horizontal lines when set in a particular type of visual context. It is generally recognised and described as a normal *illusion*. By contrast, the latter example of sensory deception clearly involves a much greater degree of misperception, based on an apparently internally generated stimulus, which has major consequences for the individual's immediate experience, his behaviour and his future circumstances. Such a misperception would generally be referred to as an example of pathological *hallucination.* This book will be primarily concerned with sensory deceptions of the latter, more severe type. However, as will become clear, it will be necessary to consider hallucinations both in relation to the more minor varieties of sensory deception and also in terms of current knowledge and thinking about the mechanisms of normal perception.

SOME HISTORICAL LANDMARKS

Sensory deception is commonplace and often represents the norm or expected normal experience in a given situation (for example, magic tricks, standard illusions, etc.). Hallucinations, a working definition of which will be outlined later, are neither commonplace nor rare. They represent a frequent (and distressing) experience for a minority of individuals but also a rare (and perhaps positive) experience for many people. As indicated above, the phenomenon of sensory deception varies in terms of both its nature and extent and also in terms of its personal and social consequences for the individual. The history of ideas about hallucinatory experiences reflects both changing conceptions about the nature of mental disorder and shifting attitudes towards those who suffer as a result.

There are numerous early references to events which, from one viewpoint or another, appear to be hallucinatory. One author (Jaynes, 1979) has gone as far as to argue that, for the ancient Greeks and earlier peoples, hallucinations were the norm. (This unlikely hypothesis is based on an analysis of the contents of the *Iliad* which, according to Jaynes, indicates that the ancient Greeks had no concept of their own consciousness, and therefore mis-attributed their own thoughts to gods and spirits.) Others have interpreted various Biblical events as hallucinatory (e.g. Bennett, 1978). Indeed, as Preuss (1975) was able to show in a careful study of early Hebrew medicine, evidence for at least a limited concept of hallucination can be traced back to before the time of Christ. However, it was the early Christian thinkers who first systematically considered the nature of hallucinatory experiences. The development of these ideas into the present-day concept of hallucination has been described in some detail by Sarbin and Juhasz (1967).

The early dominant views were those of the mystics whose ideas were enshrined in the writings of St. Augustine of Hippo (AD 354–430). St. Augustine, in his analysis of St. Paul's conversion experience (described in Corinthians), distinguished three meanings of the word 'see' corresponding to the three important levels of mystical experience. The first and lowest level was that of *corporeal* vision — that is, direct visual experience of the outside world attained through the relevant sense organs. Corporeal vision deals with objects which are located in both time and space. The second level was that of *imaginative* vision, which involves images of corporeal objects. Imaginative vision deals with objects which are located in time but not in space. Finally, the third and highest level was that of *intellectual* vision, which is concerned primarily with abstract concepts akin to those of Platonic universals such as 'love' and 'hope'. The objects of intellectual vision are located neither in time nor in space. In terms of value there was a clear progression from corporeal vision, the least reliable, through to intellectual vision, which was the most prized. Thus, the mystics assigned far greater importance to internally generated knowledge and ideas than would be likely or possible in a materialistic society.

Unlike the mystics who recognised a continuity, albeit an inverse valued one, from normal perception through imagination to intellectual reason, the scholastics argued for a sharp dividing line or discontinuity between normal perception and non-veridical perceptual experience. The important aspects of hallucinatory/imaginal experience for the scholastics, as reflected in the writings of St. Thomas Aquinas (AD 1225–1274), were source and content. For the scholastics, it was of crucial importance to decide on whether the reported experience was the work of the Devil, God, or other natural agencies or causes. Certain criteria were used in arriving at the assessment, including (a) the argument that the Devil sometimes tells falsehoods, the Holy Ghost never, (b) the argument that the Devil is more likely to appear corporeally or in the imagination than in the rational faculty, (c) the argument that if a prophecy is not confirmed, its source is not divine, and (d) the claim that the visions of those who are possessed or out of their minds are due to an unnatural partition of the imagination from the senses. It is worth noting that the second criterion is very much in line with that of the mystics in suggesting that the rational faculty (i.e. intellectual vision) is less vulnerable to trickery than the sensory or imaginative faculties.

The attitude of scholastics towards imaginative experience both kindled and reflected the philosophy underlying the inquisitorial approach of the Church. Visions and voices which were deemed to be of Satanic origin had to be dealt with in a punitive fashion, for the sake of the afflicted as much as for society as a whole. The consequences of perceptual aberration therefore became increasingly grim during the fifteenth and sixteenth centuries, leading up to and following the publication of Kramer and Sprenger's *Malleus maleficarum (The hammer of the witches)* in 1489. Kramer and Sprenger were charged by Pope Innocent VIII with the task of producing this work in order that Christendom could be defended against Satanic influences. The result was a book that advocated the widespread torture and burning of people suspected of witchcraft or possession by demons. It is apparent from Kramer and Sprenger's recommendations about how such individuals might be recognised that many of the victims of these cruel practices were people who would be regarded today as mentally ill or psychotic. Among other things it was the excesses perpetrated by the Catholic Church during this period, combined with the rediscovery of ancient Greek medicine in the guise of Galen and Hippocrates, which opened the way to the widespread acceptance of a medical, rather than a religious, conception of madness.

The conflict between religion and medicine for jurisdiction over the mentally disturbed, including those with aberrations of perception, was waged for more than 150 years before the medical viewpoint became dominant in the eighteenth century. The transfer of responsibility owed as much to enlightened and humane clerics concerned with the punitive attitudes and excesses of the inquisitorial system as it did to medical people. An influential example of the former was Teresa of Avila (AD 1515–1582). In her book *Interior Castle* she introduced the concepts of possible 'sickness' and 'lack of responsibility' in relation to individuals who were visionaries. The first task of the examiner was to decide whether certain 'natural causes' were capable of explaining the visitations, namely (a) melancholy, (b) a weak imagination, or (c) drowsiness, sleep, or sleep-like states. By forceful application of these medical-type concepts and criteria Teresa was able to save a number of nuns from the machinations of the Inquisition. In this way the Church became split into two camps, the hard-line inquisitors and the soft-line humanitarians.

It was this philosophical divide that allowed physicians to build upon Galen's conception of madness as a disturbance of bodily humours. Thus the word 'hallucination', an anglicised version of the Latin *allucinatio* (wandering of the mind, idle talk) was first introduced into English in the 1572 translation of a work by Lavater, in which the term was used to refer to a variety of strange noises, omens and apparitions. It is interesting to note that, at this time, no distinction was made between hallucinations and the phenomena now subsumed by the word 'illusion' (derived from the Latin *illusio*, meaning mocking, jeering or bantering), these terms being used interchangeably by Lavater to describe mental conditions involving the entertaining of unfounded notions or beliefs to which nothing corresponds (Sarbin and Juhasz, 1967).

With the emergence of a more humanitarian approach to insanity, and with the increasing diligence with which medical practitioners described and classified abnormal behaviour, a change occurred in the way in which the insane were treated. In England, at least, no systematic approach to the management of the insane existed at the beginning of the seventeenth century. Some became beggars, moving from town to town in search of alms, and others relied upon their families for support. Under the Poor Law Act of 1601 the majority of the insane, like other paupers, became the responsibility of the 15 000 separate parishes. Although considerable variation existed in the type and amount of aid given, most attempted to provide some form of household relief to those legally resident within the parish boundaries.

Scull (1979) has described in detail the transition from this parish-level management of the insane to the asylum-dominated approach of the nineteenth century. Although it is often assumed that this transition was a result of the defeat of the religious model of madness and its replacement by the medical model, this was only made possible by a variety of changes that occurred within the structure of society as a whole. In particular, the rise of capitalism in this period and the concentration of the population in cities led to the conditions in which it became necessary to segregate off that proportion of individuals who could not contribute usefully to the labour force. The growing interest of medical practitioners in madness served to legitimise this practice.

With the medical profession's claim of expertise in the field of madness, a variety of contrasting views of hallucinations emerged. The dominant view, expressed for example by Arnold (1806), supposed the existence of a discontinuity between 'ideal insanity' (pathological hallucination) and normal perceptual experience. Arnold argued that 'ideal insanity' was due to a defect in the bodily organs whereby incorrect information is transmitted to the brain. By contrast, Hibbert (1825), taking a more psychological approach, argued for the continuity between imagination and hallucinations, regarding hallucinations as completely natural and ordinary events.

The medical model of hallucination was consolidated by the French physician Esquirol (1832), who first made explicit the distinction between hallucinations and illusions:

> In *hallucinations* everything happens in the brain (mind). The visionaries, the ecstatics, are people who suffer from hallucin- ations, dreamers while they are awake. The activity of the brain is so energetic that the visionary, the person hallucinating, ascribes a body and an actuality to images that the memory recalls without the intervention of senses.
>
> In *illusions* on the other hand, the sensibility of the nervous extremities is excited; the senses are active, the present impres- sions call into action the reactions of the brain. This reaction being under the influence of ideas and passions which dominate the insane, these sick people are mistaken about the nature and cause of their present sensations.

The inadequacies of available psychological theories, the political requirements of the time and the need for a controlled humani- tarian approach to perceived mental instability placed natural limits on the popularity of psychological as opposed to medical theories of hallucinations and other forms of abnormal behaviour. Thus, although a pioneer of psychology of the stature of Galton (1883) could argue, on the basis of a self-report study of mental imag- ery (subjects chosen for their intellectual achievements were asked to imagine the contents of their breakfast table and describe the result), that there exists a continuity between all forms of visualisation, 'beginning with an almost absence of it, and ending in a complete hallucination', the medical view that hallucinations are almost always pathological and distinct from other kinds of mental events remained dominant.

The development of the medical approach to insanity culminated, towards the end of the nineteenth century, with the attempt to classify different categories of mental illness and, in particular, with the widespread acceptance of Kraepelin's system of psychiatric diagnosis. With a concern to appear 'scientific' rather than 'philosophical', Kraepelin attempted to identify discrete psychiatric entities on the basis of their form and course, with little regard for what the symptons of these entities might mean for the patients alleged to be suffering from them (Zilboorg and Henry, 1941). One of Kraepelin's most important contributions was the suggestion that a number of syndromes previously identified by Morel, Kauhlbaum and Hocker might be manifestations of a single disease 'dementia praecox' — later renamed 'schizophrenia' by Bleuler (1911) — which could be distinguished from the manic depressive psychoses on the basis of its poor prognosis. Existing systems of psychiatric diagnoses are derived, to a large extent, from the work of Kraepelin and other nineteenth century psychiatrists, and the medical model of madness, with its emphasis on diagnosis and classification, now enjoys such wide acceptance that even those critical of it find it difficult to avoid its terminology. From the point of view of the study of hallucinations this acceptance has had two consequences.

First, the medical model has led to the study of syndromes rather than symptoms. Most research into abnormal behaviour over the last 50 years or more has taken diagnostic categories such as 'schizophrenia' or 'depression' as independent variables. The result has been a relative dearth of studies of symptoms such as 'hallucinations' or 'delusions' (Bannister, 1968; Persons, 1986). Secondly, the view that hallucinations are medical phenomena has led to a relative lack of interest in them by psychologists, who have nevertheless had a considerable amount to say about other forms of sensory deception. Thus, as Sarbin and Juhasz (1967) have remarked:

Since the 1920s textbooks of general psychology have differentiated hallucinations from errors of perception through the simple expedient of locating them in separate chapters. They have been content to declare that errors of perception of utter convincingness, etc., were perfectly ordinary, and that hallucinations, defined in precisely the same way as errors of perception, were signs of psychosis, usually schizophrenia.

SOME CONCEPTUAL ISSUES

Sensory deceptions in general and hallucinations in particular vary considerably. This variation presents a number of conceptual problems for the researcher.

A preliminary obstacle to hallucination research is the fact that hallucination reports are, for the time being at least, objectively unverifiable. That is to say, perhaps the only reliable data about the quality and occurrence of hallucinations is the hallucinator's first-person reports. Other indications that a person is hallucinating do, of course, exist (a sudden glance towards the source of an imaginary voice, overt answering back) and have been used, for example, in ward rating scales of psychotic behaviour (e.g. Lorr's Multidimensional Psychiatric Scale; Lorr, 1953). However, although these behaviours may be reliably measured, it is not clear to what extent they can be regarded as valid indices of hallucination. Thus Patterson (cited in Falloon and Talbot, 1981) found a poor correlation between the judgement of ward staff about when patients are hallucinating and the patient's own reports of hallucinatory experiences.

For this reason (as Sarbin, 1967; Rabkin, 1970, and Al-Issa, 1978, have pointed out) the first-person reports of individuals who cannot give a good account of themselves may be particularly vulnerable to misinterpretation, especially when the mental health expert interviewing the individual lacks verbal sophistication or is unfamiliar with relevant linguistic idioms. An apocryphal story that illustrates this point concerns a Yorkshireman who tells a foreign psychiatrist that 'It's raining cats and dogs' with predictable consequences. As Sarbin notes, even in the case of the psychiatrist and the patient who share the same language, the use of phrases such as 'It's as if' (e.g. 'It's as if I saw my dead mother' rather than 'I saw my dead mother') may make all the difference.

An example which illustrates the importance of this point is provided in the form of Bender's (1970) analysis of hallucinations in children. Bender begins his account by remarking that 'It is generally accepted that young children may hallucinate communications with imaginary companions.' Although it is true that children commonly report imaginary friends, the use of the term 'hallucinate' is probably misleading in this context. Eisenberg (1962) has pointed out that a too literal interpretation of children's reported imaginings can easily lead to belief in the existence of a pathological process where none in fact is present. Bender indeed goes on to argue that such phenomena as imaginary companions may be evidence of mental pathology, although 'coaxing' and 'close questioning' may be necessary to elicit full hallucinatory reports from children.

The consequences of this approach are illustrated by one of Bender's case studies, a seven-year-old boy, Tyrone, treated with insulin coma because of his refusal to go to school, abusive behaviour, stealing and firesetting. Following an improvement in his behaviour Tyrone reported that 'there was a little boy inside him who talked to him and told him to be good'. At nine years of age Tyrone relapsed, reported that there was an object in his stomach (a little boy or grasshopper) and was given Benzedrine, Thorazine and LSD. A year later he was also given ECT. At 14 years of age Tyrone had again improved and no longer reported the little boy or the grasshopper inside him. His own account of this change is instructive:

> Last year I had a class in hygiene. They taught me about the heart and oxygen and brain. There is no place for a boy inside your heart and stomach. They taught me that common sense comes from the brain. It was my imagination that I had a boy inside me.

Bender maintained a different view: 'It is a bit disconcerting that the children never credit the psychotherapy, drug therapy, insulin or electroshock or the supportive and socialising care they receive in the hospital with clearing up their hallucinations although clinically, this is what we, the physicians, believe we can observe.

These remarks should not be taken to imply that Tyrone was not disturbed, or that children do not sometimes experience hallucinations (see Chapter 2). However, Tyrone's case does suggest that it may be particularly important to be careful when attributing hallucinations to verbally less able or easily suggestible persons in any age group. It is instructive to note that hallucinations are indeed attributed more often to such individuals. Phillips, Broverman and Zigler (1966) have reported that hallucinations, more than any other symptom, appear to be correlated with low levels of social competence. Other studies have reported that hallucinators have lower intelligence (Johnson and Miller, 1965) or poorer verbal abilities (Miller, Johnson and Richmond, 1965) than non-hallucinating psychiatric patients, although it may be that these factors play a role in predisposing people to hallucinate as well as in leading others to attribute hallucinations to them (see Chapter 4).

Not surprisingly, given these considerations, the problem of attributing hallucinations to individuals becomes particularly acute in the case of animals. This difficulty is of more than just philosophical importance because animals have frequently been used in hallucination research, particularly in research into the mode of action of hallucinogenic drugs (see Chapter 6). This problem has been carefully considered by Siegel and Jarvik (1975) who noted how easily the eye movements or crouched postures of monkeys given LSD can lead the human investigator (at the risk of being labelled hallucinating himself) to thoughts of imaginary insects or Rodin's 'Thinker'.

Siegel and Jarvik were able to find numerous reports of animals self-administering psychoactive drugs in mythology and folklore (e.g. cats eating catnip, birds in the Hawaiian Islands ingesting hallucinogenic cactus) but found ethological reports on animals' reactions to such drugs limited and unreliable. However, numerous laboratory reports of animals' reactions to hallucinogenic drugs are available. For example, Florio, Fuentes, Ziegler and Longo (1972) compared the effects of amphetamines on the behaviour of cats with their effects on the behaviour of other species. 2,5-Dimethoxy-4-methyl-amphetamine (DOM) produced backward locomotion, head nodding and the 'wet dog syndrome' (vigorous shaking of the body) in rats; searching and exploration alternating with stupor and catatonia in rabbits; and in cats 'characteristic changes in behaviour which we have designated as "hallucinatory": striking at imaginary objects in the air, sometimes exhibiting bizarre postures, staring intently at a corner of the cage, and shaking the head'. On the other hand, Dement *et al.* (1970) argued that the similar behaviour they observed in cats in their own experiments could not be regarded as hallucinatory because (a) it was not ordinarily accompanied by signs of emotion, and (b) the animals rarely exhibited visual fixation. On the contrary, they suggested that the cats' head and eye movements more properly indicated alertness, searching and expectancy.

In an attempt to clarify this issue, Siegel, Brewster and Jarvik (1974) gave saline, bromo-lysergic acid (BOL), LSD, dimethyl-triptamine, chlorpromazine, and *d*-amphetamine to rhesus monkeys. Observers blind to the drugs given studied videotapes of the animals and noted that the hallucinogenic drugs tended to produce spasms, convulsive body jerks, stereotyped behaviours, grooming behaviours and walking around with eyes closed. The hallucinogens did not produce a significant increase of behaviours that normally only occur in the presence of an appropriate stimulus (e.g. fear grimace, tracking). On the other hand, the authors argued that a hallucinogen-induced decrease in exploration time might be explained in terms of a shift of attention towards internally generated stimuli.

On the basis of their review of this kind of data, Siegel and Jarvik (1975) argued that, while the answer to the question of whether or not animals hallucinate must depend upon the extent to which the investigator is willing to make inferences from behaviour, they felt that the evidence taken as a whole was sufficient to justify a belief in animal hallucination in some cases. Moreover, they argued that, because lower organisms have a limited behavioural repertoire, it is not surprising that hallucinogen-induced behaviour appears more purposeful as observations are made higher up the phylogenetic scale. The present authors leave the reader to decide whether or not this argument is convincing for him- or herself.

Returning to hallucinations in humans, a further conceptual difficulty concerns the interacting roles of cultural values and context in determining whether a particular first-person report can be regarded as evidence of hallucination or not. Although this issue will be discussed in greater detail in a later chapter, it is worth considering, in passing, the case of ghosts and apparitions. Ghosts have been reported in most cultures and throughout history (see

Finucane, 1982, for a history). From a materialistic viewpoint ghosts are hallucinations. Yet it is unusual to regard the seeing of a ghost as a sign of mental illness, especially if this is appropriate to the cultural context.

Finally, because hallucinations share some qualities of other forms of sensory deception, indeed with normal mental imagery, the question of whether a particular event is hallucinatory may be difficult to determine, even when the person reporting the experience is able to give a good account of his or her experiences. For this reason it may be useful to consider some of the phenomenological variations that are involved in hallucinations and related experiences.

(i) Active versus passive experience

Sensory deception, whether deliberately engineered by an external agent such as a magician or arising indirectly from within in the case of a hallucinating patient, is usually viewed as a passive experience. The individual does not usually intend the experience concerned, although the response of the individual to the experience may be either positive or negative. In general, the passive experience of hallucinations tends to have a negative emotional impact on the individual concerned. However, there are social and cultural contexts in which people have or do deliberately seek to experience hallucinatory phenomena. For example youths in ancient Greece sometimes descended alone into deep caves in order to discover the truths of the world (Kouretas, 1967). Comparable examples of individuals deliberately seeking hallucinatory experiences in Western society are not uncommon. A number of the nineteenth century Romantic writers sought mind-expanding experiences through the use of alcohol (Poe, Coleridge), opium (de Quincey), hashish (Rimbaud), and nitrous oxide (Coleridge). More recently the drugs of choice for individuals in Western society have been the hallucinogens, such as mescaline, LSD and marijuana.

Given the above it is clear that a distinction needs to be made between hallucinatory experiences in which the individual is the *passive* recipient or victim and those in which the person is the *active* agent and engineer. This variable of perceived control (passive versus active) tends to influence the psychological impact of the experience. Passively received hallucinatory experiences are generally negatively valued, whereas comparable actively sought experiences are usually positively valued. This is not always the case of course as anyone who has had a 'bad trip' will readily affirm. However, in such cases the initial perceived control in setting up the experience is reportedly lost during the course of the experience itself. Thus total loss of control is experienced in association with unpleasant and frightening images.

(ii) Simple versus complex sensory deception/hallucination experience

Hallucinations, whether deliberately sought, experimentally produced or naturally occurring, differ not only in terms of the modality involved but also in terms of their complexity. Differences of complexity can be viewed along a continuum from 'simple' to 'complex' experiences.

Research work by Hebb and his colleagues at McGill University in the early 1950s indicated that normal student volunteers, when subjected to experimentally produced 'sensory deprivation' for a period of time (for example by being confined in a darkened, sound-proofed room for many hours), experience perceptual and cognitive changes including hallucinations. Although the initial suggestion was that such hallucinations represent the normal response to sensory deprivation, subsequent work has indicated that the nature of the perceptual aberrations experienced varies enormously from individual to individual. Murphy, Myers and Smith (1962) and Zuckerman (1969) opted for the more neutral terms 'reported visual sensations' (RVS) to describe visual changes and 'reported auditory sensations' (RAS) to describe changes in auditory experience. In addition, they further subdivided both of these categories into Type A and Type B subcategories. The Type A subcategory included all 'simple' changes in sensory experience such as perceived flashes of light, spots, simple geometric figures, clicks, hums, tones, etc. while the Type B subcategory included 'complex' experiences of integrated and meaningful events. Moreover, the available evidence suggests that there is a natural tendency for such experiences to progress from 'simple' to 'complex' with increasing duration of exposure to the experimental procedure (cf. Zuckerman, 1969; Slade, 1984).

The perceptual effects of hallucinogenic drugs, such as psilocybin, mescalin and LSD-25, have shown a similar degree of variation. However, the drug-induced experiences tend to be richer and more commonly visual in nature, whereas those of sensory deprivation are equally experienced in the auditory and visual modality. These differences notwithstanding, the perceptual experiences reported following ingestion of hallucinogenic drugs appear to range along a continuum from (a) simple, meaningless and unstructured sensations (e.g. distortions of colour, shape and size of objects), through (b) more structured, simple sensations which Kluver (1942) described as 'form-constants' (e.g. various geometric shapes, lattice-work, cobwebs, etc.), to (c) the experience of meaningful and integrated objects and scenes (e.g. Walt Disney characters in action). The phenomenology of drug-induced hallucinations will be described in more detail in Chapter 5. For the moment it is worth noting that, as with 'sensory deprivation', the perceptual changes induced by hallucinogenic drugs tend to demonstrate a progression over time in terms of complexity. Not surprisingly, they also appear to be influenced by drug-dosage level (cf. Zuckerman, 1969; Slade 1976b).

Visual and auditory hallucinations are also frequently present in temporal lobe epilepsy, either during the aura or during the attack itself, whereas they are relatively uncommon in epileptic states stemming from lesions in other areas of the brain. As with hallucinations induced by sensory deprivation or hallucinogenic drugs, those directly initiated by a temporal lobe epileptic focus vary in structure and complexity from simple, elementary sensations to more meaningful and integrated perceptions (see Chapter 2).

(iii) Private versus public perceptual experiences

Hallucinatory and related perceptual experiences are essentially private and subjective. That is, at the instant in time at which the experience occurs, no other person shares the same experience. The privacy of the event may persist indefinitely or the individual may communicate the fact of the experience to others, either through direct self-report or through his/her own behaviour (for example, by arguing with the hallucinatory voices). Whether or not the individual's perceptual experience will remain private or be communicated to others will depend on both the quality of the experience and the concerns and motivations of the percipient.

Sarbin (1967), in a highly original analysis of the concept of hallucination, argued that the reasons for an hallucinator's public disclosure remain one of the major unanswered questions in the field. He put forward four possibilities, namely:

(a) the individual's need for clarification of an unusual experience, through external validation,
(b) the individual's wish to share a valued experience with others,
(c) the individual's attempt at self-upgrading through the announcement of a new status (for example, as a distinguished military hero), and
(d) the presence of an appropriate audience.

The second of these possibilities is often observed in clinical practice and was clearly exemplified by a schizophrenic patient seen regularly by the first author. This patient had daily 'messages from God' which he was instructed to pass on. He carefully wrote down word-by-word accounts of what he heard and gave them to the author. When questioned, he said that he felt very relieved once he had passed on the messages, as his responsibility in the matter was then fulfilled. Unfortunately, the author was not able to make much sense out of the messages, which consisted of a repetitious mixture of German and Yiddish commands. Further communication between the author and the source of the messages was therefore seriously curtailed.

Sarbin's list of reasons for 'going public' is obviously not comprehensive, as Sarbin himself has pointed out. One other factor that comes across strongly in clinical experience is that of *fear*. Patients often confide the nature of an unusual experience to mental health professionals because they are afraid of what the experience means for their integrity. They seek reassurance and help. Some, in addition, are motivated by fear of the content of their hallucinations. This may occur, for example, when a patient hears voices discussing means of bringing about his or her death or destruction.

The question of why people 'go public' with their hallucinations begs the further question of how many people may have similar experiences but prefer to keep them 'private'. Are such experiences perhaps the norm rather than the exception? This is an issue which will be addressed in Chapter 3.

(iv) Types of sensory deception/hallucination experience

Sensory deception can take many forms. As well as recognising the previously described distinctions it is useful to discriminate between varieties of aberrant perceptual experience on other grounds. As already indicated, one of the earliest distinctions to be made was that between 'hallucinations' and 'illusions', first made by Esquirol (1832). For Esquirol, hallucinations were exclusively the product of internal processes whereas illusions resulted from a combination of internal and external influences. Such a distinction has carried through into current thinking in which illusions are deemed to be misperceptions of real events whereas the term 'hallucination' is usually reserved for a perceptual experience in the absence of an appropriate external stimulus.

Another distinction that has been made is between 'hallucinations' and 'pseudo-hallucinations' (e.g. Baillarger, 1846; Kandinsky, 1885; Jaspers, 1911; Sedman, 1966; Hare, 1973; Kraupl-Taylor, 1981). Following earlier writers, Jaspers (1911) distinguished true hallucinations from pseudo-hallucinations on the grounds that the latter occur in 'inner subjective space' whereas true hallucinations have an objective reality of their own. Sedman (1966) used different criteria to distinguish 'inner voices', which he considered to be forms of pseudo-hallucination, from experiences which he regarded as true hallucinations. For Sedman, the major criterion for making this distinction was that of the realistic quality of the experience. He therefore argued that, unless an experience is sufficiently vivid and compelling to be considered a true perception at the time by the percipient, the term pseudo-hallucination should be used in preference. Or, to put it another way, the percipient must lack insight into the false nature of the experience for it to qualify as an example of true hallucination. In fact, as Kraupl-Taylor (1981) has pointed out, these two criteria need not necessarily be connected and the term 'pseudo-hallucination' has been used in two ways — to refer to hallucinations that are recognised by the percipient to be non-veridical (i.e. not corresponding to a real object) and to refer to introspected images of great clarity. Kraupl-Taylor suggested that the former be referred to as 'perceived pseudo-hallucinations' and that the latter be referred to as 'imagined pseudo-hallucinations'. The reality characteristics of hallucinations and related experiences have been explored by Aggernaes and his colleagues in the 1970s, and this work will be described in some detail further on in this chapter.

The other distinction that has been made is between true hallucinations on the one hand and various kinds of mental imagery on the other. Maury (1848), for example, was one of the first to describe explicitly the various forms of vivid mental imagery which can occur during the transition from wakefulness to sleep, which he named 'hypnogogic imagery'. The related waking phenomenon has since come to be known as 'hypnopompic imagery'. These forms of vivid imagery are distinguished from true hallucinations on the basis of both the context in which they occur and the individual's lack of conviction in their realistic nature. The same is true for dreams and other dream-like experiences.

Another type of mental imagery is that which occurs during remembering or imagining, when the individual is able to produce a vivid representation of an event at will. It would seem that the crucial distinguishing feature that separates these kinds of experiences from hallucination is voluntary control. (The interested reader is referred to the book by Kosslyn, 1983, for a review of the literature on mental imagery.)

In sum, true hallucinations have been distinguished from illusions, pseudo-hallucinations and various forms of vivid mental experience. However, it should be noted that many observers, while accepting the validity of these distinctions, have tended to view them as points on a continuum, with mental imagery at one end and true hallucinations at the other (e.g. Jaspers, 1911).

(v) Reality characteristics of hallucinatory and related experiences

As alluded to above, one of the major criteria for distinguishing between true hallucinations and other related experiences involves the notion of 'reality characteristics'. One of the most extensive and fruitful attempts to define these difficult qualities has been made by Aggernaes and his colleagues (Aggernaes, 1972a, 1972b; Aggernaes and Nyeborg, 1972; Aggernaes and Myschetzky, 1976; Aggernaes, Haugsted, Myschetzky, Paikin and Vitger, 1976).

In his first study, Aggernaes (1972a) defined seven reality characteristics which could be assessed by means of a structured interview. Each of these characteristics could be defined in terms of a bi-polar contrast as follows:

(a) A quality of 'sensation' versus a quality of 'ideation' (i.e. perception versus imagination).
(b) A quality of 'behavioural relevance' versus a quality of 'no behavioural relevance' (an indication of the extent to which the experience has immediate importance to the person).
(c) A quality of 'publicness' versus a quality of 'privateness' (the extent to which the person feels his or her experience is shared with others).
(d) A quality of 'subjectivity' versus a quality of 'objectivity'. (An experienced event has a positive quality of objectivity if the individual feels that under favourable conditions he or she would be able to experience the event in more than one modality.)
(e) A quality of 'existence' versus a quality of 'non-existence'. (An experienced event is said to have a positive quality of existence if the person feels certain that the event would also occur when nobody experiences it at all.)
(f) A quality of 'independence' versus a quality of 'dependence'. (An event is said to have a positive quality of independence if the person feels certain that the experience is not simply the result of himself or herself being in a quite unusual mental state, where 'quite unusual mental state' refers to such conditions as psychosis, bad nerves, intense emotional states, intoxicated states or drug withdrawal.)
(g) A quality of 'involuntarity' versus a quality of 'voluntary'. (An experience is said to have a positive quality of involuntarity if the person feels that it is impossible or extremely difficult to alter or dismiss the experience simply by wishing.)

Aggernaes gave examples of questions which may be used to elicit

20

Table 1.1: Studies of the experienced reality of hallucinations and related phenomena
Key: + Positive; — Negative; D/C Doubtful or changing

Study and target experience	1. Quality of sensation	2. Quality of behavioural relevance	3. Quality of publicness	4. Quality of objectivity	5. Quality of existence	6. Quality of independence	7. Quality of involuntary
1. AGGERNAES, 1972 (a) Study of hallucinations in 41 chronic schizophrenic patients: 41 auditory, 3 visual, 1 tactile	+=42 (93%) D/C=2 (4%) —=1 (3%)	+=38 (84%) D/C=0 (0%) —=0 (0%)	+=13 (29%) D/C=2 (0%) —=30 (67%)	+=35 (78%) D/C=3 (6%) —=7 (16%)	+=36 (80%) D/C=4 (9%) —=5 (11%)	+=44 (98%) D/C=0 (0%) —=1 (2%)	+=38 (84%) D/C=3 (6%) —=4 (10%)
2. AGGERNAES, 1972 (b) Study of hallucinations in 29 LSD drug abusers: 15 visual, 11 auditory	+=25 (95%) D/C=1 (4%) —=0 (0%)	+=16 (62%) D/C=7 (26%) —=3 (12%)	+=2 (8%) D/C=20 (77%) —=4 (15%)	+=9 (35%) D/C=12 (46%) —=5 (19%)	+=9 (35%) D/C=14 (54%) —=3 (12%)	+=1 (4%) D/C=14 (54%) —=11 (42%)	+=11 (42%) D/C=12 (46%) —=3 (12%)
3. AGGERNAES et al. 1976 Study of 15 non-psychotic patients: predominant ratings							
A. Actual perceptions of a thing or voice:	+	+	+	+	+	+	+
B. Thinking of an existing thing:	—	+	+	+	+	+	—
C. Thinking of a non-existing item:	—	—	—	—	—	+	—

and assess these qualities. For example, in order to assess the quality of 'objectivity' of verbal hallucinations the examiner might ask, 'Are the emitters of the voices persons in flesh and blood which can be eventually found and seen or touched?' In his first paper, Aggernaes applied these criteria to 45 hallucinations (41 auditory, three visual, one tactile) reported by 41 male schizophrenic patients. The findings are presented in the upper section of Table 1.1 where the number and percentage of experiences judged to be positive, negative and doubtful or changing are shown. Very few responses were in fact classified as doubtful or changing (4.4 per cent overall). Moreover, Aggernaes observed that none of the hallucinations examined within 24 hours of their occurrence fell into this category. The other main finding was that, for six of the seven reality characteristics, most of the hallucinations were judged to have positive qualities: that is, they were like actual perceptions. The one exception was that of the quality of publicness, two-thirds of the hallucinations being judged as having the quality of privateness.

In a second study (Aggernaes, 1972b) the reality characteristics of 26 hallucinations (15 visual, 11 auditory) experienced during LSD intoxication by young drug abusers were studied and compared with the characteristics reported by the schizophrenic patients. The findings are presented in the middle section of Table 1.1. One clear point of contrast emerges in relation to the number of hallucinations judged to be doubtful or changing (44 per cent overall). Also, the number of positive qualities reported were generally lower, particularly in relation to the characteristic of independence. Thus, the profile of reality characteristics, as determined by this method, highlights differences in the experiential quality of different types of hallucination.

In a later publication (Aggernaes *et al.*, 1976) an eighth quality named the 'involuntarity of an experienced item' was added, distinct from the seventh item of 'involuntarity of an item' on the original list. An experience is said to have this quality if the percipient feels that it is impossible for him or her to alter the *object* experienced (and not just the experience) simply by wishing it altered. The authors described the results of applying this extended system to the 'normal' experiences of 15 non-psychotic patients. The responses for three such experiences are presented in the lower section of Table 1.1. In terms of the original seven reality characteristics, the experience of an *actual perception* (of a thing or a voice) is judged to be positive for all the qualities. The experience of *thinking* of an existing object lacks the positive qualities of sensation and involuntarity of the experience. Furthermore, thinking of a non-existing item, for example a fairy, was judged to lack all of the positive qualities with the exception of independence.

These studies represent a bold attempt to define and measure the subtle phenomenological parameters of sensory deceptions and hallucinations. Whereas the system that Aggernaes and his colleagues have developed has clear applications in the context of research, it has not been generally adopted for clinical purposes, probably because of the substantial amount of time that would be required for its routine use.

A WORKING DEFINITION OF HALLUCINATION

In the previous section an attempt was made to dissect some of the dimensions of sensory deception in general and hallucinatory experiences in particular. It is now possible to propose a working definition of hallucination which will be used throughout the rest of this book. A hallucination may be defined as:

> Any percept-like experience which (a) occurs in the absence of an appropriate stimulus, (b) has the full force or impact of the corresponding actual (real) perception, and (c) is not amenable to direct and voluntary control by the experiencer.

It is worth considering each aspect of this definition in turn.

(i) A percept-like experience in the absence of an appropriate external stimulus

This is the criterion used by Esquirol and others since to distinguish between hallucinations and illusions. A key term in the definition is that of the 'appropriate external stimulus'. With very few exceptions (for example extreme sensory deprivation) there is usually some form of external sensory stimulation impinging on the individual. An experience may be considered a hallucination only where such stimulation fails to provide the appropriate sensory stimulus for the experienced response. This would be exemplified in the case of the person who hears a voice when the only available auditory stimulus is running water.

(ii) A percept-like experience having the full force and impact of an actual perception

This is the criterion used by various authors, for example Sedman, to distinguish between true hallucinations and pseudo-hallucinations. This criterion is not a simple one; rather it is clearly multifaceted. In Aggernaes' system this criterion is divisible into at least five qualities (sensation, behavioural relevance, publicness, objectivity and existence).

In the case of an individual who has experienced many hallucinations over a period of time, this criterion can pose something of a problem. Although an experience may have the full force and impact of an actual perception, the person may well have learnt from previous similar experiences that it is actually hallucinatory. For this reason it seems reasonable to require only that the experience resembles in all respects the corresponding actual perception and not that the individual necessarily believes it to be real.

(iii) A percept-like experience which is not amenable to direct and voluntary control

This criterion serves to distinguish between hallucinations and other kinds of vivid mental imagery. In Aggernaes' system it corresponds to the criterion of involuntarity of the experience.

In practice, the inability of the hallucinator to call up, modify or terminate his or her experience is probably the single most important factor contributing to fear and distress. Arguably, if the experience could be controlled and terminated at will, its emotional impact would be dramatically reduced.

HALLUCINATIONS, DISORDER AND THE HUMAN MIND

The study of sensory deceptions in general and hallucinations in particular has important implications for the understanding of mental disorder and also, less obviously, for the understanding of the human mind in general. To conclude the present chapter it will be useful to give brief consideration to these implications.

(i) Hallucinations and mental disorder

With respect to abnormal psychology, it is obviously the case that a comprehensive account of hallucinations could lead to remedies for those who are tormented by unremitting voices or visions. Such individuals are relatively common, both on psychiatric wards and in the community, and are routinely seen by psychiatrists, clinical psychologists, social workers and nurses. A major advance in psychiatric care would be achieved if these professionals could be given techniques to enable them to help the chronic hallucinator. Although existing research into the psychological treatment of hallucinations is limited, one purpose of the present book will be to outline what is known in this respect and to indicate likely directions of future progress.

If a comprehensive account of hallucinations can be constructed, it will have to address a number of issues of general importance to the psychopathologist. First, there is the vexed question of finding a dividing line between those forms of sensory deception which may be considered normal and those which may be considered pathological. As will already be obvious, this problem has so far proved difficult to resolve. According to one viewpoint there is in fact no clear dividing line that can be drawn (see Chapter 3).

A second, equally vexed question concerns the relationship between hallucinations and diagnosis. In this respect, as will be shown in the next chapter, the modality and form of hallucinatory experiences have generally been considered of special diagnostic importance. The validity of this viewpoint, however, will have to be considered within a wider context pertaining to the validity of the currently employed diagnostic categories which have evolved from the work of Kraepelin in the nineteenth century.

A final question which must be addressed with respect to abnormal psychology concerns the relationship between the form and content of psychopathology. Hallucinations are experiences which may vary both in form and content. These variations are open to study but unfortunately little empirical research has been pursued in this direction. It is likely that attempts to address this issue will have implications for psychopathology as a general science.

(ii) Hallucinations and the normal mind

Less obvious are the benefits to be gained for psychology in general by studying hallucinations. Yet, in other areas such as the biological sciences, the simultaneous study of the normal and the abnormal has proved a rich source of discovery.

Progress in psychology has been impeded by considerable conceptual as well as empirical barriers to the understanding of human nature. Early systematic psychologists of the introspection-ist schools attempted to naively analyse raw experiences and came unstuck as a result of the unreliability of their methods. For example, using introspection some psychologists maintained that there was 'imageless thought' whereas others disagreed. As they were arguing about subjective experiences there was no way in which they could resolve this dispute. In this respect, Watson's (1913) philosophy of behaviourism (the doctrine that psychology should model itself on the physical sciences and study the publicly observable, i.e. behaviour) was a considerable step in the right direction, an approach that allowed psychologists to resolve their differences by the inspection of data.

It is not our purpose here to repeat the often stated but ill-founded claim that the rise of behaviourism led to a sterile psychology that ignored the importance of events within the organism (cf. Bentall, 1985). Watson did not banish internal events from psychology altogether, as is often assumed, but instead advocated that they be studied by reference to objective criteria. However, some of Watson's followers did create an intellectual climate in which most psychology experiments consisted of the presentation of a stimulus and the measurement of a response with only a limited concern for what went on in between. Within this context the private world of the psychotic seems to pose particular difficulties. At the end of the Second World War the development of the digital computer led to attempts to describe models of information-processing mechanisms within the organism and subsequently to modern cognitive psychology (Gardner, 1985). However, it is not clear that these efforts have solved many of the problems presented by the difficult phenomena observed in the psychiatric clinic.

The implications of hallucinations for psychology are therefore considerable. As extreme forms of perceptual aberration they present extreme tests for theories of perception. More importantly, hallucinations might cast some light on precisely that area of psychology which is most difficult to illuminate: consciousness. It is, after all, in the individual's consciousness that hallucinations are rooted.

The subject of consciousness has recently made something of a return to psychology after a period of banishment by some of Watson's more enthusiastic followers (Ornstein, 1979; Dixon, 1981). The reasons for this return are various but include a general sense of dissatisfaction with the results of the more limited kinds of stimulus–response research and, at the same time, a confidence that the lessons of behaviourism having been learnt, experimental psychology is now ready to take on this most baffling object of investigation. Whether this confidence is warranted remains to be seen. Certainly, formidable philosophical obstacles remain in wait for the psychologist who holds aspirations in this direction (see, for example, Borst, 1970; Armstrong and Malcolm, 1984). To some extent the study of hallucinations may call forth these obstacles and reveal them and, in so much as hallucinations and other bizarre phenomena of the psychiatric ward succeed in doing this, at least some progress will be made towards a general understanding of the human mind.

2

Pathology and Hallucination

Hallucinations have been found to occur in association with a wide range of organic and emotional states. Consequently hallucinations have come to be viewed as predominantly forms of abnormal or pathological perceptual experience. In this chapter we will be concerned with outlining some of the pathological processes and conditions which are commonly associated with the experience of hallucination. These conditions include disorders of the sensory systems; basic physiological variations such as increases in temperature and lack of water; disorders of the central nervous system; and psychiatric conditions such as schizophrenia and the manic depressive psychoses. A particular issue we will concern ourselves with is the question of whether the type of hallucination reported is related to the type of pathology observed. With respect to physiological disorders and variations this is a relatively simple problem to address as the type of pathology suffered by the individual can be determined independently of the type of hallucination experienced as a result. For example, the presence of a lesion in the temporal lobe may be determined by radiological examination; body temperature may be determined by a thermometer. In the case of psychiatric conditions, however, this issue is more complicated because psychiatric diagnosis depends primarily upon *symptoms* (what the patient says about his experiences) rather than *signs* (clear evidence of pathology observed by the clinician). In the absence of an identifiable biological substrate underlying a condition, therefore, the only way of identifying a syndrome is by the detection of a cluster of traits occurring together (Wing, 1978). For this reason, as Kendell (1975) and Blashfield (1984) have pointed out in extensive analyses of the merits of psychiatric diagnosis, there is considerable debate about whether psychiatric patients can be divided into groups suffering from separate syndromes or whether, on the contrary, some other approach to the classification of abnormal behaviour is required. The persistence of this debate without an agreed resolution makes the issue of the relationship between hallucinations and psychiatric disorders particularly difficult to unravel; it will only be possible to consider this problem in the light of a number of conceptual problems relating to the use of diagnosis in psychiatry in general.

HALLUCINATIONS AND AGE

As a starting point for our examination of the relationship between hallucinations and various kinds of physiological and mental pathology it will be useful to consider whether there is any connection between hallucinations and age. This is because different conditions are more likely to occur in people of different ages.

In fact, very little evidence pertaining to the age prevalence of hallucinations exists. Hallucinations are most often associated with the diagnosis of schizophrenia, and a substantial body of evidence indicates that this diagnosis is most often given to individuals aged between late adolescence and approximately 40 years (Hamilton, 1984; Warner, 1985). None the less, hallucinations are found to some extent at both ends of the age scale.

Garralda (1984) studied 20 psychotic children with hallucinations. The mean age of her sample was 13.6 years and the youngest hallucinator was ten years of age. Most of the hallucinations were auditory and located in 'inner space' (i.e. they were 'imagined pseudo-hallucinations' according to Kraupl-Taylor's definition given in the previous chapter). A substantial proportion of the hallucinatory voices made suicidal instigations. When compared with other psychotic children, the children with hallucinations had more symptoms of depression and anxiety. Garralda's failure to find a hallucinating child below the age of ten years is of particular interest. Other studies of childhood psychoses have also failed to reveal convincing evidence of hallucination in very young children (Kolvin, Ounsted, Humphrey and McNay, 1971; Eggers, 1973, 1982). Of course, the identification of hallucinations in children poses special problems, as indicated in the previous chapter. In this context it is interesting to note that young children's conceptions of 'reality' and 'imagination' are quite different from those of adults. For example, children below the age of eight years often report dreams as objectively real (Piaget, 1974) and younger children have only a very limited understanding of the distinction between 'appearance' and 'reality' (Flavell, 1986). Research to be described in Chapter 8 also indicates that the skill of discriminating between the real and the imaginary does not completely develop until after the age of six years (Foley, Johnson and Raye, 1983). It may therefore be muddled thinking to suppose that hallucinations could occur before about this age.

There can be no doubt that some kinds of hallucination are quite common in the elderly. For example, Berrios and Brook (1984) examined 150 consecutive referrals to a psychogeriatrician and found that 44 out of their sample experienced visual disturbances of one sort or another. Of these, the most common were hallucinations of people (either faces, shadows or complete figures) or hallucinations of small animals (spiders, dogs, monkeys, etc.). Seven of their sample were found to experience a new type of sensory disorder, which Berrios and Brook termed 'the picture sign' and which consisted of mistaking a television image or a newspaper photograph for a three-dimensional object and treating it accordingly (for example by talking to it). Berrios and Brook hypothesised that this kind of disorder was a form of sensory delusion. However, in most cases, the visual experiences reported by the hallucinators were described as 'ghostly, fleeting and mundane', and it is notable that only 12 of the patients believed in the objective reality of their perceptions. Why hallucinations should be so common among the elderly is not clear; however, it seems likely that sensory defects or defects of the central nervous system may be involved and these will be considered separately below.

SENSORY DEFECTS

Hallucinations have been reported in conjunction with various defects of the sensory systems. Reductions in visual or auditory acuity, in particular, seem to lead to hallucinations in the damaged modality, especially in the elderly.

A number of authors have reported auditory hallucinations in association with progressive deafness (Ross, Jossman, Bell, Sarbin and Geschwind, 1975; Ross, 1978; Miller and Crosby, 1979; Barraquer-Bordas, Pena-Casanova and Pons-Iraz'abal, 1980; Hammeke, McQuillen and Cohen, 1983). For example, Hammeke *et al.* describe two representative cases, that of a 75-year-old retired female schoolteacher and that of an 80-year-old nun. In both patients the hallucinations began after several years of progressive deafness, and included both unformed (simple sensations) and formed (detailed and vivid experiences) components. The formed components included musical passages (e.g. hearing someone singing 'Jingle bells') and voices, including voices remembered from childhood. The hallucinations occurred most often during periods of low ambient noise, and could be controlled to some extent by concentration or subvocalisation. Neither patient was completely deaf; in the case of the schoolteacher, hearing was spared to the extent that conversation was possible with the aid of a hearing aid, whereas, in the case of the nun, there was severe hearing loss in one ear and only moderate hearing loss in the other. Attempts to reduce the hallucinations by antipsychotic or anticonvulsant medication failed. As a patient reported by Ross (1978) had been suffering from similar hallucinations for over 20 years, it might be thought that this kind of hallucination, once acquired, is permanent. However, in a case of auditory release hallucination associated with central deafness following stroke, described by Barraquer-Bordas *et al.* (1980), hallucinations lasted for only a week following the onset of deafness, indicating that recovery is sometimes possible. Similar visual hallucinations have been reported in association with progressive blindness or other visual defects (Cogan, 1973; Brust and Behrens, 1977; White, 1980; McNamara, Heros and Boller, 1982) or following visual loss resulting from damage to the optic nerve or optic chiasma (Jacobs, Karpik, Bozian and Gothgen, 1981). This phenomenon is sometimes known as the 'Charles Bonnet' syndrome after the philosopher who first described the syndrome in his grandfather (Berrios and Brook, 1982; Damas-Mora, Skelton-Robinson and Jenner, 1982).

No consensus of opinion exists about the causes of hallucinations associated with sensory defects; however, a number of authors have postulated that sensory deprivation is the

31

neuropsychological mechanism primarily involved. According to this hypothesis, low levels of stimulation cause the disinhibition of perception-bearing circuits in the nervous system with the result that perceptual traces of previously experienced events are released into consciousness (Cogan, 1973; West, 1975; Brust and Behrens, 1977). For this reason hallucinations associated with sensory deficits are sometimes known as 'release hallucinations'. (The possible role of sensory deprivation in hallucinations will be discussed in more detail in Chapters 4 and 5.) Other authors have hypothesised that some kind of disorder of the central nervous system is also necessary for hallucinations to be experienced following sensory deficits. The evidence pertaining to this controversy is somewhat mixed. Thus, Hammeke *et al.* (1983) reviewed the available literature and found 15 reported cases of auditory release hallucinations. Of these, only five had been assessed using EEG, and in three of these cases central nervous system abnormalities were detected. Berrios and Brook (1984), on the other hand, in their sample of 44 elderly patients suffering from visual hallucinations, could find no consistent relationship between EEG or CT scan results and the presence of hallucinations, although hallucinations were highly correlated with eye pathology (present in 47 per cent of hallucinators) and delusions (present in 32 per cent of hallucinators). The possible role of central nervous system disorders in hallucinations will be considered in some detail below.

PHYSIOLOGICAL VARIATION

One kind of physiological variation which is conducive to hallucination is an abnormality of body temperature. It is commonly recognised that fevers involving high brain temperature often produce hallucinatory-type experiences. However, it seems that a low brain temperature can also have a similar effect. In one study, for example, Fay (1959) found that hallucinations occurred at brain temperatures approaching a high of 40°C or a low of 34°C.

Food and water deprivation are also generally recognised as conducive to the experience of hallucination. A common image in folklore is that of the severely dehydrated refugee, crawling across a sandy desert under a blazing hot sun, hallucinating a mouthwatering oasis. Some less extreme examples of physiological-deprivation-induced hallucinations have been described by Forrer (1960), who concluded that 'The circumstance of hunger and thirst which accompanied each benign hallucination suggests an ultimate physiological origin for the phenomenon itself.' Again, however, it is not only physiological deprivation but also excess which is associated wih hallucinations. Noonan and Ananth (1977), for example, described the case of a compulsive water drinker who, as an apparent consequence of water intoxication, experienced extended auditory and visual hallucinations.

As we will see in subsequent chapters, the effects of extreme physiological variation are paralleled by the effects of extreme levels of external sensory stimulation. Conditions which lead to substantially *reduced* stimulation (such as sensory, perceptual and social deprivation) are found to be associated with an increased frequency of aberrant perceptual experiences, including halluci-nations. Similarly, conditions which are associated with stimulation *overload* (such as sleep deprivation) are also associated with an increased frequency of hallucinations (see Chapter 4).

A final example of the way in which basic physiological variations can affect the tendency to hallucinate concerns breath-ing patterns. Allen and Agus (1968) studied two patients with a history of both auditory and visual hallucinations, one of whom was diagnosed as suffering from schizophrenia, the other remaining undiagnosed. During a number of sessions the investigators experimented with hyperventilation, instructing their subjects to breath rapidly and deeply. They found that, after between 10 and 15 minutes of this, both the subjects reported visual and auditory hallucinations. Allen and Agus then instructed their two subjects to return to a normal pattern of breathing with the result that the hallucinations rapidly disappeared.

As with the previous examples of the effect of physiological variations, reduction in respiration rate has also been associated with an increase of hallucination. The first author and associates (Slade, Judkins and Fonagy, 1976) found a decrease in respiration rate or sometimes even total withholding of breath in association with the onset of auditory hallucinations in predisposed indi-viduals.

MEDICAL CONDITIONS

As Asaad and Shapiro (1986) have observed in a review of clinical aspects of hallucinations, hallucinatory experiences can occur in association with many different types of medical conditions and treatments. Examples include open-heart surgery (Freyhan, Giannelli, O'Connell and Mayo, 1971; Meyendorf, 1982); incipient cardiovascular accident (Fletcher, Vardi, Allelov and Streifler, 1978); haemodialysis (Buchanan, Abram, Wells and Teschan, 1977–78); hypothyroidism (Jain, 1972); and legionnaire's disease (Gregory, Schaffner, Alford, Kaiser and McGee, 1979). Such is the ubiquitous nature of the phenomenon in physical disease that a number of investigators have been encouraged to seek medical causes of psychiatric disorder in general and hallucinations in particular.

One of the larger-scale studies of this type was carried out by Hall, Popkin and Faillace (1978). Hall *et al.* studied a sample of 658 consecutive psychiatric outpatients using careful medical and biochemical evaluation. Medical disorder was considered causative of psychiatric symptoms if: (a) psychiatric symptoms abated significantly with medical treatment; (b) medical symptoms seemed clearly related to the onset of psychiatric symptoms; or (c) the presence of medical disorder, even though untreatable, explained the patient's symptom pattern. Using these criteria Hall judged 9.1 per cent of the patients to have a medically induced psychiatric disorder. Hall went on to identify 100 patients with symptoms having a medical aetiology; of these 18 per cent presented with auditory hallucinations and 12 per cent with visual hallucinations. Medical conditions associated with psychiatric disorder, in order of importance, were: (a) cardiovascular and endocrine disorders; (b) infections; (c) pulmonary disease; (d) gastrointestinal disorders; (e) haematopoietic (anaemic) disease; (f) CNS disorder; and (g) malignancy. Twenty-eight per cent of the index group were diagnosed as having a functional psychotic disorder, including auditory or visual hallucinations, or both.

CENTRAL NERVOUS SYSTEM DISORDER

As might be expected, those medical conditions which have a

34

direct effect on central nervous system functioning are usually regarded as having the greatest hallucinatory consequences. Such neurological precipitants include the post-concussion syndrome (Lloyd and Tsuang, 1981); the migraine syndrome (Hachinski, Porchawka and Steele, 1973); meningiomas of various types (Bollati, Galli, Gandolfini and Marini, 1980; Hunter, 1968); neurocysticercosis (tapeworm) in children (Lefevre, Diament and Valente, 1969); viral encephalitis (Mize, 1980); and a rare condition known as palinacousis (Malone and Leiman, 1983) involving hearing a voice, music or random noise repeated after the event.

Disorders of nervous system functioning produce hallucinatory experiences which vary in duration, modality, form, content and intensity. The nature and quality of hallucination is related, to some extent, to the kind of neurological insult and its location. It is therefore worth briefly considering the types of CNS disorders which have been specifically investigated in terms of their hallucinatory consequences.

(i) Focal lesions of the brain

Although no single, therapeutically created lesion reported by neurosurgical investigators has been found to be invariably and exclusively associated with the production of hallucination, various sources of evidence suggest that certain areas of the brain are more closely involved than others. One relevant source of evidence results from the study of drug/lesion interactions. Baldwin, Lewis and Bach (1959) administered LSD-25 to a group of chimpanzees, with the consequent production of bizarre, psychotic-like episodes. These episodes were not affected by lobectomies, either unilateral or bilateral, of the frontal, parietal or occipital lobes, nor by unilateral temporal lobectomy. However, they did not occur following bilateral temporal lobectomy. It therefore seems possible that the existence of an intact temporal cortex is necessary for the production of psychotic-like behaviour, presumably including hallucinations. In a related study, Holden and Itil (1970) compared the responses to LSD-25 administration of a group of 13 chronic schizophrenic patients who had undergone pre-frontal lobotomy many years previously with a matched group of unoperated chronic schizophrenic patients. The pre-frontal loboto-mised patients exhibited markedly more severe psychotic features, including more severe auditory, visual and tactile hallucinations, than the control patients. One possible explanation suggested by Holden and Itil is that a frontal lesion can trigger temporal and occipital lobe symptomatology, including hallucinations, by means of fronto-temporal and fronto-occipital association tracts.

A second source of evidence which suggests the importance of the temporal cortex for hallucinatory activity stems from the clinical investigation of focal epileptic states. Visual and auditory hallucinations are frequently present in temporal lobe epilepsy, either during the aura or during the attack itself, while being relatively uncommon in epileptic states involving focal lesions in other areas of the brain. In fact the association of hallucinations with temporal lobe epilepsy is sufficiently strong for the former to serve as a useful localising sign of the focal lesion responsible. As with other kinds of hallucinatory states the hallucinations of temporal lobe epilepsy vary in structure and complexity from simple, elementary sensations and patterns to those of more meaningful and integrated percepts. In general it appears that the more posterior the lesion in the temporal cortex, the more complex and structured the hallucinatory experience (Mayer-Gross, Slater and Roth, 1975).

A third source of evidence concerning the role of temporal lobe structures has come from work pioneered by Penfield and his associates involving direct electrical stimulation of the exposed cortex under local anaesthesia (Penfield and Rasmussen, 1950; Penfield and Jasper, 1954; Penfield and Perot, 1963). In studies of a total of 520 epileptic patients suffering from focal temporal lobe lesions, Penfield observed that meaningful auditory and visual hallucinations occurred *only* following electrical stimulation in or near the temporal lobe. However, hallucinations did not invariably occur as a result of stimulation of this region. In fact only 40 patients (i.e. 7.7 per cent) reported such experiences. Similar studies have been carried out by other investigators. Mahl, Rothen-burg, Delgado and Hamlin (1964), using electrical stimulation of the deeper structures of the temporal cortex, obtained frequent reports of auditory hallucinations but no visual hallucinations from a single epileptic patient. In another study, Horowitz and Adams (1970) subjected 16 patients with intractable temporal lobe epilepsy to depth stimulation of the temporal lobe structures. Meaningful visual hallucinations and pseudo-hallucinations were reported by 12 of their patients, although out of a total of 1509 separate stimulations only 1.7 per cent produced hallucinatory experiences. There therefore appears to be some variability not only in the number of patients reporting hallucinations from temporal lobe stimulations but also between the results of repeated stimulations in the same patient.

Because of the hazards involved in craniotomy, almost all of the direct electrical stimulation studies in humans have been carried out during therapeutic surgery on patients with focal epileptic lesions. They have therefore involved electrical stimulation of diseased tissue which may produce a different response to that of neurologically healthy tissue. However, a Japanese group (Ishibashi, Hori, Endo and Sato, 1964) have reported the results of a depth stimulation study carried out on 17 chronic schizophrenic patients with hallucinations. In four of their patients they obtained reports of visual hallucinations on stimulation of the deep temporal structures. It would therefore appear that direct electrical stimulation of apparently healthy temporal lobe structures may have the same effects as the stimulation of structures with focal lesions (although the assumption that chronic schizophrenics are neurologically healthy might not be entirely justified, cf. Seidman, 1984).

Some of the electrical stimulation studies have also provided evidence relating to laterality effects. Penfield and his colleagues found that hallucinatory reports were slightly more frequent with stimulation of the right (non-dominant) temporal lobe than with the left, although the difference was not statistically significant. Baldwin and Frost (1970) analysed the data obtained from 919 stimulations in 139 human craniotomies (79 left hemisphere, 60 right hemisphere) and concluded that hallucinations originated mainly from stimulation of the right side. Horowitz and Adams (1970), on the other hand, found no difference in the frequency of meaningful, structured hallucinations between the hemispheres, although stimulation of the right hemisphere produced a slightly greater frequency of simple, elementary sensations.

In summary, it would appear that, while no single focus in the brain invariably and exclusively produces hallucinations, such experiences are most commonly associated with damage to the temporal lobes, especially the deeper and more posterior structures.

37

From the small amount of evidence available on laterality effects, it seems that hallucinations can be evoked with a slightly greater frequency from the right as opposed to the left hemissphere.

(ii) Acute organic brain syndrome and delirium

A second example of hallucinations being associated with identifiable brain dysfunction concerns the acute organic brain syndrome or delirium. Such a state is characterised by a general disturbance of consciousness which includes impairments of thinking, comprehension, memory, perception and attention, which commonly fluctuate over time (Lipowski, 1967). Disorientation for time (year, month, day and date), place (current environment) and personal identity (name, age, etc.) are the most useful diagnostic features of this condition. As a rule, disorientation for time tends to precede disorientation for place or personal identity.

Delirium is a consequence of a wide range of illnesses which directly or indirectly affect the normal functioning of the brain. Such illnesses may range from cerebral infections, trauma and neoplasms through respiratory, endocrine and renal diseases, to the effects of poisons and drugs. Given that such a broad range of conditions can produce the acute organic brain syndrome it is not surprising that delirium is a relatively common phenomenon by medical standards. Lipowski (1967) reported evidence suggesting that approximately 30 per cent of adults will experience an episode of delirium during their lifetimes. Moreover, in a later publication, Lipowski (1975) noted that both young (children) and elderly patients are more vulnerable to becoming delirious than those in intermediate age groups.

Hallucinations occur fairly frequently in delirium but are usually fleeting and almost invariably visual in nature. They tend to be worse at night and the phenomenon of 'sundowning' has been particularly noted in the elderly. That is, the delirious state, including visual hallucinations, tends to become more prominent when the lights are turned down and communication with others stops.

(iii) Alcoholic states

Another example of hallucinatory activity apparently having an organic basis is to be found in the acute alcoholic psychoses. Psychotic states occur in a small proportion of chronic alcoholic patients, usually during or subsequent to a period of sudden withdrawal of alcohol (Victor and Hope, 1953; Saravay and Pardes, 1967). Two main categories are usually distinguished in which hallucinations are considered a primary feature: delirium tremens and alcoholic hallucinosis. Despite the considerable problems of definition and differentiation of these two states (see Gross, Halpert and Sabot, 1963, 1968), most authorities seem to agree that delirium tremens is characterised by tremulousness, a delirious state involving clouding of consciousness, and primarily visual and haptic hallucinations. Alcoholic hallucinosis, on the other hand, is characterised by mainly auditory hallucinations, occuring in more or less clear sensorium, and accompanied by associated delusional features. Both conditions but especially the latter are relatively uncommon. For example, Benedetti (1952) collected cases of alcoholic hallucinosis from many hospitals in Switzerland and found only 113 such patients in 30 years. Similarly, May and Ebaugh (1953) found only 99 cases in 31 years in an American study while Scott (1967) found only 32 cases treated at the Maudsley Hospital in London over a 12-year period.

In spite of its rarity, alcoholic hallucinosis has aroused considerable interest because of the similarity of its principal features to those seen in functional schizophrenic states. Bleuler (1911) in fact suggested that in these cases there is almost invariably an underlying schizophrenic illness which is unmasked by the effects of the alcohol. However, the evidence relating to this proposition is in general contradictory. Follow-up studies by Victor and Hope (1953), Benedetti (1952) and Gross, Halpert, Sabot and Polizos (1963) have shown that patients suffering from alcoholic hallucinosis have a very different course, prognosis and outcome from patients suffering from schizophrenia. Scott (1967) and Schuckit and Winokur (1971) found that the incidence of schizophrenia in the families of such patients was no different from that in the population at large.

The auditory hallucinations which occur in acute alcoholic psychoses vary in their degree of structure and meaningfulness,

39

much as they do in other hallucinatory states. For example, as in the case of those sensory defects associated with ageing, two classes of alcoholic hallucinations are usually distinguished: 'elementary hallucinations' and 'formed hallucinations', the former including prolonged or sustained sounds (e.g. buzzing, humming and whistling) and short phasic sounds (e.g. shots, bangs, clicks, etc.) while the latter include experiences of voices and music. Gross, Halpert, Sabot and Polizos (1963) found that many of the prolonged 'elementary' sounds experienced could be explained by the 51 per cent incidence of sustained tinnitus (a middle ear disorder) in their group of alcoholic patients. Saravay and Pardes (1967) obtained evidence for a similar explanation of the short phasic 'elementary hallucinations' in their patients. Moreover, Gross, Halpert, Sabot and Polizos (1963) found that an increasing severity of hallucinations (both auditory and visual, 'elementary' and 'formed') was significantly correlated with the presence of tinnitus and also with the presence of a general neurosensory hearing loss. It therefore appears that in acute alcoholic psychoses, as in the case of hallucinations associated with ageing, a disturbance of the perceptual processes may be partly responsible for the occurrence of hallucinatory experiences.

Further evidence relating to the mechanisms of alcoholic hallucinosis and delirium tremens comes from a series of analogue studies reported by Alpert and Silvers (1970) and Maletzky (1976). The former used continuous injections of ditran (a pharmacological compound with hallucinogenic properties) in an attempt to simulate the effects of alcohol and drug withdrawal. In a group of 14 volunteer patients, they found that ditran produced auditory hallucinations in two out of four with a history of alcoholism and in one out of ten with a history of drug abuse. They then carried out a series of three individual case investigations with alcoholic volunteers, involving an injection of ditran followed by continuous parallel monitoring of subjective experiences, clinical state and physiological responses over a two-to-three-hour period. Behavioural and mental changes were noted in the order of vague prodromata, through hallucinations to delirium, the various changes being dose-related. In all three patients, the drug administration was followed by a steady increase in respiration rate up to a certain point, followed by a gradual reduction and return to the starting level. In two of the patients similar parallel changes were noted in pulse rate, mean arterial blood pressure and electromyographic (EMG) indices. Visual hallucinations were reported by two of these patients during the period of elevated respiration rate. Thus the hallucinatory experience seemed to be temporally related to a state of increased physiological arousal induced by the drug.

Maletzky (1976) selected a sample of 22 alcoholic patients presenting with a history of violent or bizarre behaviour under the influence of alcohol. Inclusion criteria included a history of more than one episode of such behaviour under the influence of alcohol, absence of such behaviour when sober, amnesia for such episodes, and no evidence of neurological disorder based on history, neurological examination and EEG. These patients agreed to take part in an experiment involving the intravenous injection of 25 per cent alcohol in 5 per cent glucose in water. Following infusion, the behaviour of the subjects was closely monitored. Four types of reaction were observed: (a) a violent reaction characterised by inappropriate rage (nine subjects); (b) a psychotic reaction characterised by hallucinations, delusions and distortions (four subjects); (c) a mixed reaction involving both the above (two subjects); and (d) a normal reaction characterised by signs of alcohol intoxication alone (seven subjects). Thus hallucinations, both auditory and visual, were observed in 27 per cent of these subjects in response to intravenous alcohol. As the work of Alpert and Silvers suggests, this finding implies that, in predisposed individuals, hallucinations can be triggered by interventions producing a change in physiological arousal level.

FUNCTIONAL PSYCHIATRIC DISORDERS

Hallucinations of one form or another are said to occur in all the major functional psychotic states. In addition it is commonly held that the form and content of such hallucinations vary in accordance with the diagnostic category of the patient and that the nature of the hallucinatory experience therefore has a special diagnostic significance. The two characteristics of hallucinations which have been most widely studied in this context are modality and form.

Before considering the evidence for this argument it is worth briefly considering the general problem of relating any symptom to any psychiatric diagnosis. As alluded to at the beginning of the

41

chapter, this problem is quite different from the problem of relating symptoms to various types of physical disorder. Whereas, in the case of a physical disorder, diagnosis can be determined independently of symptomatology by reference to a number of objective signs (the results of radiological examination, histological analysis, biochemical analysis, etc.), there are no objective signs in psychiatric disorders other than the patient's behaviour (Alpert, 1985). As psychiatric diagnosis can only be determined on the basis of symptomatology, the investigator interested in the relationship between symptoms and diagnosis must avoid the folly of circular reasoning (defining the symptoms of a condition in advance, only to discover that people said to be suffering from that condition have those very same symptoms). For this reason, there is some doubt about whether psychiatric patients can be divided into discrete groups suffering from different mental illnesses in the same way that general medical patients can be divided into discrete groups suffering from essential hypertension, coronary thrombosis, lung cancer, rubella, the common cold, etc. (with perhaps a few patients suffering from more than one condition). Various alternatives to the discrete diagnostic categories of Kraepelin and his followers have been proposed (Blashfield, 1984). These include dimensional models in which patients are said to be located on various continuous personality dimensions such as 'neuroticism', 'psychoticism', etc. (see for example Eysenck, Wakefield and Friedman, 1983; Claridge, 1985); hierarchical models in which neurosis is seen as a less severe form of psychosis (see for example Foulds and Bedford, 1975); and random symptom models in which different psychiatric symptoms are regarded as having nothing much to do with each other (see for example Slade and Cooper, 1979). The relative merits of these different models continue to be hotly debated (Kendell, 1975; Blashfield, 1984). To illustrate this controversy it will be helpful to examine an early study that indicated only a minimal relationship between symptoms and diagnosis.

Zigler and Phillips (1961) collected data on the symptomatology and diagnoses of 793 patients admitted to a large American mental hospital over a 12-year period. The results of their investigation can be seen in Table 2.1.

It will be observed that most symptoms were found to some extent in all four of the major diagnostic categories used in the

Table 2.1: Percentage of hospital patients in four diagnostic categories manifesting particular psychiatric symptoms. From Zigler and Phillips (1961)

Symtom	Total sample (N=793)	Manic depressive (N=75)	Neurotic (N=152)	Character disordered (N=279)	Schizophrenic (N=287)
Depressed	38	64	58	31	28
Tense	37	32	46	33	36
Suspiciousness	35	25	16	17	65
Drinking	19	17	14	32	8
Hallucinations	**19**	**11**	**4**	**12**	**35**
Suicidal attempts	16	24	19	15	12
Suicidal ideas	15	29	23	15	8
Bodily complaints	15	21	21	5	19
Emotional outburst	14	17	12	18	9
Withdrawn	14	4	12	7	25
Perplexed	14	9	9	8	24
Assaultative	12	5	6	18	5
Self-depreciatory	12	16	16	8	13
Threatens assault	10	4	11	14	7
Sexual preoccupation	10	9	9	6	14
Maniacal outburst	9	11	6	7	12
Bizarre ideas	9	11	1	2	20
Robbery	8	0	3	18	3
Apathetic	8	8	8	4	11
Irresponsible behaviour	7	3	7	9	7
Headaches	6	7	10	4	5
Perversion (except homosexuality)	5	0	5	10	2
Euphoria	5	17	2	2	5
Fears own hostile impulses	5	4	9	5	2
Mood swings	5	9	5	4	4
Insomnia	5	11	7	3	5
Psychosomatic disorders	4	7	6	3	5
Does not eat	4	9	4	2	4
Lying	3	0	1	7	0
Homosexuality	3	3	3	8	2
Rape	3	0	3	8	1
Obsessions	3	8	3	1	4
Depersonalisation	3	4	1	0	6
Feels perverted	3	0	3	1	5
Phobias	2	4	5	0	2

hospital. For example, hallucinations were found to be most prevalent among those diagnosed as schizophrenic (35 per cent) but were also found in those diagnosed as manic depressive (11 per cent), psychoneurotic (4 per cent) and character disordered (12 per cent). By statistical analysis, Zigler and Phillips were able to demonstrate significant relationships between symptoms and diagnoses. For example, hallucinations were over-represented among the schizophrenics and manic depressives and under-represented among the psychoneurotics and the character disordered. However, the magnitude of these relationships was generally found to be so small that Zigler and Phillips were forced to reach the rather stark conclusion that 'Membership in a diagnostic class conveys only minimal information about the symptomatology of the patient.' Because of this it is not clear, at least on the basis of Zigler and Phillips' data, that the four different diagnoses correspond to discrete disease entities. The same relationship between symptoms and diagnoses could probably be achieved if symptoms were randomly distributed among patients and if those patients with predominantly anxiety-related problems were assigned to the category of psychoneurosis, those with predominantly hallucinatory and delusional symptoms were assigned to the category of schizophrenia, and so on (Zigler and Phillips were unable to test for this possibility).

Of course, Zigler and Phillips' study was carried out some time ago and it is possible that the development of more refined methods of diagnosis based on standardised psychiatric interviews, together with the discovery of more sophisticated statistical techniques, would yield quite a different picture if the study were repeated today. In fact, modern data pertaining to this issue will be described towards the end of the chapter. Bearing this continuing controversy in mind, however, it will now be useful to examine in detail some studies that have tried to assess the importance of hallucinations for psychiatric diagnosis. It is only after examining these data that it will be possible to assess their significance.

(i) Modality differences

It has commonly been suggested that, whereas medical and organic conditions can give rise to visual hallucinations, auditory hallucinations tend to be related fairly exclusively to the functional psychotic disorders, particularly schizophrenia. In this respect the following two propositions are commonly advanced: (a) auditory hallucinations are common in schizophrenia whereas visual hallucinations are rare; and (b) the opposite is true for patients suffering from organic brain syndromes and affective disorder.

Evidence pertaining to the first proposition is presented in Table 2.2. It can be seen from the table that, of the 16 studies which have specifically addressed this issue, all have found a higher incidence of auditory than visual hallucinations in samples of patients diagnosed as suffering from schizophrenia. In fact, while the overall incidence of auditory hallucinations is approximately 60 per cent, that of visual hallucinations is only about 29 per cent. With respect to the proposition that the hallucinations of organic brain syndromes and affective disorders are predominantly visual rather than auditory in nature, however, the evidence is less clear cut.

In an early study carried out in the USA, Bowman and Raymond (1931) found a relatively low incidence of both kinds of hallucinations in groups of manic-depressive patients and patients suffering from general paresis, with a slight tendency for auditory hallucinations to be more common. In a more recent study also carried out in the USA, Goodwin, Alderson and Rosenthal (1971), on the other hand, found a high incidence of both auditory (82 per cent) and visual (72 per cent) hallucinations in a group of 28 selected patients suffering from primary affective disorder, although in a group of nine patients with organic brain syndromes visual hallucinations were more than twice as common as auditory hallucinations (89 per cent as opposed to 44 per cent). In a subsequent British study, Lowe (1973) looked at the diagnostic significance of hallucinations in four groups of paranoid, schizophrenic, manic-depressive and organic patients, each group consisting of 15 subjects. Using discriminant function analysis (a statistical technique for identifying which symptoms discriminate between different diagnostic groups) based on 15 parameters of hallucinatory activity he found that the variables of frequency and duration were among the best predictors of diagnosis whereas that of modality was relatively poor. In discussing his results, however, Lowe noted that paranoid hallucinations were predominantly auditory, whereas manic-depressive hallucinations were predominantly visual.

45

Table 2.2: The comparative incidence of auditory and visual hallucinations in schizophrenia

Study	Country	Sample	N	Type of hallucination		
				Auditory	Visual	Other
Bowman and Raymond (1931)	USA	Acute schizophrenics	1408	53%	21%	Tactile=1% Gustatory=2% Olfactory=1% Somatosensory=4%
Feinberg (1962)	USA	Acute schizophrenics	19	84%	4% (estimated)	
Malitz et al. (1962)	USA	Chronic schizophrenic	100	50%	9%	
Vitols et al. (1963)	USA	Acute (white) schizophrenics	110	35%	13%	
Vitols et al. (1963)	USA	Acute (negro) schizophrenics	128	57%	30%	
Goldberg et al. (1965)	USA	Acute schizophrenics	74	34%	16%	
Goldberg et al. (1965)	USA	Acute schizophrenics	270	45%	18%	
Mott et al. (1965)	USA	Acute schizophrenics	50	66%	24%	
Small et al. (1966)	USA	Acute schizophrenics	50	66%	30%	
Holmboe and Astrup (1967)	Sweden	Acute schizophrenia and schizophreniform psychoses	255	79%	25%	Tactile=28%
Jansson (1968)	Sweden	Young (15–24 years) schizophrenics	293	25%	13%	
Goodwin et al. (1971)	USA	Acute schizophrenics	13	69%	46%	Tactile=54% Gustatory=46% Olfactory=23%

Study	Country	Diagnosis	N			Modality
Goodwin et al. (1971)	USA	Chronic schizophrenics	32	94%	72%	Tactile=53% Gustatory=6% Olfactory=19%
Zarroug (1975)	Saudi Arabia	Acute schizophrenics	69	68%	62%	
McCabe (1976)	USA	Chronic schizophrenics	25	52%	20%	Tactile=36% Gustatory=4% Olfactory=4%
Deiker and Chambers (1978)	USA	Functional psychosis (mainly schizophrenia)	28	86%	64%	Tactile=71% Gustatory=32% Olfactory=39%
Total:			2924			
Mean:				60.19%	29.19%	
SD:				19.93%	20.76%	
Range:				34–94%	4–72%	

Unfortunately no figures for the actual frequencies of various types of hallucinations were provided by Lowe.

In contrast to Lowe's observations, Taylor and Abrams (1975) studied a group of patients with acute mania and found a 47 per cent prevalence of auditory hallucinations as opposed to only a 23 per cent prevalence of visual hallucinations. However, in a study which focused on the slightly different issue of the quality of visual hallucinations in schizophrenic, organic and affective psychoses, Frieske and Wilson (1966) found that visual hallucinations in schizophrenia always occurred in conjunction with other types, mainly auditory, whereas 33 per cent of organic and 7 per cent of affective patients experienced visual hallucinations alone. On the basis of this evidence, therefore, it would seem to be the unique occurrence, rather than the relative prevalence, of visual hallucinations that is characteristic of organic and affective disorders.

A related proposition to those already considered is that auditory hallucinations in general, and certain types in particular, are characteristic of schizophrenia to the point of being pathognomic. The latter part of this proposition will be dealt with below. The evidence concerning the former is again contradictory. Lowe (1973), as mentioned above, found that the modality of hallucination is a relatively poor indicator of differential diagnosis. In a similar vein, Goodwin et al. (1971), who initially studied a series of 116 consecutively admitted patients with hallucinations as a prominent feature, also found that modality was a relatively non-specific feature of hallucinations. For example, of all the patients who had experienced hearing 'voices', only 35 per cent were diagnosed as suffering from schizophrenia: the other 65 per cent were placed in one of four other categories: affective disorder, alcoholism, organic brain syndrome and hysteria. In contrast to these results, however, two further studies have reported a strong association between hallucinations and a diagnosis of schizophrenia.

Lewinsohn (1968), in a study of 175 acute schizophrenics and 134 non-schizophrenic psychiatric patients, found that, while only 30 per cent of schizophrenics were reported to have hallucinations, the inverse probability (i.e. of being diagnosed schizophrenic when hallucinations are present) was 0.84. On this basis he suggested that 'In some previous studies in which subjects were chosen on the basis of the presence of hallucinations, predominantly schizophrenics were (probably) selected.' A similar conclusion concerning the diagnostic implications of auditory hallucinations came from a large-scale, cross-cultural study conducted by the World Health Organization, the International Pilot Study of Schizophrenia (WHO, 1975). Elaborate and lengthy psychiatric interviews were conducted on a total of 1202 patients suffering from functional psychotic disorders in nine different countries (Colombia, Czechoslovakia, Denmark, India, Nigeria, Taiwan, USSR, UK and USA). Great pains were taken to train the interviewers in each of the nine field research centres in the conduct and scoring of the various standardised interview schedules, resulting in reasonably high inter-rater and inter-centre reliabilities for diagnosis and the identification of symptoms. By means of various clinical and computer techniques, a core schizophrenic group was isolated, numbering 306 patients who met a range of diagnostic criteria. Auditory hallucinations were found to be present in 74 per cent of this group.

Clearly the empirical findings in this area are conflicting. However, it must be said that the larger-scale and better-controlled studies seem to support the diagnostic significance of hallucinations. On the other hand, it must be added that by far the majority of these studies have been carried out in developed countries. The significance of this observation will become apparent when cultural differences in hallucination are considered in the next chapter.

(ii) Form and content

Auditory hallucinations may take many forms. For example, some are non-verbal, consisting of noises and music, and others are exclusively verbal.

Kurt Schneider (1959) proposed a set of practical diagnostic criteria for schizophrenia which have been particularly influential and which all involve some form of delusional or hallucinatory experience. The three specifically hallucinatory 'first-rank symptoms' described by Schneider are: (a) the patient hearing a running commentary on his or her own actions; (b) voices speaking about the patient in the third person; and (c) the patient hearing his or her own thoughts spoken aloud — 'Gedankenlautwerden'.

49

Table 2.3: The diagnostic significance of different types of hallucinations in the International Pilot Study of Schizophrenia (WHO, 1975)

Symptom	N	Schizophrenic and paranoid psychoses ($N=876$)	Manic psychoses ($N=79$)	Depressive psychoses, neuroses, etc. ($N=229$)
(1) Voices speaking to patient (2nd-person voices)	332	0.91	0.05	0.03
(2) Voices speaking about patient (3rd-person voices)	172	0.95	0.03	0.02
(3) Running commentary by voices on patient's behaviour	136	0.97	0.03	0.02

In the World Health Organization study of schizophrenia (WHO, 1975) referred to in the previous section the diagnostic significance of these Schneiderian symptoms was investigated. The results are shown in Table 2.3. It can be seen that two of the three forms of hallucination described by Schneider — running commentaries and third-person voices — were indeed found to be diagnostic. A third non-Schneiderian form of hallucination was also found to be of diagnostic significance, however. This was voices in the second person, a symptom generally considered to be indicative of a depressive illness in Great Britain. Nevertheless, despite this finding, the results taken as a whole seemed to match reasonably well with Schneider's analysis. On this evidence at least, there does appear to be a close agreement between an internationally agreed method of diagnosing schizophrenia and the presence of certain forms of verbal hallucination.

The content of psychotic hallucinations varies considerably from individual to individual (Hamilton, 1984, 1985). Sometimes the voices of patients talk disjointedly or mention odd phrases which seem to have no relevance to their lives. At other times the voices may talk about the patient's private thoughts or guilty secrets. Quite often, the auditory hallucinations of patients diagnosed as schizophrenic, whether they consist of short phrases or more extensive monologues, are abusive in nature. Thus, a patient encountered by the second author heard voices shouting 'Roderick is a queer!' (i.e. homosexual). Another patient experienced third-person voices which exchanged very negative judgements about any decisions he made. Less frequently, the voices may be neutral in attitude towards the patient or even reassuring. Such voices are most often heard by chronically disturbed patients who have a long history of psychiatric disorder. Visual hallucinations are equally variable in content but are again usually affect-laden. For example, a patient described by Hamilton (1984) both heard and saw large numbers of patients being tortured, while a middle-aged female patient encountered by the second author saw repeated visions of the Virgin Mary who had come to prophesy doom.

The functional significance of hallucination-content is a much ignored topic of research but it seems reasonable to assume that, even when hallucinations are caused primarily by biological factors, their content may reflect important psychological concerns or conflicts. Within the psychiatric literature it has been suggested that the mood congruence of hallucinations may be important, particularly with respect to distinguishing between schizophrenic and affective disorders (APA, 1980; Hamilton, 1984).

(iii) The significance of symptom–diagnosis relationships

It is now necessary to assess the significance of these kinds of findings in the light of the controversy surrounding the existence of discrete psychiatric disease entities. Data from research into schizophrenia relevant to this controversy have previously been reviewed by the second author (Bentall, 1986; Bentall, Jackson and Pilgrim, 1988). In fact, the existence or not of a unitary schizophrenia disease entity has been a matter of some debate for many years (see, for example, van Praag, 1976; Sarbin and Mancuso, 1980). With respect to the study of hallucinations, the problem can be stated in this way: given that there is a relationship between the type of hallucination experienced by a patient and his or her psychiatric diagnosis, different hallucinations may reflect or even be caused by different discrete psychiatric disease entities; on the other hand, the reasoning behind this argument may prove to be circular and patients may receive different diagnoses *because*

51

they suffer from different types of symptoms. It is actually quite difficult to devise tests that distinguish between these two possibilities. However, as Wing (1978) has pointed out, the first criterion of a disease entity must be a cluster of traits that tend to occur together. In other words, if certain groups of symptoms tend to be associated with each other but not with other symptoms, it is reasonable to assume that those groups represent meaningful syndromes perhaps caused by different underlying disorders. If, on the other hand, all psychiatric symptoms turn out to be equally related to each other, there are no grounds for confidence about the existence of discrete disease entities, and a dimensional, hierarchical or even random model of symptom distributions may be more appropriate. A slightly different version of this argument has been suggested by Kendell (1975) who noted that, if symptoms belong to discrete psychiatric disease entities, patients suffering from the symptoms of more than one entity should be very rare.

A number of multivariate statistical techniques can be used to evaluate the associations between symptoms. The simplest approach involves testing Kendell's assertion that patients suffering from the symptoms of more than one psychiatric disorder should be rare. The method of discriminant function analysis can be used to study groups of patients with different diagnoses to evaluate the extent to which they share common symptoms. A more difficult approach involves collecting symptom data from patients without respect to diagnosis and using techniques such as factor analysis or cluster analysis to evaluate the extent to which symptoms correlate (in the case of the former) or patients are divisible into groups with common symptoms (in the case of the latter). This approach is a more sophisticated version of the approach used by Zigler and Phillips (1961) described above.

Although Kraepelin distinguished between the manic-depressive psychoses and dementia praecox (renamed 'schizophrenia' by Bleuler) on the basis of outcome, the differential diagnosis of the two conditions has remained problematic. A particular source of difficulty has been the existence of large numbers of patients who apparently suffer from the symptoms of both conditions. Following Kasanin (1933), these patients have often been described as suffering from 'schizo-affective' conditions. Kliest, Leonard and other continental psychiatrists have maintained that these disorders constitute a third variety of psychosis, distinct from both schizophrenia and manic depression (Hamilton, 1984). Beck (1967), on the other hand, has argued that the schizophrenic and affective psychoses exist at either end of a spectrum with the schizo-affective psychoses in the middle. Ollerenshaw (1973), noting a similarity between schizophrenic thought disorder and the manic phase of manic depression, has suggested a third possibility: that schizophrenia and mania are essentially identical. Attempts have been made to establish whether or not a natural dividing line exists between the schizophrenic and affective psychoses using discriminant function analysis. Kendell and his colleagues (Kendell and Gourlay, 1970; Brockington, Kendell, Wainwright, Hillier and Walker, 1979; Kendell and Brockington, 1980) carried out such analyses on symptoms and data collected from large groups of patients with schizophrenic, affective or schizo-affective diagnoses. In none of the studies was it possible to identify clear cut-off points between schizophrenic and manic-depressive conditions.

Attempts to distinguish between schizophrenic and affective symptoms on the basis of outcome have also failed to yield clear evidence of a difference between the two types of condition. It will be recalled that Kraepelin held that schizophrenic patients generally had a very poor outcome whereas the prognosis for manic-depressive patients was held to be more favourable. In fact, the outcome of schizophrenia has proved to be highly variable. Ciompi (1980), for example, studied the lives of 288 patients over a minimum follow-up period of 37 years after admission to hospital. During this period 27 per cent had experienced complete recovery whereas only 22 per cent were judged to have experienced a severe outcome. Similar results were obtained in follow-up studies by Manfred Bleuler (1978) and by Huber, Gross, Schuttler and Linz (1980). More carefully controlled but shorter-term studies have supported these observations. In the USA Strauss and his colleagues (Strauss and Carpenter, 1974a, 1974b; Hawke, Strauss and Carpenter, 1975) followed a group of 131 patients diagnosed as schizophrenic over a five-year period, finding no difference in outcome between groups of patients with different sets of schizophrenic symptoms (e.g. paranoid versus non-paranoid). Moreover, when Strauss and his colleagues compared their schizophrenic group with a small group of hospitalised patients with other diagnoses, only a marginal difference in outcome was discovered.

As discussed earlier, a second method of identifying discrete

53

psychiatric disease entities involves the use of factor analysis or cluster analysis procedures. Factor analysis is a method of evaluating inter-correlations between different traits and has been used to estimate the extent to which symptoms occur in association with each other. Blashfield (1984), in a review of the factor analytic data on psychotic symptoms, has shown how the results obtained reflect difficulties in assessing symptoms and in choosing between a range of available methods of factor analysis. As a result, no consistent picture of the structure of psychotic traits has emerged from the various studies which have been carried out. A further problem with this kind of data has been pointed out by Slade and Cooper (1979), who argued that apparent associations between symptoms might emerge as a result of selection factors. For example, patients with multiple symptoms may come to the attention of psychiatrists more readily than those with few or only one symptom. By using a mathematical procedure in order to take this possibility into account, Slade and Cooper were able to show that, on the available evidence, it was not possible to reject the hypothesis that psychotic symptoms are randomly associated. As Slade and Cooper pointed out, this finding does not prove that a schizophrenia syndrome does not exist but it does suggest that substantial correlations between symptoms can be generated from random data given certain constraints (which may or may not be operating in the real world). Clinical evidence does seem to suggest that certain kinds of symptoms tend to go together. Thus, many authors have argued that delusions often occur following hallucinations as the patient struggles to explain his or her disturbing experiences (Maher, 1974; Hamilton, 1985). Crow (1980a), on the other hand, has argued on biological grounds that separate schizophrenic syndromes of positive symptoms (hallucinations and delusions) and negative symptoms (anhedonia, social withdrawal) can be identified (see Chapter 6). While these kinds of claims cannot meet many of the objections raised by Blashfield or by Slade and Cooper without further empirical evidence, patients exhibiting a combination of delusions and hallucinations do seem to be quite frequently encountered in clinical practice. In this regard, it is interesting to note that a recent factor analysis of psychotic symptom data collected using a well validated psychiatric interview schedule (the Present State Examination) revealed three psychotic syndromes corresponding to positive symptoms (delusions and hallucinations), negative symptoms and disordered thought (Liddle, 1987).

Cluster analysis has been used to address this problem in a rather different way. Instead of measuring the degree of association between symptoms, techniques of cluster analysis can be used to divide patients into groups with similar symptoms. If such groups match diagnoses, there is strong evidence for the existence of discrete forms of psychiatric disorder. In one such analysis carried out as part of the International Pilot Study of Schizophrenia, schizophrenic patients were spread across the ten clusters revealed (WHO, 1975). In a similar analysis carried out by Everitt, Gourlay and Kendell (1971), clusters suggestive of the manic and depressive phases of manic depression, paranoid schizophrenia and, less convincingly, chronic schizophrenia were found; however, the association between diagnosis and clusters was weak and over 60 per cent of the patients fell into two poorly defined clusters containing patients from nearly every diagnostic group.

Of course, the results of these kinds of investigations depend on the quality of the available symptom data. It might therefore be argued that more sophisticated studies would yield different results. It should also be noted that both factor-analytical and cluster-analytical procedures have a number of statistical problems attendant on them which make interpretation of the findings rather difficult (Kendell, 1975; Blashfield, 1984). Nevertheless, those studies that have been carried out suggest that the existence of discrete psychiatric entities is equivocal. If the borderlines between different diagnoses do prove to be arbitrary, it may be that the association between different types of hallucination and diagnoses occurs simply because patients with different types of hallucinations tend to be given different labels.

CONCLUSIONS

Extremes of brain temperature, water intake and breathing pattern have been associated with hallucinations. Abnormalities of physiological functioning should therefore always be considered as a possible explanation for clinically observed hallucinatory experiences.

It would seem that many medical conditions can result in

55

hallucinations or other psychiatric symptoms. Indeed, it is perhaps not surprising that many physicians have been encouraged to look for medical causes of psychiatric disorder. Nevertheless, in the largest study to address this issue so far (Hall *et al.*, 1978), only 9.1 per cent of psychiatric patients were judged to suffer from a medical disorder. Medical disorder must, however, be considered as a possible cause of any hallucinatory experience.

With respect to the relationship between functional psychiatric disorder and hallucination, the following conclusions appear warranted. First, auditory hallucinations are more than twice as common as visual hallucinations in patients diagnosed as schizophrenic, at least in developed countries. Secondly, the opposite is not necessarily true for patients diagnosed as suffering from organic or affective disorders, although visual hallucinations do seem to be more common in patients suffering from these conditions. Finally, as the evidence pertaining to the existence of discrete psychiatric disease entities is equivocal, it is at least possible that auditory hallucinations tend to be associated with schizophrenia because patients suffering from them tend to be labelled schizophrenic.

Certainly, it is difficult to disagree with Asaad and Shapiro (1986) who have argued that, given the wide range of conditions implicated in hallucination, hallucinations of any sort should not be accepted as pathognomic of schizophrenia. One implication of this view is that hallucinations should be studied in their own right, rather than as part of larger psychiatric syndromes.

3

The Social Context of Hallucination

The question of whether or not hallucinations are related to normal mental events has been a matter of dispute over a period of centuries. In the last chapter the traditional medical approach to hallucinations, prevalent in much of the existing literature, was outlined and an attempt was made to relate the phenomenology of different hallucinatory experiences to different types of physical and mental disorder. An assumption underlying much of the work subsumed by this approach is that hallucinatory experiences are strictly pathological in nature. One implication of this assumption is that, with perhaps a few exceptions, hallucinations only occur in mentally or physically ill individuals. A further implication that might be drawn is that hallucinations should be considered qualitatively distinct from normal mental events, although there is less than unanimous agreement among psychopathologists on this latter question. In the present chapter this issue will be examined in further detail. In particular an attempt will be made to discern whether hallucinations are inevitably a sign of illness. In order to address this issue three sources of evidence will be examined: (a) data pertaining to the question of whether hallucinations are related to less pathological forms of experience; (b) data pertaining to the experience of hallucinations in 'normal' individuals; and (c) evidence relating to cultural variation in the experience of hallucinations.

THE CONTINUITY BETWEEN HALLUCINATORY AND OTHER EXPERIENCES

In Chapter 1 it was shown that one of the major conceptual issues to be resolved with respect to hallucinations concerns the extent to which they can be considered continuous with normal mental imagery. Hallucinations certainly do seem to share much in common with dreams, hypnogogic and other forms of imagery, and consistent with this observation some early theorists (e.g. Hibbert, Galton) maintained that these kinds of experiences are related. Others (e.g. Arnold) took a quite different view, arguing that hallucinations are strictly pathological in nature and hence quite distinct from normal mental experiences.

Until quite recently, this question had not been studied using empirical methods. In the last 20 or so years, however, there has been considerable interest in the possibility that a continuum exists between normal and abnormal experiences, fuelled by the suspicion that the study of borderline states might yield important information about mental breakdown, particularly in the case of those patients diagnosed as schizophrenic. Thus, although the idea that mental illness might be dimensional in nature can be traced in the psychiatric literature at least as far back as the work of Kretschmer (1925), one of the earliest psychologists to systematically propound this view with respect to schizophrenia was Meehl (1962). Meehl observed that, while it is generally accepted that schizophrenia has a genetic component, it is also generally believed that not all individuals inheriting a vulnerability to schizophrenia actually become schizophrenic. Meehl therefore proposed that what was inherited was a disposition to schizophrenia, which he labelled *schizotaxia*. Meehl went on to argue that, even in individuals who do not become schizophrenic, schizotaxia may manifest itself in the form of *schizotypal* personality traits. (A rather similar idea to Meehl's was later proposed by Eysenck (Eysenck and Eysenck, 1976) on the basis of research into normal variations in human personality. Eysenck argued that three dimensions of personality — which he labelled extraversion, neuroticism and psychoticism — could be identified and measured by questionnaire. However, Eysenck's psychoticism scale has been a subject of controversy, mainly because it has been argued that it measures antisocial traits rather than psychoticism (Claridge, 1985). Evidence for this viewpoint includes the actual items in the scale, which make little reference to psychotic features of personality or experience, and the fact that socially deviant individuals such as criminals and drug addicts score higher on the scale than psychiatric patients.)

A series of attempts at detecting schizotypal individuals by means of psychometric measures were made in the 1960s and 1970s, using such instruments as the Object Sorting Test, the Rorschach, and the Minnesota Multiphasic Personality Inventory. One strategy used involved looking for particular patterns of questionnaire scores from the non-schizophrenic relatives of schizophrenics (individuals presumably at high risk for schizotypy). Grove (1982) carefully reviewed much of this literature, arguing that, on close examination, differences between high-risk groups and controls on these scales have proved evanescent with the result that 'Construction of single scales or batteries of scales to assess dimensions of differences between schizotypes and non-schizotypes has not delivered on early promises.'

Grove noted that these early attempts to identify schizotypy were based on Bleuler's (1911) conception of schizophrenia which emphasises cognitive disorganisation rather than overt symptomatology. Early tests designed to measure schizotypy therefore shunned overt symptoms such as hallucinations, perhaps on the assumption that non-psychiatrically diagnosed individuals would be unwilling to divulge information about such experiences. In contrast, more recent research into schizotypy has attempted to tap overt symptoms directly (see Grove, 1982; Claridge and Broks, 1984).

Much of the current interest in overt schizotypal symptoms originates from the Danish–American adoption studies of Rosenthal, Wender and Kety. Two types of study were carried out. In one set of studies the biological and adoptive relatives of adopted children who became schizophrenic were traced in an attempt to see whether the biological parents were more likely to be schizophrenic than the adoptive parents or the parents of control adoptees (Kety, Rosenthal, Wender and Schulsinger, 1968; Kety, Rosenthal, Wender, Schulsinger and Jacobsen, 1975). In a second series of studies, the adopted-away offspring of schizophrenic and non-schizophrenic parents were traced and examined for evidence of schizophrenic breakdown (Rosenthal, Wender, Kety, Welner

59

and Schulsinger, 1971; Haier, Rosenthal and Wender, 1978). Although the results of these studies have generally been taken as unequivocal evidence of an inherited predisposition to schizophrenia, closer analysis reveals a number of methodological problems which make interpretation of the data problematic (see Lidz and Blatt, 1983; Lidz, Blatt and Cook, 1981; and Chapter 6). Of particular relevance to the present discussion was the failure of the studies to produce evidence of the inheritance of schizophrenia when only data of breakdowns and hospitalisation were included in the analysis. The investigators therefore broadened their criteria of schizophrenia to include various borderline states which they described as *schizophrenia spectrum disorders*. Using this concept, they claimed a greater prevalence of these disorders in the biological relatives of their target groups, and therefore claimed evidence of the inheritance of a schizotypal disposition.

Because Kety and his colleagues were not confident of their ability to identify the cues to which they had been responding when making a diagnosis of schizophrenia spectrum disorder, Spitzer, Endicott and Gibbon (1979) tried to operationalise the criteria for this diagnosis. In consultation with Kety and others they were able to develop a set of criteria which seemed to discriminate, on the basis of case-note data, between individuals Kety and others had diagnosed as suffering from a schizophrenia spectrum disorder and those they had not so diagnosed. These criteria, which are listed in Table 3.1, were later incorporated into the third edition of the American Psychiatric Association's *Diagnostic and Statistical Manual* (DSM-III; APA, 1980) under the name: *schizotypal personality disorder.*

Spitzer *et al.* were also able to discern a second type of personality disorder, the *borderline personality disorder* frequently referred to in the psychiatric literature, and devised a second set of operational criteria for this form of personality organisation, also listed in Table 3.1. In a less than perfectly controlled questionnaire study to which over 800 American psychiatrists responded (out of over 4000 approached) Spitzer *et al.* found that their criteria seemed to identify those patients the psychiatrists had themselves determined to be schizotypal or borderline. Although the two types of personality organisation were found to be statistically independent, over half of the patients evaluated in the study reached the criteria for both disorders. Claridge and Broks (1984)

60

Table 3.1: DSM-III criteria for schizotypal and borderline personality disorders (APA, 1980)

Criteria for schizotypal personality disorder

A. At least four of the following:

1. Magical thinking, superstitiousness, clairvoyance, telepathy, '6th sense', 'others can feel my feelings' (in children and adolescents, bizarre fantasies or preoccupations).
2. Ideas of reference.
3. Social isolation, e.g. no close friends or confidants, social contacts limited to essential, every-day tasks.
4. Recurrent illusions, sensing the presence of a force or person not actually present (e.g. 'I felt as if my dead mother were in the room with me'), depersonalisation, or derealisation not associated with panic attacks.
5. Odd speech (without loosening of associations or incoherence), e.g. speech that is digressive, vague, overelaborate, circumstantial, metaphorical.
6. Inadequate rapport in face-to-face interaction due to constricted or inappropriate effect, e.g. aloof, cold.
7. Suspiciousness or paranoid ideation.
8. Undue social anxiety or hypersensitivity to real or imagined criticism.

B. Does not meet the criteria for schizophrenia.

Criteria for borderline personality disorder

A. At least five of the following are required:

1. Impulsivity or unpredictability in at least two areas that are potentially self-damaging, e.g. spending, sex, gambling, substance use, shoplifting, self-damaging acts.
2. A pattern of unstable and intense interpersonal relationships, e.g. marked shifts of attitude, idealisation, devaluation, manipulation (constantly using others for one's own ends).
3. Inappropriate intense anger or lack of control of anger, e.g. frequent displays of temper, constant anger.
4. Identity disturbance manifested by uncertainty about several issues relating to identity such as self-image, gender identity, long-term goals or career choice, friendship patterns, values and loyalties.
5. Affective instability, marked shifts from normal mood to depression, irritability or anxiety lasting a few hours and only rarely more than a few days, with a return to normal mood.
6. Intolerance of being alone, e.g. frantic efforts to avoid being alone, depressed when alone.
7. Physically self-damaging acts, e.g. suicidal gestures, self-mutilation, recurrent accidents or physical fights.
8. Chronic feeling of emptiness or boredom.

B. If under 18 years does not meet the criteria for identity disorder.

have subsequently devised two brief questionnaires to detect cognitive and personality traits hypothesised to be important in determining vulnerability to schizotypal and borderline personality disorders.

A rather different symptom-orientated approach to schizotypy was simultaneously developed by Chapman and Chapman and their co-workers, who attempted to design scales to measure individual symptoms they believed to be important in schizophrenia and the schizotypal personality. The Chapmans and their co-workers (Chapman, Chapman and Raulin, 1976) began by developing scales to measure physical and social anhedonia (lack of interest in physical and social pleasures, respectively) and went on to devise scales to measure body image and perceptual aberrations and magical thinking (Chapman, Edell and Chapman, 1980). Preliminary research with normal subjects has indicated a relationship between high scoring on these scales and reports of psychotic-like experiences, difficulty in concentrating, social withdrawal and abnormal responses on the Rorschach inkblot test (Chapman, Edell and Chapman, 1980; Miller and Chapman, 1983).

Before focusing on hallucinations, it is worth placing the concept of schizotypy in perspective. First, it should be noted that the concept of schizotypy has been derived from the diagnostic concept of schizophrenia, the general utility of which has been questioned (see Chapter 2). Secondly, it should be recalled that early attempts to identify psychometric indicators of schizotypy were mostly unreplicated. Thirdly, one current formulation of the schizotypy concept (that incorporated in DSM-III) has been derived from research (the Danish–American adoption studies) which has been criticised on methodological grounds. On the other hand, these objections do not necessarily imply that the concept of schizotypy is not useful, and the more recently developed schizotypy scales of Claridge and the Chapmans show considerable promise as research tools. In particular, it is possible that the study of schizotypal traits will yield information relevant to psychiatric taxonomy and may help to resolve some of the disputes about diagnosis referred to in the previous chapter. Indeed, it seems likely that schizotypy, like schizophrenia itself perhaps, will prove to be a multidimensional phenomenon. Chapman, Edell and Chapman (1980) found that scores on their anhedonia scales were essentially uncorrelated with perceptual aberration scores, suggesting that these two types of schizotypy are unrelated. Muntaner and Garcia-Sevilla (1985), using the Chapman anhedonia scales, Eysenck's P (psychoticism) scale, and Claridge's scales for schizotypal and borderline personality, extracted three factors from data collected from a large group of Spanish students. These factors appeared to reflect positive symptoms, social withdrawal and antisocial behaviour. More recently, the present authors (Bentall, Claridge and Slade, 1988) have collected data from normal subjects using a questionnaire made up of the Eysenck Personality Questionnaire (designed to measure his three personality dimensions of extraversion, neuroticism, and psychoticism, and including a lie scale) and fourteen published scales measuring schizotypal traits or symptoms. These latter scales included those designed by the Chapmans, Claridge's scales, a scale designed by the first author to measure disposition towards hallucinations (the LSHS — see below) and various other scales designed to measure psychotic states or traits (e.g. delusions, attentional difficulties) gleaned from the psychiatric and psychological literature. When the data were factor-analysed, three factors were identified which appeared to be similar to those obtained by Liddle (1987) (described in the previous chapter) from psychiatric subjects given the Present State Examination. Two of the factors seemed to correspond to positive symptom traits (disposition towards hallucinations and delusions) and anhedonia. The third factor seemed to reflect social anxiety and cognitive disorganisation. Of particular interest in the present context is the apparent association observed between hallucinatory and delusional experiences.

Whatever the ultimate virtue of the concept of schizotypy, research in this area, particularly the more recent, symptom-orientated studies, has successfully drawn attention to mental states and behaviours which appear to exist on the borderline between psychosis and normality. Indeed, there can be little doubt that such states exist, and there is no reason why they cannot be investigated without prejudging the question of whether clusters of such states are associated with high risk for schizophrenic breakdown.

A number of relevant studies have been carried out to investigate the relationship between hallucinations and normal experiences. It should be noted that the argument for a continuum

Table 3.2: Examples of scoring criteria for assessing psychotic-like auditory and visual experiences to be used in conjunction with standard psychiatric interview schedules (e.g. Schedule for the Affective Disorders and Schizophrenia — Lifetime version; SADS-L). From Chapman and Chapman (1980), where additional criteria can be found for scoring other hallucinatory and non-hallucinatory psychotic-like experiences

---

Voice experiences and other auditory hallucinations

(Do not score single words, such as hearing one's name called, and do not score hypnogogic and hypnopompic experiences except where specified.)

Item	*Score*

A. S has heard a hallucinatory outer voice that recites a running commentary on his behaviour (a blow-by-blow commentary on a sequence of behaviour as it occurs) or hears two or more outer voices discussing something.

    1. S believed for more than a few minutes that this voice was produced by others. — 10

    2. S suspected for more than a few minutes that the voice was produced by others (or felt this even though he knew better). — 7

    3. S has always attributed the origin to himself. — 5

B. S has heard hallucinatory outer voices other than God, devil, angels and spirits that speak intelligible phrases or sentences other than above.

    1. S believed for more than a few minutes that this voice was produced by others. Example: S reports that last summer she often heard the voice of a man she had once worked for, and for a while believed he really was speaking to her. — 8

    2. S suspected for more than a few minutes that the voice was produced by others (or felt this even though he knew better). — 6

    3. S has always attributed the origin to himself. Example: S heard an outer voice of a friend at frequent intervals over a 3-month period, but reports always being aware that the experience must be her own imagination. — 4

C. S has heard hallucinatory outer voices of God, the devil, angels, or spirits that speak intelligible phrases or sentences.

    1. S believed for more than a few minutes that the voice was produced by others. Example: S regularly hears 'spirit guides' speaking outside the head, giving advice and information. — 6–8

    2. S has suspected for more than a few minutes that the voice was produced by others (or felt this even though he knew better). Example: S heard outer voices that he thinks may be the devil or may instead be his own imagination. — 4–6

3. S has always attributed the origin to himself. Example: S hears an outer voice that sounds like God's voice but S knows it could not be, and that he must himself be responsible.   3–5

Visual hallucinations and other visual experiences

A. S saw hallucinatory objects outside of self, other than when resting or meditating.
    1. S believed the experience was veridical for more than a few minutes.
        (a) The hallucinatory percepts were very brief. Example: S has hallucinated people in brief flashes. He attributes the experience to his psychic power.   6
        (b) The hallucinatory percepts were longer than a moment. Example: S has trouble driving because she hallucinates automobiles which are not there.   8
    2. Same experience as 1 above, but the perception has subcultural support.
        (a) Brief.   3
        (b) Not brief. Example: S sees a coloured 'aura' around people he meets. The interviewer has a blue aura which is a 'good' aura.   4
    3. Same experience as either 1 or 2 above, but S merely suspected that the experience was veridical (or felt it was even though he knew better) for more than a few minutes.   3
    4. Same experience as 1 or 2, but S believed that the experience was veridical no longer than a few minutes, or never believed it was veridical. Example: S often catches brief glimpses of little animals which she then realises are not there.   2

---

between hallucinatory and 'normal' experience rests on two separate but related claims: first, that there are experiences which lie between hallucinations and, say, vivid imagery in terms of phenomenology; secondly, that these hallucinatory and borderline events are related in the sense that individuals prone to experiencing one type of event may also be prone to experiencing the other.

Evidence for the first claim has been provided by Strauss (1969), who studied patients' responses during the Present State Examination (Wing, Cooper and Sartorius, 1974), the structured psychiatric interview used in the International Pilot Study on Schizophrenia. Strauss concluded that a significant number of patients report experiences intermediate between strict hallucinations and normal mental states (e.g. when a patient reports that he or she thinks he or she has seen the shadow of a man next to his

Table 3.3: Items from the Launay–Slade Hallucination Scale (LSHS) from Launay and Slade (1981). In the original study by Launay and Slade, items were scored as either 'applies to myself' or 'does not apply to myself'. In subsequent studies by Bentall and Slade (1985a, b) and Young, Bentall, Slade and Dewey (1986, 1987) a five-point scoring system was employed (0='certainly does not apply to me'; 1='probably does not apply to me'; 2='unsure'; 3='probably applies to me'; and 4='certainly applies to me'). Also shown are the number and percentage of subjects scoring each item as 'certainly applies to me' in the studies by Bentall and Slade (1985a) and Young *et al.* (1986)

	Subjects scoring items as 'certainly applies to me'			
	Bentall and Slade (N=136 males)		Young *et al.* (N=101 males and 103 females)	
	N	%	N	%
1. Sometimes a passing thought will seem so real it frightens me.	27	19.9	44	21.5
2. Sometimes my thoughts seem as real as actual events in my life.	36	26.5	49	24.0
3. No matter how much I try to concentrate on my work, unrelated thoughts always creep into my mind.	67	49.3	106	51.9
4. In the past I have had the experience of hearing a person's voice and then found that no one was there.	21	15.4	27	13.2
5. The sounds I hear in my daydreams are usually clear and distinct.	26	19.1	28	13.7
6. The people in my daydreams seem so true to life that I sometimes think they are.	11	8.1	24	11.7

7.	In my daydreams I can hear the sound of a tune almost as clearly as if I were actually listening to it.	56	41.2	77	37.7
8.	I often hear a voice speaking my thoughts aloud.	24	17.7	28	13.7
9.	I have been troubled by hearing voices in my head.	0	0.0	4	1.9
10.	On occasions I have seen a person's face in front of me when no one was in fact there.	4	2.9	3	1.4
11.	I have heard the voice of the devil.	4	2.9	2	0.9
12.	In the past I have heard the voice of God speaking to me.	2	1.5	11	5.3

car). On the basis of this observation, Strauss suggested that both normal and pathological mental states (he considered delusions as well as hallucinations) varied along four major dimensions that can be viewed as criteria for degree of pathology: (a) the strength of the individual's conviction in the objective reality of his or her experiences; (b) the extent to which there is an absence of direct cultural or stimulus determinants (e.g. the absence of a fundamentalist religious background in a person who thinks that the devil is influencing his or her behaviour); (c) the amount of time spent preoccupied with the experience; and (d) the implausibility of the experience (e.g. seeing a man from Mars as compared with mistaking seeing a car outside one's house).

Chapman and Chapman (1980) subsequently designed a simple method of rating the point at which such experiences fall on the continuum between normality and abnormality. Descriptions of a series of experiences relating to a range of psychiatric symptoms were submitted to judges who rated them on an 11-point scale on which zero indicated minimal deviancy from normality. Sufficient consistency was found in the judges' responses to allow the modal ratings to be used in the final scales, designed for rating responses given during structured psychiatric interviews. Examples of rating values for several types of hallucinatory experience are shown in Table 3.2. In assigning these scores to interview responses, raters are allowed to subtract or add a point according to whether the interviewee comes from a background that encourages or discourages the experiences in question. Even so, the Chapmans have discouraged the use of these scales with individuals from markedly non-Western or highly religious (e.g. spiritualist) backgrounds, thus highlighting the importance of cultural events in determining the attribution of pathology to abnormal experiences (see below).

Evidence also exists relating to the second claim to be considered — that vivid non-pathological experiences and hallucinations are psychologically related in the sense that individuals prone to the former will also be vulnerable to the latter. Launay and Slade (1981) gave statements relating to both types of experience to individuals suffering hallucinations and to control subjects. Launay and Slade were able to identify 12 items which discriminated between the two groups. Of these items, a number referred to non-hallucinatory experiences (e.g. 'No matter how hard I concentrate on my work, unrelated thoughts always creep into my mind' and 'In my daydreams I can hear the sound of a tune almost as clearly as if I were actually listening to it'). These items were subsequently compiled into the Launay–Slade Hallucination Scale (LSHS; see Table 3.3) which was tested on a group of 200 prisoners and 54 normal subjects (prison psychologists). When data from these subjects were analysed, it was found that responses to the scale fitted a mathematical model devised by Rasch (1966) to test whether items measure related events; in other words, individuals were more likely to score on the non-pathological items on the scale if they scored on the pathological items. Research carried out using the LSHS will be described in more detail below and in subsequent chapters.

HALLUCINATIONS IN NORMAL INDIVIDUALS

If, as has been suggested, hallucinations are not necessarily associated with a particular psychiatric diagnosis, and if hallucinations exist on a continuum with normal mental events, it is logical to enquire into the prevalence of true hallucinatory experiences in normal individuals. In fact, one implication of abandoning a strictly medical model of schizophrenia is that psychotic symptoms should be represented to some extent in individuals who are not mentally ill.

The available evidence suggests that the prevalence of symptoms of mental disorder is surprisingly high among people living within the community who do not consider themselves to be in any way odd or deranged. For example, in the famous Midtown study of mental health in the community, carried out in Manhattan in the late 1950s, only about a quarter of all those interviewed were considered to be completely free from psychiatric impairment (Srole, Langner, Michael, Opler and Rennie, 1961). Although the Midtown team did not investigate the prevalence of specific symptoms, approximately 6 per cent of the individuals in their sample were judged to reach the criteria for psychotic disorder as assessed from their questionnaire responses (Langner and Michael, 1962). Comparable results have been obtained in other community surveys (Dohrenwend and Dohrenwend, 1974) and in questionnaire studies carried out in the UK (Cochrane and Stopes-Roe, 1980).

A few attempts have been made to assess the prevalence of specifically hallucinatory experiences in the general population. Of these, most (not surprisingly, given the widespread acceptance of the pathological model) have been motivated by an interest in religious or parapsychological phenomena. Without exception the sampling methods employed leave much to be desired. None the less, they are worth considering in some detail because the results obtained consistently cast doubt on the notion that hallucinations are exclusively associated with mental or physical pathology.

The earliest and most extensive of these studies was carried out by Sidgewick et al. (1894) on behalf of the Society for Psychical Research. In total, 7717 men and 7599 women were interviewed by a large team of correspondents to the project. Although the selection of subjects was not random, people suffering from obvious signs of mental or physical illness were excluded. Of the total sample, 7.8 per cent of the men and 12 per cent of the women reported at least one hallucinatory experience in their lifetime. Hallucinations appeared to occur most frequently among subjects aged between 20 and 29 years (subsequently discovered to be the maximum risk period for the diagnosis of schizophrenia, see

Hamilton, 1984), and visual hallucinations were more common than auditory hallucinations (in contrast with patients recently diagnosed as schizophrenic for whom the reverse is the case, at least in developed countries — see below). The most common type of hallucination, as classified by content, was of living persons absent at the time of the experience. Hallucinations with a religious or supernatural content formed a small but significant minority of the phenomena recorded. In an attempt to establish the psychical significance of hallucinations, Sidgewick argued that a small proportion of the experiences reported were veridical (i.e. depicted some distant event that later turned out to be true).

The Sidgewick study was followed up by West (1948) who was interested in the possibility that, with the lapse of 50 and more years and in a technologically more sophisticated era, hallucinations would be less common. West used the 'Mass Observation' organisation to distribute a questionnaire designed to cover the same topics as those covered in the interviews carried out by Sidgewick. The replies were often less than satisfactory, and many of the respondents did not complete the questionnaire adequately. However, the results, such as they were, lent general support to those of Sidgewick. Of 1519 subjects who replied, 217 or 14.3 per cent reported having experienced hallucinations. As before, female respondents reported hallucinations more often than males, and hallucinations were more often reported in the visual rather than the auditory modality. As Sidgewick had found, multimodal hallucinations were comparatively rare (11.6 per cent in 1894; 8.4 per cent in 1948). Moreover, in contrast to Sidgewick, West found that none of the hallucinations reported was convincingly veridical.

The first report of a modern census of hallucinations was made by McKellar (1968), who questioned a group of 500 'normal' people and found that 125 reported at least one hallucinatory experience. Although McKellar gave few details in his account it is clear that the experiences reported were genuine hallucinations:

Some of the visual hallucinations related to early life, and some had religious content, for example, 'seeing an angel in church during the service', and, 'early in adolescence I saw God (conventional white-robed with beard) ... and the Devil', equally conventional. Others were auditory, frequently of voices speaking and one of 'sounds of a dog known to be dead'. Tactile hallucinations, for example 'feeling a tap on the shoulder' were also reported by some subjects, together with hallucinations of smell, such as the 'smell of food cooking when nothing to account for it'.

Similar findings have recently been reported by Posey and Losch (1983), who questioned a sample of 375 college students. No less than 71 per cent of their subjects reported some experience of at least brief, occasional hallucinated voices during periods of wakefulness. Thirty-nine per cent reported the Schneiderian symptom of hearing thoughts spoken aloud. Five per cent of the subjects reported holding conversations with their hallucinations.

A slightly different approach to investigating hallucinations in normal individuals involves the use of standardised scales, similar to the schizotypy scales discussed earlier in the chapter. A standardised measure of disposition towards hallucination that is currently available is the Launay–Slade Hallucination Scale (LSHS), the construction of which was described above. Three studies carried out by the present authors involved testing samples of normal individuals on this scale. Although the choice of sample in each case left something to be desired, the results are consistent with the earlier research.

In Launay and Slade's original study a control group of 54 prison psychologists were asked to score each of the items on the LSHS as applying to themselves or not applying to themselves. In a second study by Bentall and Slade (1985a) 136 male undergraduate students were required to complete two parallel forms of a modified version of the scale in which each of the 12 items had to be scored on a five-point scale ('certainly applies', 'possibly applies', 'unsure', 'possibly does not apply', and 'certainly does not apply'). In the final study Young *et al.* (1986) gave the modified LSHS to 203 male and female undergraduate students.

Data from the latter two studies are given in Table 3.3, which shows the number and percentage of subjects scoring each of the items as 'certainly applies'. The findings of the studies were highly consistent, showing that a considerable proportion of individuals were prepared to score even some of the most 'pathological' items as applying to themselves. For example, the percentages of subjects scoring the Schneiderian item 'I often hear a voice speaking my thoughts aloud' as certainly applying to themselves were 17.7

71

per cent and 13.7 per cent in the studies by Bentall and Slade and by Young *et al.*, respectively. Bentall and Slade were able to investigate the distribution and reliability of scores on the LSHS. As shown in Figure 3.1, scores on the scale were approximately normally distributed, suggesting that the disposition to hallucinate varies on a continuum. The reliability of the scale, as assessed by the subjects' responses on a parallel form after a period of several weeks, was acceptable, suggesting that the scale may measure a reasonably stable trait. In the final study of the series, Young *et al.* compared the LSHS scores of male and female subjects and found that the female subjects scored, on average, slightly but significantly higher on the scale. This result is consistent with the sex differences in reported hallucinations found by Sidgewick (1894) and West (1948).

Further evidence that hallucinations are not strictly pathological phenomena can be found in studies of hypnotic suggestion. Barber (1970) noted that, while textbooks of hypnosis often state that auditory and visual hallucinations can be induced in hypnotised subjects by means of suggestion, it is not always clear what is meant by this assertion because the criteria for hallucination are usually ill-defined and the nature of hypnosis remains something of a mystery. In fact, the concept of 'hypnotism' is particularly problematic because no physiological correlate of a trance state has been demonstrated, nor is it clear that hypnotised subjects do things that they would not otherwise do given an appropriate incentive. For this reason, some theorists have suggested that hypnosis is a social–psychological phenomenon and that the behaviour of hypnotised subjects should be seen as a form of compliance to unusual social pressure (Barber, 1969; Wagstaff, 1983).

For example, in order to test whether hypnotically induced hallucinations are genuine hallucinations, Rosenthal and Mele (1952) presented hypnotised subjects with grey cards and suggested that the cards were a particular colour (e.g. red). They then asked the subjects to report the colour of a second grey card on the hypothesis that, if the subjects had genuinely hallucinated the suggested colour, they should see the negative afterimage (green) on the second card. In fact, the four subjects all reported such an afterimage. In a more complex study by Underwood (1960), however, subjects were asked to positively or negatively

Figure 3.1:

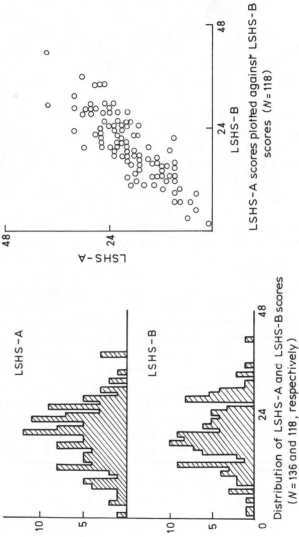

Distribution of LSHS-A and LSHS-B scores
(*N* = 136 and 118, respectively)

LSHS-A scores plotted against LSHS-B
scores (*N* = 118)

hallucinate critical parts of various illusion figures; a significant effect on the reporting of the illusions was achieved for only one of the three figures, and then only for the subjects in the deep-trance condition. A general problem with this kind of research is that the subjects involved have been selected for their suggestibility. In order to demonstrate that there is something to hypnosis beyond social compliance, it is necessary to show that a trance state is required to achieve these kinds of results.

A number of studies have been carried out by Barber and his colleagues in order to investigate the effects of suggestions to hallucinate in the absence of a hypnotic induction procedure. Barber and Calverley (1964) tested 78 secretarial students using the suggestion, 'I want you to close your eyes and hear a phonograph record with words and music playing "White Christmas". Keep listening to the phonograph record playing "White Christmas" until I tell you to stop.' After 30 seconds the subjects were asked to check a rating scale with the following options: (a) they had not heard the record; (b) they had had a vague impression of hearing the record; (c) they had clearly heard the record but they had not believed that it was being played; and (d) they had clearly heard the record and had believed that it was being played.

Barber and Calverley found that no less than 49 per cent of their subjects reported that they had clearly heard the record and 5 per cent stated that, in addition, they had believed the record was being played. On a similar visual task in which the subjects were asked to see a cat sitting in their lap, 31 per cent reported seeing the cat and 2.5 per cent reported believing that the cat existed.

Surprising though this result may seem, it has been replicated by Bowers (1967), who used 40 undergraduate students as subjects, and by Spanos and Barber (1968), who used 98 female nurses. Using a method of scoring in which a score of 1 indicates not reporting perception of the suggested stimulus; 2 indicates reporting a vague perception of the suggested stimulus; 3 indicates reporting a clear perception of the suggested stimulus; and 4 indicates reporting both perception of the stimulus and belief in its existence, the subjects in these two studies actually obtained higher scores on average than those obtained by Barber and Calverley (see Table 3.4, taken from Barber, 1970).

Considerable research has been carried out in an attempt to delineate the parameters of this phenomenon. For example,

Table 3.4: Mean scores of subjects in three studies using the Barber and Calverley (1964) test. Scoring for both auditory and visual items was on a four-point scale (4=saw or heard suggested item and believed it had been presented; 3=saw or heard suggested item but knew it was not there; 2=saw or heard a vague impression of suggested item; 1=did not see or hear suggested item). From Barber (1970). See text for details

Study	Mean auditory hallucination score	Mean visual hallucination score
Barber and Calverley (1964) (N=78)	2.31	1.97
Bowers (1967) (N=40)	2.50	2.05
Spanos and Barber (1968) (N=90)	2.33	1.95

Thorne (1967) selected hypnotically susceptible subjects and found no difference between a hypnotised group and an instructed group in terms of their ability to hallucinate a song as measured by the song's interference with a memory task. Sarbin and Andersen (1963) attempted to replicate Underwood's (1960) results using randomly selected subjects and instructions rather than hypnotic induction; whereas only 3 per cent of Underwood's subjects had achieved the deep trance state necessary to produce hallucinatory responses, 9 per cent of Sarbin and Andersen's subjects reported perceiving the required visual illusion.

In an attempt to look at the role of social variables in suggested hallucinations, Bowers (1967) and Spanos and Barber (1968) considered the possibility that the task demands of the Barber and Calverley procedure might make subjects report a greater conviction in the reality of the suggested stimulus than they really felt. In both studies groups of subjects were exposed to demands for honesty (a short lecture to the effect that the subjects should be honest and not report experiences just to please the experimenter) and task-motivating instructions (instructions to the effect that the subjects should try and 'control their minds' and perform well). The demands for honesty did not reduce the percentage of subjects willing to report belief in the reality of the suggested stimuli. The task-motivating instructions, on the other hand, had the effect of increasing the number of subjects prepared to report belief in the stimuli *unless* they were accompanied by the demands for honesty, in which case they had no effect at all.

One factor that may be of particular importance in this procedure is the wording of the rating scale used. McPeake and Spanos (1973), using Barber and Calverley's visual paradigm, provided subjects with a rating scale in which they were given the opportunity to state that they clearly 'imagined' rather than 'saw' the cat. The result was a reduction in the percentage of subjects willing to state that they had believed in the existence of the cat, although some subjects (approximately 1 per cent) continued to report this, a result replicated by Spanos, Ham and Barber (1973). This finding is particularly interesting given Sarbin's (1967) suggestion that an individual's description of his or her own imaginings may make all the difference in determining whether or not that person is labelled as a hallucinator. Obviously the social context of the experiment is also important. Spanos (1986) remarked that

> While responding to a hallucination suggestion, subjects are operating on the basis of normative expectations that encourage the interpretation of imaginings as 'real events'. However, when the suggestion is terminated, a new set of expectations comes into play. Both the experimenter and the subject know that it is appropriate for the subject now to acknowledge that the suggested object was never really there. On the other hand, when implicit norms encourage (rather than discourage) continued belief in the nonself, unintended origin of imaginings, then retrospective undoing need not occur.

It seems clear from this observation, and from the results of the questionnaire studies cited above, that many more people at least have the capacity to hallucinate than a strictly medical model implies should be the case. Of course, it might be objected that the results obtained by Barber and Calverley and those who have used their method are precisely a product of a rather unusual social context. However, there is at least some evidence to suggest that these findings relate to every-day experiences. For example, Foulkes and Fleisher (1975) interrupted normal subjects during periods of relaxed wakefulness and questioned them about their imaginings. Nineteen per cent of those questioned reported images which they believed to be real at the time of their occurrence.

HALLUCINATION AND CULTURE

A final source of evidence that calls into question the view that hallucinations are strictly pathological phenomena emerges from the study of cultural variation in hallucinatory experience.

Wide cultural variations in attitude towards hallucination have been noted by a number of authors (Bourguignon, 1970; Rabkin, 1970; Al-Issa, 1977, 1978) and were briefly considered in Chapter 1. As Rabkin has pointed out, in many societies hallucinations, far from being regarded as evidence of a deranged mind, are actively sought out, often by resort to extreme and perhaps dangerous measures (e.g. by ingestion of toxic substances or by pushing the body to the point of extreme exhaustion). Bourguignon noted that 'trance' states, in which individuals apparently perceive and commune with spirits, are particularly valued in many so-called 'primitive' cultures. In a survey of the anthropological literature pertaining to 488 societies, Bourguignon found that, in 62 per cent of his world-wide sample, such hallucinations play a major role in ritual practices. In the majority of cases, these hallucinations were not induced by the ingestion of psychoactive chemicals.

Communication with spirits may have a number of functions and, in such societies, the nature of the communication may determine whether or not the experience of the hallucinator is regarded as pathological. When guidance is sought from a spirit, the experience of the spirit's presence may be particularly valued. When the spirit imposes itself on the individual to correct some cultural wrong-doing, the spirit can usually be exorcised by the individual mending his ways or making some form of atonement.

For example, it is taboo for a Mohawk Indian to eat his own game, and if he does so he will be haunted by the spirits of his kill until he makes suitable reparation (Bourguignon, 1970). Experiences of this sort may prove clinically important. For example, McDonald and Oden (1977), clinical psychologists working in Hawaii, were asked to treat two members of the indigenous population, both male students, who suffered from hallucinations of dead relatives. After failing with a variety of behavioural techniques, including desensitisation (see Chapter 7), they decided to enquire into the cultural significance of these experiences. Although the people they approached for information (mostly native Hawaiian friends and colleagues) showed some reluctance to discuss the issue, McDonald and Oden were able to establish that confrontations with dead ancestors (called *aumakua*) were relatively common among the Hawaiians (approximately 40 per cent of the people they approached said they had experienced them) and typically resulted from the violation of a cultural taboo. The function of the *aumakua* was to prompt the individual into mending his ways. On further investigation, McDonald and Oden found that their two patients had indeed transgressed cultural laws, and the instruction to make amends was sufficient to bring the hallucinations to an end.

Of course, the haunting of sinners by ghosts is a familiar theme within our own culture (Finucane, 1982). Sometimes, especially if the hauntings persist and are accompanied by other symptoms, the victim may come to the attention of the psychiatric services. As Kroll and Bachrach (1982) have pointed out, hallucinations of a religious nature appear to be particularly associated with self-destructive acts. They illustrated their case with such examples as a young man who shot himself after he failed to heed his voices which were telling him to bring his extended family together; and a young woman who cut off her right hand with a power saw in response to a vision of Henry Kissinger as the Antichrist.

Notwithstanding the data described in the previous chapter, there is at least some evidence of differences in the type of hallucinatory experience reported to psychiatrists in different countries (Al-Issa, 1977, 1978). As detailed in the last chapter, in Western societies auditory hallucinations are comparatively common and visual hallucinations are comparatively rare among psychiatric patients. In non-Western societies, however, this may not be the case. In the one study cited in Table 2.2 not carried out in the West, Zarroug (1975) in Saudi Arabia found that just over 50 per cent of hallucinations reported by patients diagnosed as schizophrenic were in both the auditory and visual modality. A further 12 per cent of hallucinators reported purely visual hallucinations, and only 17 per cent suffered purely auditory hallucinations. Similar results were found by Murphy, Wittkower, Fried and Ellenberger (1963) in Africa and the Near East; by Rubenstein (1976) for psychiatrically disturbed Cuban immigrants to the USA; by Krassioevitch, Perez-Rincon and Suarez (1982) for schizophrenic patients in Mexico; and by Ndetei and Singh (1983) for patients diagnosed as schizophrenic in a Kenyan mental hospital. A different pattern still was discovered by Collomb (1965) who found that, among psychiatrically disturbed Senegalese patients, hallucinations of transient sounds or odours were particularly common. As this book was being completed, the preliminary results of the World Health Organization Collaborative Study on Determinants of Outcome of Severe Mental Disorders (a follow-up to the International Pilot Study of Schizophrenia) were reported (Sartorius, Jablensky, Korten, Ernberg, Anker, Cooper and Day, 1986). Symptom profiles of psychotic patients were collected from twelve centres world-wide. Complete analyses of this substantial data set have yet to be published, but the initial analysis allowed a comparison of the symptom profiles of first-admission psychotic patients in developed and undeveloped countries. Although the profiles were generally similar, a greater incidence of visual hallucinations was noted in the developing countries, a result consistent with the data already reviewed above. Not surprisingly, some authors have argued that a lack of awareness of cultural differences in hallucination can lead to patients from ethnic minority groups being misdiagnosed as suffering from schizophrenia (Liss, Welner, Robins and Richardson, 1973).

The possibility that the quality of hallucinations may vary with time as well as geography must be considered. Jablensky and Sartorius (1975) have argued that it is particularly difficult to carry out historical studies of psychotic symptoms for periods before the nineteenth century because of the paucity of the available data. However, Kroll and Bachrach (1982) compared the religious hallucinations of 23 contemporary psychiatric patients with 134 reports of visions collected from the writings of medieval European scholars. Although the medieval visions were not considered as examples of insanity at the time, they were similar in many ways to the hallucinations reported by the modern patients. Leinz (1964), on the other hand, analysed psychiatric records in Vienna for a 100-year period and found a steady fall in the number of visual hallucinations reported, matched by a comparable increase in the reporting of auditory hallucinations. Diethelm (1956) reported a similar result from an analysis of the records of a North American psychiatric clinic. It is interesting to note that comparable changes have been reported for other types of psychotic symptoms and syndromes. This, it has often been observed that catatonic (motor disturbance) symptoms of schizophrenia have become less common during the past century (Cooper and Sartorius, 1977; Hare, 1983). Moreover, it is possible that the severity of psychotic symptomatology has generally decreased with time. Zubin, Magaziner and Steinhauer (1983), on the basis of a review of a series of studies on the outcome of schizophrenia, have argued that the course and prognosis of schizophrenia have become progressively more benign since the turn of the century.

The causes of these cultural and historical differences are difficult to assess. As Al-Issa (1977, 1978) has observed, one factor of importance may be the degree of tolerance that a culture shows to reports of perceptions which cannot be publicly verified. In some cultures, the reporting of hallucinations is positively reinforced whereas in other cultures (particularly the West) it may lead to less than pleasant consequences. Moreover, as Kroll and Bachrach (1982) have noted, the folk theory of visions and voices adopted by a culture may be important in determining whether a hallucination is viewed as veridical or as evidence of insanity. Medieval visions, though often similar to the experiences of modern-day schizophrenics, were typically classified as true perceptions of heavenly or satanic events. Indeed, medieval writings on insanity make few references to hallucination and instead take overt evidence of disturbed behaviour (e.g. babbling, wandering aimlessly, thrashing, biting) as diagnostic of madness. In this respect, it is interesting to note that comparable trends in the seeing of ghosts can be identified. Finucane (1982), in his extensive social history of ghosts, noted, for example, that apparitions were relatively common in Victorian England in comparison with today.

It is unlikely that differences in attitude towards the reporting of hallucinations is the whole story, however. For example, it is difficult to see how this could account for as many as 40 per cent of native Hawaiians observing *aumakua* (McDonald and Oden, 1977) whereas at the most between 10 and 20 per cent of British adults have experienced hallucinations. The observed cultural and historical variations in modality of hallucination are also difficult to account for purely in terms of reporting bias. (Some of the historical variations in hauntings are similarly difficult to explain in terms of cultural differences in attitude towards reporting them. For example, Finucane has shown that the ghosts of ancient Greece were generally powerless and pitiable, whereas Roman ghosts were threatening and dangerous.) Given that these observations do reflect genuine differences in the frequency and quality of hallucinations in different areas of the world and at different times, it would appear that we must seek the causes of hallucination, at least in part, in the social and historical environment of the hallucinator.

CONCLUSIONS

There can be no doubt that hallucinations are often pathological in the sense that they are associated with an underlying disturbance or disease. In the present chapter an attempt was made to find out whether this is invariably the case.

It seems clear that hallucinations are related to non-pathological mental phenomena. Experiences which are 'hallucination-like' but which are not usually regarded as indicative of mental illness are statistically associated with full hallucination reports. There can also be little doubt that hallucinations occur to a limited extent in individuals who are not otherwise mentally ill. The implication of these findings is that hallucinations will only be understood in the context of an understanding of normal cognitive processes. Finally, the social context of the hallucinator also appears to be important, both in determining the reporting of hallucinations and in determining the attribution of mental pathology to the hallucinating individual. It would appear, therefore, that a full understanding of hallucinations must appeal not only to normal cognitive processes but also to the social roots of decisions about what is real and what is imaginary.

4

Variables Affecting the Experience of Hallucination

In the preceding chapters, a number of important conceptual issues have been examined. In the present chapter, the role of variables that seem to affect the occurrence of hallucinations will be considered. Data about the effects of these variables constitute the raw information that any model of hallucination must attempt to explain.

A number of variables have been found to affect the probability that a given individual will hallucinate in a given situation. These variables include environmental events, constitutional factors and learning effects. Because many of the relevant data have been collected from subjects suffering from psychotic hallucinations, caution may be necessary when attempting to extrapolate findings about these variables to other types of hallucinatory experience (e.g. drug-induced hallucinations).

Some years ago the first author outlined a working model which was essentially a functional analysis of auditory hallucinations (Slade, 1976a). In this model the important antecedents of hallucinatory behaviour were hypothesised to be psychological stress, degree of hallucinatory predisposition and environmental stimulation. In addition, it was proposed that hallucinations are affected by their reinforcing consequences for the hallucinator. This hypothetical four-factor model or functional analysis is outlined in Figure 4.1.

The model suggests that 'stress events' (factor 1) lead to a generalised elevation and disturbance of mood which can be characterised as a state of high internal arousal. This state of high internal arousal was viewed as interacting with the individual's

Figure 4.1: A functional analysis of hallucinations (from Slade, 1976a)

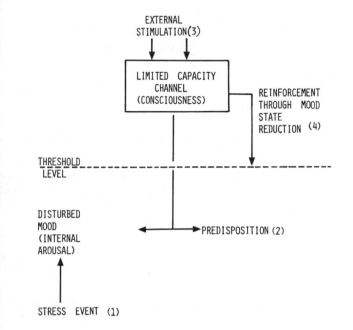

current level of hallucinatory predisposition (factor 2). If the outcome of this interaction is sufficient to raise the hallucinatory tendency above a critical threshold level, it was argued, a hallucinatory experience will be triggered in consciousness. Thus the two critical antecedents (stress and individual predisposition) were viewed as interactive. Minimal stress, it was argued, may trigger hallucinations in highly predisposed individuals while severe stress would be necessary to trigger a comparable experience in a mildly predisposed person.

According to this model, other factors may influence both the occurrence and future probability of hallucinatory experiences. One of these, it was argued, is the prevailing level of environmental stimulation (factor 3) to which the individual is currently responding. Given a limited channel capacity model of consciousness (with all its philosophical problems — see the next chapter) it was suggested that hallucinatory experiences may only gain access to consciousness at the expense of the individual attending to external sources of stimulation. On this view, relevant external stimulation may block the experience of internally generated events such as hallucinations.

The final factor in the hypothetical model was reinforcement. On the argument that at least some patients report improved mood following a hallucinatory episode, it was suggested that this may serve to reinforce the experience, thereby increasing its probability of occurrence on future occasions. In Figure 4.1 this is shown as operating by lowering the threshold level for the individual. Thus, with many repeated hallucinatory experiences, it was predicted that the individual patient's threshold for hallucination will be brought down to a low level such that virtually any stressful stimulus (however mild) will be capable of triggering a hallucinatory experience. In essence, it was proposed that factor 2 (predisposition) may be modified by factor 4 (reinforcement). Another implication of the model is that 'acute' and 'chronic' hallucinations may be subject to different controlling stimuli.

In the 1976 paper the then existing support for the four-factor model was described. In considering variables affecting hallucination in the present context, it will be useful to take this model as a framework and to update the empirical evidence relating to each of the four factors.

PSYCHOLOGICAL STRESS

The term 'stress' has been used in a variety of ways in psychology, for example to describe classes of environmental stimuli, particular types of physiological and psychological responses, and intervening (cognitive or emotional) variables (Cox, 1976). In the paper referred to above, a 'stress event' was conceived of as any event, of either external (situational) or internal (cognitive) origin, which gives rise to a relative elevation and disturbance of mood state, specifically of tension and anxiety. The essential feature of this definition is that it is response-based rather than stimulus-based. It therefore follows that a stimulus event which is perceived and responded to as threatening by one individual may not be so by another individual.

In spite of the need to recognise individual differences in

response to the same or similar stressors, it is still possible to denote general types of 'stress event' which have the potential for triggering hallucinatory activity. A useful fourfold classification of general stressors is based on two kinds of distinction (see Table 4.1). The first distinction is between (a) discrete, traumatic (acute) stress and (b) continuous, moderate (chronic) stress. Studies on the social psychiatry of psychoses have highlighted the relevance of both acute, traumatic stress (life events) and chronic, continuous stress (particularly high expressed emotion on the part of a key relative) on both schizophrenic breakdown and relapse. Birley and Brown (1970), for example, found a quadrupling in the number of independent life events (acute stressors) reported by 50 schizophrenic patients in the three-week period immediately preceding breakdown or relapse. This compared with a steady rate of stressful life events reported by a control sample of 325 factory workers over a 12-week period. This finding has generally been replicated in subsequent studies, although Rabkin (1980), noting a number of methodological problems inherent in this kind of work, has argued that the relationship between stress events and schizophrenic breakdown may be weaker than earlier authors had suggested.

Brown, Birley and Wing (1972) also developed a method of measuring the 'expressed emotion' (EE) of key relatives of schizophrenic patients using a structured interview approach. Three specific indices were found to be strongly related to the overall measure of expressed emotion: (a) the number of critical comments made by family members; (b) manifest hostility; and (c) emotional over-involvement by family members. Applying these measures to the key relatives of 101 schizophrenic patients, they found that 58 per cent of those with high EE relatives relapsed

Table 4.1: A four-fold classification of stress events

Type of stress	Situational	Cognitive
Discrete	e.g. life events	e.g. ruminations about life events
Continuous	e.g. expressed emotion of relatives	e.g. worries about high expressed emotion relatives

during the follow-up period as compared with only 16 per cent of patients with low EE relatives.

In a subsequent paper Vaughn and Leff (1976) reported on the nine-month relapse rates of a sample of 128 schizophrenic patients, focusing particularly on the interaction between the protective value of tranquilliser medication and the stressful effects of expressed emotion (see Figure 4.2). They found that, when key relatives were rated low on EE, the relapse rate was also low and no advantage was obtained from medication; however, when relatives were rated high on EE, they found that medication did significantly reduce the likelihood of relapse. One other variable that was found to be relevant to relapse in patients from high EE families was the amount of time spent in direct face-to-face contact. Where this was more that 35 hours per week, relapse rates were particularly high, rising to 92 per cent among patients not receiving medication. This clearly demonstrates the importance of continuous, moderately disturbing stress events to such patients over and beyond the more easily identifiable acute, traumatic forms of stress. Subsequent research has generally borne out this observed relationship between expressed emotion, medication and relapse (Barrowclough and Tarrier, 1984; Atkinson, 1985).

Leff and Vaughn (1980), in an attempt to formulate an integrative model of stress effects on the course of schizophrenia, brought together data from both life-event and expressed-emotion studies and concluded that patients on regular medication are protected against either *acute* stress (life events) or *chronic* stress (high EE relatives) but *not* both. Thus, while distinguishing between acute and chronic stressors, Leff and Vaughn argued that the two may interact in such a way as to render medication ineffective. It should be noted, in passing, that this kind of model may not only be applicable to patients diagnosed as schizophrenic. For example, the role of life stress in depression has long been appreciated (Brown and Harris, 1978), and two studies have indicated that familial high expressed emotion may be predictive of relapse in depressed patients (Vaughn and Leff, 1976; Hooley, Orley and Teasdale, 1986).

There is at least some evidence suggesting that particular kinds of stress event may elicit hallucinatory experiences. The clearest example of this concerns hallucinations following bereavement. Reese (1971), in a study of recently widowed men and women,

Figure 4.2: Percentage schizophrenic patients suffering relapse within 9 months of discharge as affected by expressed emotion (EE) of family, contact with family (greater or less than 35 hours per week) and neuroleptic medication. From Vaughn and Leff (1976)

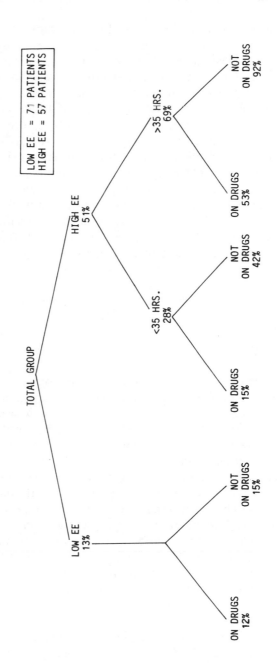

estimated that no less than 13.3 per cent of his sample had experienced hallucinations of their deceased spouse's voice. Other authors have noted the occurrence of visual hallucinations associated with grief in the elderly. Wells (1980) described two grieving patients suffering from hallucinations of the self (autoscopic phenomena), and Alroe and McIntyre (1983) described three cases of elderly patients with ocular disorders who suffered from the Charles Bonnet syndrome shortly following loss of a spouse. The finding of a relationship between hallucination and grief has also been replicated across cultures; Matchett (1972) observed that, among the Hopi Indians of North America, non-psychotic people often hallucinate the presence of a recently deceased family member. He noted the similarity between this phenomenon and 'appearances' described in Western literature, for example the ghost of Hamlet's father (Shakespeare) and the ghost of Jacob Marley (Dickens).

Other examples of visual hallucination have been noted in association with life-threatening or potentially life-threatening situations. Comer, Madow and Dixon (1967) described the experiences of two miners trapped in darkness for a period of two days; their hallucinations, which appeared to relate to their predicament, included visions of doorways and stairs and even of the Pope (perhaps symbolising a more powerful source of help). Belenky (1979) described visual hallucinations occurring in soldiers taking part in sustained military operations (without sleep) over several days. Finally, Siegel (1984) reviewed the available psychiatric literature on hostage victims and found that, of 31 persons for whom sufficient information was available, eight victims experienced hallucinations varying from simple geometric shapes to complex memory images. Isolation and life-threatening stress seemed to be particularly predictive in this respect.

Ongoing, moderate stress tends to figure in the case reports of hallucinating psychiatric patients. For example, in two individual cases reported by the first author (Slade, 1972, 1973) the patients concerned reported that certain situations were difficult for them and caused them distress and anxiety. In the first case the stressful situation was the patient's home life and particularly the patient's relationship with his father. In the second case the stressors were interpersonal situations outside the family. These are more subtle forms of stress and therefore more likely to be overlooked or dismissed by comparison with traumatic forms of life event.

The second distinction made in Table 4.1 is between 'situational' and 'cognitive' stressors. The former are generally readily identifiable (e.g. life events, expressed emotion) and have been briefly described above. However, clinical and research experience demonstrates that individuals can be stressed not only by presenting situations but also by 'cognitions' about such situations. This was true for the first patient described above (Slade, 1972), who reported as much distress when on a bus thinking about his father as he experienced when confronting his father at home.

With respect to the mode of action of psychological stress in eliciting hallucinations, it would seem that increased physiological arousal is involved. For example, Allen and Agus (1968) found that they could reliably induce hallucinations in two patients with a history of hallucination by making them hyperventilate.

Several authors have attempted to assess the role of arousal in hallucination more directly, using pyschophysiological techniques. Stern, Surphlis and Koff (1965) attempted to measure arousal during a word-association task and found that schizophrenic patients with a history of hallucination of unpleasant content, as measured by the Inpatient Multidimensional Psychiatric Scale (Lorr, 1953), exhibited impaired electrodermal responsiveness. In a rather better controlled study, Toone, Cooke and Lader (1981) found that hallucinating patients had higher levels and greater fluctuations of skin conductance than controls, both indicative of high internal arousal. A previously unpublished case study carried out by the first author illustrates the way in which a systematic relationship may exist between psychophysiological activity and the onset of auditory hallucinations (Fonagy and Slade, 1986). The study involved a patient who reported a total of 463 voices during three 45-minute sessions. Throughout these sessions the patient was monitored by means of a polygraph measuring skin conductance (SC), finger pulse volume (FPV), respiration rate (RR) and heart rate (HR). Data on these four psychophysiological measures were averaged for 10-second intervals during the 60 seconds preceding the onset of reported hallucinations, for the duration of the hallucinations, and over the 60 seconds following their cessation. The results are presented graphically in Figure 4.3.

It can be seen from Figure 4.3a that there is a steady increase in

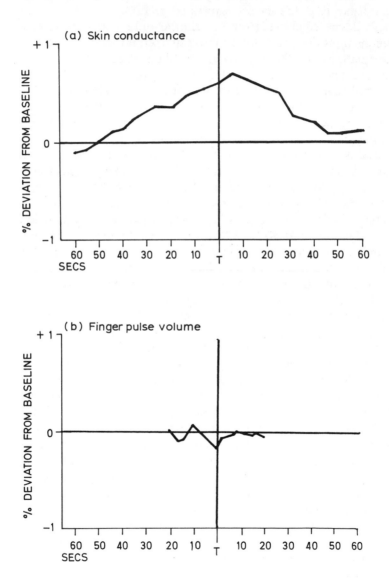

Figure 4.3: Mean skin conductance (SC), finger pulse volume (FPV), respiration rate (RR), and heart rate (HR) in a patient before, during and after reported auditory hallucinations ($N = 463$)

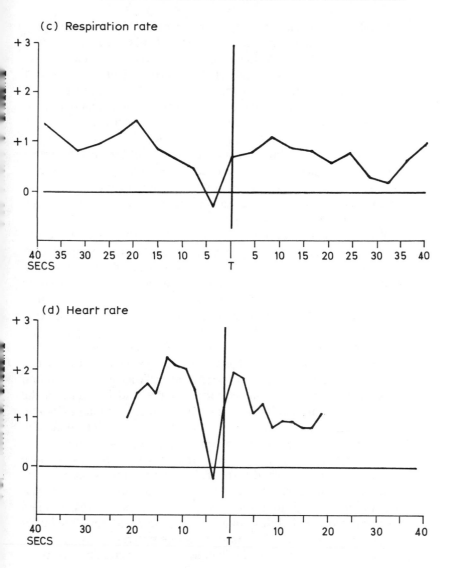

(c) Respiration rate

(d) Heart rate

skin conductance, relative to baseline, over the 60-second period preceding hallucinatory activity (T), followed by a gradual return to baseline. There is also a parallel decrease in finger pulse volume (Figure 4.3b) over the 20-second period preceding hallucinatory activity, followed by a subsequent increase following hallucinations.

91

Both of these results are consistent with an increase in sympathetic autonomic nervous system arousal prior to hallucination. However, the observed changes in respiration rate (Figure 4.3c) and heart rate (Figure 4.3d) show a different pattern. Instead of a continuous increase in these parameters up to the point of hallucination, an initial increase is demonstrated which is then followed by a fairly sharp decrease which commences at around 15 seconds (RR) or 10 seconds (HR) prior to the report of hallucinatory experience. One possible explanation for this observed pattern of increased skin conductance combined with respiration rate/heart rate decrease is that it reflects an anticipatory response on the part of the patient, similar to that described by Lacey (1967) in reaction-time experiments.

A larger-scale attempt to relate electrodermal activity to the onset and cessation of auditory hallucinations has been reported by Cooklin, Sturgeon and Leff (1983), who studied fluctuations of skin conductance in 15 schizophrenic hallucinators. For ten of the subjects there was sufficient inter-rater agreement about the onset and offset of hallucinations to allow an analysis to be carried out. However, non-verbal indices of hallucination (e.g. eye movement, inclination of the head into a listening position, movement of the lips) were used, although subjects were requested to indicate when they could hear voices. A significant relationship was found between the onset of hallucinatory episodes and increases in the spontaneous skin conductance fluctuation rate. Although Cooklin *et al.* noted that they could not rule out the possibility that such increases were merely concomitants of the behaviours selected to indicate hallucination, they argued that this was unlikely because the behaviours concerned were slight compared with the postural changes that occurred frequently during recording. Nevertheless the authors noted that they were still unable to discriminate between two possibilities: that an increase in arousal facilitates hallucination or that hallucinations are themselves arousing.

Of course, these two possibilities are not mutually exclusive. However, when the evidence reviewed above is taken as a whole, it is difficult to avoid the conclusion that stress, mediated by autonomic arousal, can facilitate hallucination in appropriately predisposed individuals.

PREDISPOSING FACTORS

One of the most obvious features that emerges from the literature on hallucinations, whether experimentally induced hallucinations in normal individuals or occurring spontaneously in pathological states, is the observation of individual differences. Some people hallucinate under specifiable conditions and others do not. This observation indicates that there may be constitutional differences which predispose individuals to hallucinatory experience. These differences may be reflected in biological history (genetic factors) or in psychological dispositions as measured by various tests. The genetic evidence on hallucinations will be discussed in Chapter 6, and the present discussion will focus on psychological factors. One appropriate research paradigm for investigating such factors involves the comparison of a group of people having a history of hallucinations with another group without such a history but matched in terms of as many other relevant variables as possible. Although this paradigm is an obvious one, very few studies of this type have been carried out.

(i) Intelligence and language skills

In order to compare the intelligence of hallucinating and non-hallucinating patients, Johnson and Miller (1965) examined the performance of hospitalised soldiers on a standard battery of tests given on admission to the US Army. The hallucinators, on average, had a significantly lower premorbid intelligence compared with the non-hallucinators. Moreover, the differences could not be attributed to social class, education, age, urban vs. rural upbringing or any of a range of other variables. Furthermore, on average the hallucinators' premorbid performance IQ was significantly lower than their verbal IQ as estimated from a vocabulary test, although this was not the case for the non-hallucinators. In a subsequent study, Miller, Johnson and Richmond (1965), hypothesising that their original verbal test gave an inadequate indication of their subjects' verbal abilities, found that a group of hallucinators performed significantly worse than a matched group of non-hallucinators on a range of tests measuring descriptive language skills (descriptive style, sensitivity to connotative meaning in the

93

selection of metaphors, and verbal fluency). More recently, Heilbrun and Blum (1984) found that hallucinators were significantly poorer than non-hallucinating psychiatric controls on a vocabulary task measuring the subjects' familiarity with unusual word meanings (see 'Other cognitive measures' below).

The implications of these findings are not clear. As noted in Chapter 1, it seems likely that verbally unsophisticated people are sometimes mistakenly diagnosed as hallucinating. Equally, it is possible that verbally unsophisticated people are particularly vulnerable to believing that their imaginings are real. Finally, of course, the possibility that low IQ and hallucinations both reflect some kind of underlying neuropathology cannot be ruled out. Although there are no data available at present which will allow a choice to be made between these hypotheses, they are, in any case, not mutually exclusive.

(ii) Personality differences

Lewinsohn (1968) carried out a series of studies aimed at investigating personality differences between hallucinating and non-hallucinating schizophrenic patients. In one study he found, contrary to expectation, no difference in social withdrawal/isolation between the groups. In fact, on some measures hallucinators were judged by their peers to be significantly more friendly, less defensive and more likeable, and were wanted more as roommates than non-hallucinating schizophrenic patients. In a second study, Lewinsohn compared similar groups of patients on the Minnesota Multiphasic Personality Inventry (MMPI) and found only two significant differences: hallucinating patients scored higher on the F Scale (one of the validating scales) and lower on Barron's Ego-strength Scale (Barron, 1953). Lewinsohn concluded that 'the direction of the differences suggests that the hallucinated patients admit to a greater number of outright psychotic symptoms i.e. they present themselves as being more disturbed'.

In a more recent study which bears on this finding, Chapman, Edell and Chapman (1980) investigated psychosis-proneness in college students using two of their schizotypy scales, the Physical Anhedonia Scale (measuring lack of interest in physical pleasures) and the Perceptual Aberration Scale (measuring, for the most part, disturbances of body image). The two scales had a small negative correlation, indicating that they measured independent traits. When examined using a modified structured psychiatric interview, the subjects scoring highest on perceptual aberration reported more psychotic-like experiences (including auditory and visual experiences) and were more socially withdrawn than controls. The subjects scoring high on physical anhedonia did not report more psychotic-like experiences than the controls but were more socially withdrawn.

The first author (Slade, 1976c) carried out a study using the Eysenck Personality Inventory (Eysenck and Eysenck, 1973) in which a small group of patients with a history of auditory hallucinations was compared with a matched group of patients without such a history and with a group of normal controls. No significant differences were found between the three groups on either the neuroticism (N) or the extraversion–introversion (E) dimensions of the scale. However, significant differences were found between all three groups on the psychoticism (P) scale. The hallucinators scored significantly higher than the non-hallucinators, who in turn scored above the normal controls. In general hallucinators endorsed more items indicative of interpersonal problems (including paranoid and aggressive items) and, in addition, exclusively endorsed three items which appear to reflect 'unconventional attitudes'. It was also noted that the mean P score of the hallucinators was above that of any of the normative groups of hospital patients and equivalent only to those of male and female prisoners. Launay and Slade (1981) subsequently investigated the relationship between EPI P scores and scores on the Launay–Slade Hallucination Scale (LSHS) in a population of male and female prisoners (the N and E EPI subscales were not administered); a significant relationship was observed between P and LSHS scores.

Subsequent research, using a later version of Eysenck's scale (the Eysenck Personality Questionnaire; Eysenck and Eysenck, 1976) has tended to emphasise the importance of the neuroticism subscale in identifying individuals prone to hallucination. Ramanathan (1984a,b) found a relationship between scores on the N scale of the EPQ and measures of the extent to which schizophrenic patients experienced interference by and coped with auditory hallucinations. In a later study, Ramanathan (1986) measured various aspects of hallucinatory activity in hallucinating schizophrenics and found that high N scores were related to anxiety prior to hearing voices, anticipation of voices, anger expressed when hearing a voice, and the degree of interference experienced in occupational and social activity as a result of the hallucinations.

A recent study by the present authors (Young, Bentall, Slade and Dewey, 1986) also suggested a relationship between neuroticism as measured by the EPQ and hallucination. EPQ scores were correlated with LSHS scores for a sample of 203 student subjects; a significant correlation was found between N and LSHS scores but not between P and LSHS scores. The discrepancy between these results for the P scale and earlier results may be more apparent than real as the P scale underwent substantial revision, with a removal of the more obviously psychotic items, during construction of the EPQ (Eysenck and Eysenck, 1976). The observed relationship between hallucination scores and neuroticism may be of some theoretical interest, however. On the one hand, as Ramanathan (1986) has suggested, high neuroticism scores may reflect the degree to which individuals are disturbed by their psychotic or psychotic-like experiences. On the other hand, as Claridge and Broks (1984) have observed (following the discovery of a correlation between N and their schizotypy scale), the self-reporting of psychotic-like experiences may reflect the kind of emotional instability (and, presumably, vulnerability to stress) measured by the N scale.

Following the observation that hallucinators tend to endorse paranoid and aggressive items on the original (EPI) P scale, Judkins and Slade (1981) investigated the relationship between auditory hallucinations and hostility, using the Hostility and Direction of Hostility Questionnaire (HDHQ; Caine, Foulds, and Hope, 1967) in a group of 26 hallucinating patients. Total hostility scores were higher than those obtained from a combined paranoid and non-paranoid non-hallucinating schizophrenic sample. In addition to a total hostility score, the HDHQ yields a direction of hostility score designed to measure whether an individual directs his or her aggression primarily towards others (extrapunitiveness) or inwards in the form of self-criticism and guilt (intrapunitiveness). When the hallucinating subjects were classified according to the duration, location (pseudo vs. real hallucination) and quality (abusive and hostile vs. friendly and reassuring) of their voices, the location of the voices was found to be related to direction of hostility scores such that those with auditory pseudo-hallucinations tended to score as intrapunitive. The quality and duration of the voices appeared to be correlated, both relating to total hostility scores so that patients who reported predominantly abusive voices experienced them for a shorter duration and scored higher on total hostility that those with predominantly pleasant voices.

(iii) Suggestibility and responsiveness to instructions

In Chapter 3 research indicating that subjects given simple suggestions will sometimes report hallucinations was described. For example, Barber and Calverley (1964) found that, if instructed to close their eyes and listen to the record 'White Christmas', roughly 5 per cent of their subjects (secretarial students) would subsequently report believing that the record had been played. This finding would seem to have implications for the explanation of hallucinations in psychiatric patients. Suggestibility and the willingness to believe in the reality of an event on instruction might conceivably be an important determinant of hallucination. In this context, it is interesting to note that the hallucination-like experiences that have been reported during sensory deprivation seem to be, at least in part, a function of overt suggestion (Jackson and Kelly, 1962; Schaefer and Bernick, 1965) and the explicit demand characteristics of sensory deprivation experiments (Orne and Scheibe, 1964).

One early finding seemed to indicate that suggestions have less effect on hallucinators than on non-hallucinators. Sarbin, Juhasz and Todd (1971) gave hallucinating schizophrenics, non-hallucinating schizophrenics and college student controls suggestions that several samples of distilled water contained varying concentrations of salt. The college students reported tasting salt more often than the non-hallucinating schizophrenics, who reported the taste of salt more often than the hallucinators. In a second experiment, the subjects were told to hear voices against a white-noise background; although no significant differences were found between the three groups, a non-significant trend similar to that found in the first experiment was observed.

In contrast, subsequent research has tended to support the view that hallucinators are peculiarly responsive to instructions to see or hear non-existent events. Mintz and Alpert (1972) tested hallucinating schizophrenics, non-hallucinating schizophrenics and normal controls on Barber and Calverley's 'White Christmas' test and found that hallucinators were more likely than controls to report hearing the record (75 per cent of hallucinators) and to believe that it had been played (10 per cent). Consistent with these findings, Buss, Larson and Nakashima (1983) examined a group of auditory hallucinating schizophrenics and reported that approximately 60 per cent of their sample were 'excellent hypnotic subjects'. Buss *et al.* hypothesised that much of the symptomatology of these patients was generated by 'spontaneous self-hypnosis'. This explanation has limited theoretical value, however, if only because hypnosis is a phenomenon that has resisted explanation except, perhaps, in social–psychological terms (see Chapter 3).

In a recent study, Alpert (1985) gave groups of hallucinating schizophrenics, non-hallucinating schizophrenics and hallucinating alcoholics suggestions to hear voices as they listened to white noise. The hallucinating patients were much more likely to report hearing complex stimuli (e.g. voices) than the non-hallucinators, who typically reported simple sounds. When weak suggestions were compared with strong suggestions in two groups of hallucinating schizophrenics, it was found that the strong suggestions increased the frequency with which voices were reported, but not the quality of the voices. Jakes and Hemsley (1986) obtained similar results with normal subjects selected according to scores on the Launay–Slade scale. Subjects watched a random dot display on a television monitor and were given suggestions to see objects. Responses were classed according to whether they were reports of simple shapes or reports of complex stimuli (the Type A and Type B classification advocated by Zuckerman — see Chapter 1). A significant correlation was found between Type B responses but not Type A responses and LHSH scores.

In an attempt to assess whether these results indicate that hallucinators are generally more suggestible than controls, the present authors (Young, Bentall, Slade and Dewey, 1987) gave the Barber and Calverley auditory suggestion task (the subjects were instructed to close their eyes and hear a tape recorder playing 'Jingle Bells' rather than 'White Christmas') and its visual equivalent (in which subjects are instructed to see a cat on their lap) together with two measures of suggestibility to groups of students scoring low or high on the LSHS. The two suggestibility scales used were Barber's Hypnotic Suggestibility Scale (Barber and Calverley, 1963), consisting of a series of suggestions (e.g. to experience thirst, to levitate arms) and detailed scoring criteria, and Gudjonsson's (1983) Interrogative Suggestibility Scale, designed to identify individuals who, under the influence of leading questions and interpersonal pressure, are likely to make statements in accordance with the expectations of an interrogator. Differences between the groups similar to those observed by Mintz and Alpert (1972) were found for both the auditory and the visual suggestion tasks (although all the subjects tended to be relatively conservative in their judgements compared with those of Mintz and Alpert) but no differences were found between the groups on either measure of suggestibility. In a second experiment the authors went on to apply the same methodology to groups of hallucinating and non-hallucinating psychiatric patients; differences between the groups were again found on the Barber and Calverley auditory task but not on the visual task. Again, no differences were found on either of the two more general measures of suggestibility.

From these results it seems clear that hallucinating individuals seem particularly influenced by information given in the form of instructions when describing their perceptions. However, it is not obvious that hallucinators are responsive to *any* instructions. On the contrary, on the balance of the evidence collected to date, it seems that they are more influenced than others only by information pertaining to the domain of their perceptions. The importance of this finding will be discussed in Chapter 8.

(iv) Other cognitive measures

A variety of other cognitive measures have been used to identify factors predisposing individuals to hallucinate. As many of these have been studied in attempts to evaluate specific theories of hallucination, they will be discussed in detail in the next chapter. However, it would be wrong to proceed further without considering the work of Heilbrun and his colleagues.

Heilbrun (1980) hypothesised that hallucinators mistake the

source of their experiences so that they misattribute self-generated experiences (thoughts, imaginings) to an external agent. In an attempt to test this hypothesis, he assessed the ability of hallucinating patients and non-hallucinating controls (mostly diagnosed as schizophrenic in both groups) to recognise their own thoughts. The opinions of the patients were elicited on five topics (e.g. 'What are some of the important things to look for in a friend?') and tape recorded. These verbatim statements were used in individualised multiple-choice tasks in which the alternatives were either lexically different (the same statement but with synonyms substituted), semantically different (statements of more or less adequate approximate meaning to that of the patient) or syntactically different (statements in which the clause structure of the patient's original statement had been altered to varying degrees). Attempts were made to control for the patients' verbal memory, stability of opinions and communication skills, and the test sessions were conducted one week after the elicitation of opinions. Hallucinating subjects were found to be significantly poorer at recognising their own statements (using a combind score for lexical, semantic and syntactic items) than the controls.

In a second study, Heilbrun, Blum and Haas (1983) investigated preferred mode of mental imagery and spatial location of sounds in hallucinating and non-hallucinating patients. As mental imagery theories of hallucination are dealt with in detail in the next chapter, this aspect of their results will not be discussed here. The subjects' ability to locate sounds spatially was assessed using a task in which the subjects sat surrounded by an opaque screen. The experimenter placed himself at different points outside the screen and asked, 'Where am I?'. The subjects were required to state a number relating to the location at which he or she felt the experimenter to be. No restrictions were placed on the subjects' head movements except that they were required to orient themselves in a particular direction at the start of each of the 24 trials. Hallucinated patients diagnosed as reactive schizophrenics (sudden onset of psychosis, good premorbid personality) performed worse on this task than their non-hallucinated controls, who were matched for age, education, drug type and dosage.

In a final study, Heilbrun and Blum (1984) studied perception of meaning in hallucinating and non-hallucinating patients. Heilbrun and Blum argued that the initial phase of hallucination might be characterised by a considerable degree of ambiguity about the meaning of a perceived stimulus. On this view, the ability of the percipient to reach a valid judgement about the meaning of ambiguous stimulation and a willingness to defer assignment of meaning in unclear cases would seem to be important factors in the judgement process. Rapid assignment of meaning would be particularly likely to lead to misjudgements in individuals who failed to consider alternatives.

Tolerance of ambiguity was assessed by requiring the subjects to guess the meaning of repeated monosyllabic words spoken against decreasing levels of noise; scores were calculated according to the number of trials on which subjects withheld a guess. (An attempt was also made to assess the subjects' ability to consider alternative meanings by employing an unusual meanings vocabulary test; although hallucinators performed less well than controls on this test, it seems likely that this difference reflects a deficiency in verbal skills — see above.)

Reactive patients showed less tolerance of ambiguity than process (slow onset, poor premorbid personality) patients but, although reactive hallucinators scored lower on this measure than any other group, the interaction between process vs. reactive status and hallucinatory status failed to reach significance. However, Heilbrun and Blum noted that since quick, accurate identification of words could be misinterpreted as low tolerance of ambiguity on their measure, error scores needed to be taken into account. When they looked at these scores they found that the reactive hallucinators performed significantly worse than the subjects in any other group, suggesting that they had a tendency to make rapid, inaccurate judgements. This analysis is consistent with the findings of three other studies that need to be considered in the present context.

In their study employing the 'White Christmas' test, Mintz and Alpert (1972) also reported results obtained with an additional procedure, which they described as a measure of 'reality testing' (the skill of distinguishing between real and imaginary events — see Chapters 5 and 8). Subjects were asked to listen to voices against a white noise background and were required to guess what the voices were saying and to rate their confidence in their judgements. Mintz and Alpert hypothesised that a low correlation between the accuracy of the subjects' guesses and their confidence in them would be indicative of poor reality testing. Hallucinators

101

showed a poorer relationship between confidence and accuracy than either non-hallucinating schizophrenics or normal controls.

In a more recent study, Schneider and Wilson (1983) measured the reaction times and accuracy of schizophrenic patients and normal individuals on an auditory and a visual discrimination task; the normal subjects were generally more accurate than the schizophrenics but, on the auditory task, current auditory hallucinators generally performed better than schizophrenics who had hallucinated in the past or who had never hallucinated. More importantly from the present perspective, the hallucinators showed faster reaction times on this task than the other subjects.

Finally in this respect, Alpert (1985) described a study in which hallucinating and non-hallucinating psychiatric patients were asked to describe recordings of brief phrases played through a low-pass filter so that they were intelligible to varying degrees; the hallucinators produced errors that were more semantically constrained than those of the non-hallucinators, and were inappropriately confident about their judgements.

Taken together with the results obtained by Heilbrun and Blum, these three studies seem to indicate that hallucinators make rapid and over-confident judgements about their perceptions; on simple discrimination tasks such as those employed by Schneider and Wilson this need not be at the expense of accuracy, but on more complex verbal tasks accuracy may suffer as a result.

In his most recent experiment, Heilbrun and his colleagues (Heilbrun, Diller, Fleming and Slade, 1986) investigated disattentional strategies (means of avoiding aversive stimulation) in schizophrenics who were either process hallucinators, reactive hallucinators, or non-hallucinating (reactive and process schizophrenics combined). Subjects listened to a series of adjectives on a tape and were assigned to one of three conditions: 'switching' (concentrating on a visual stimulus), 'holding' (concentrating on the first word on the tape to the detriment of those that followed) or a control condition (no disattentional strategy). The efficacy of the two strategies for the different groups of patients was later assessed by using a recognition task for words on the tape. A condition by group interaction was found to be significant, with recognition most impaired by the switching strategy in the case of the process hallucinators and by the holding strategy in the case of the reactive hallucinators. Heilbrun *et al.* suggested that the efficacy of these strategies might reflect the extent to which the patients employed them in their every-day lives and that both strategies might result in an increased vulnerability to hallucinations. Thus, it was argued that increased attention to the visual modality at the expense of the auditory modality might result in a lack of familiarity with lexical thought. On the other hand, reactive schizophrenics, according to this argument, would be more likely to perceive their thoughts as real because of their increased attention to them. Unfortunately, although the control group of non-hallucinating schizophrenics showed no significant effects as a result of either disattentional strategy, the fact that they were patients of both reactive and process schizophrenics raises the possibility that the differences observed were due to premorbid status and prevents the drawing of firm conclusions about the role of disattentional strategies in hallucinations.

As already indicated above, investigators have employed a range of other cognitive tests in studies of hallucination. This is particularly true with respect to measures of 'mental imagery' and 'reality testing'. However, these will be considered in the next chapter in the context of particular psychological theories of hallucination.

ENVIRONMENTAL STIMULATION

The probable role of environmental stimulation in hallucination has already been discussed at various points in the preceding chapters. Some of the studies described under the topic of stress (above) involved a degree of reduced sensory stimulation or isolation, for example in the context of being trapped in a mine (Comer et al., 1967) or being taken hostage (Siegel, 1984). Visual hallucinations associated with isolation and relative sensory poverty have also been reported by mountain climbers, arctic explorers and lone sailors.

In Chapter 1, the reporting of hallucinations in sensory deprivation experiments was briefly mentioned. Research into sensory deprivation has waned in recent years and it now seems clear that the extent to which hallucinations occur in normal subjects as a result of these procedures was exaggerated by early researchers (Zuckerman and Cohen, 1964; Zuckerman, 1969;

Reed, 1979; Slade, 1984). For example, in a careful review of 54 data sets involving nearly 1000 subjects, Zuckerman (1969) found that, whereas approximately 50 per cent of subjects reported simple (Type A) sensations in both the auditory and visual modalities, only about 20 per cent of subjects reported complex visual experiences and only about 15 per cent reported complex auditory experiences. As already noted, suggestion appears to play some role in these kinds of report. Thus, only a minority of individuals subjected to sensory deprivation procedures appear to have experiences approaching true hallucination, and it seems likely that these subjects may be predisposed to hallucinate in some way (Slade, 1984). None the less, the finding that some subjects can be led to hallucinate by a relative absence of sensory stimulation is of theoretical interest.

Harris (1959) reported the results of an empirical study of sensory deprivation with 12 schizophrenic patients. Each patient lay on a couch in a sound-proofed cubicle, wearing opaque goggles and gloves fitted with cardboard cuffs for brief periods of time (approximately half an hour). Harris noted few changes in mental state following this procedure. However, some patients reported that their auditory hallucinations ceased, and others said that their voices had become less vivid and less troublesome. These changes were specific to the sensory deprivation situation and there was no carry-over to the ward environment. Given the short periods involved (most sensory deprivation studies with normal subjects last for days) and the poorly controlled nature of the study, it is difficult to know what to make of this finding. (For example, it is possible that the reduction of hallucinations resulted simply from disorientation as the subjects adjusted to their new and unusual circumstances.) Moreover, subsequent studies using sensory deprivation with schizophrenic individuals (e.g. Cleveland, Reitman and Bentinck, 1963; Robertson, 1964) produced conflicting results, some indicating improvement while others indicated no change or even a worsening of symptomatology.

The phenomenon of release hallucinations associated with sensory loss, discussed in Chapter 2, may be of relevance in this respect. Of particular interest is the observation that these kinds of hallucination are particularly likely to occur following progressive but incomplete sensory loss, and especially during periods of stimulation. Thus, in Hammeke et al.'s (1983) two cases, described in Chapter 2, auditory hallucinations seemed to occur most often during periods of low ambient noise whereas, in the three cases of visual release hallucination described by White (1980), visions of brightly coloured stereotyped figures (animals or objects) occurred during the initial phases of progressive eye disease and tended to be provoked by light. The common factor that seems to be relevant in these examples is a low ratio of signal (stimulus strength) to sensory noise.

Experimental evidence pertaining to the role of environmental stimulation in hallucination has been collected in two studies by Slade (1974) who required two hallucinating patients to report the occurrence or non-occurrence of hallucinations during successive 20-second time periods. During each period one of six conditions was implemented: a no-activity (control) condition; three shadowing conditions in which the subjects were required to repeat letters presented randomly through earphones at differing rates; a reading condition in which the subjects were required to read a series of letters from a printed sheet as quickly as possible; and a writing condition in which the subjects were required to write down letters read from a sheet. For both subjects, the frequency of hearing voices decreased in an orderly fashion with an increase in the rate at which the verbally presented information was processed. The voices were also reduced by the reading and (to a lesser extent) the writing conditions.

In a subsequent study, Margo, Hemsley and Slade (1981) used a similar procedure with seven schizophrenic hallucinators. In this study, nine conditions were employed: (1) a contol condition with no stimulation; (2) a reading aloud condition; (3) and (4) two listening conditions in which the subjects were required to listen to recorded passages judged to be interesting and boring, respectively; (5) a pop-music condition; (6) a condition in which the stimulation consisted of regular electronic blips; (7) a condition in which the subjects listened to a passage read in Afrikaans (which none of them understood); (8) a condition in which the stimulation consisted of irregular electronic blips; (9) a 'sensory restriction' condition in which the patients sat wearing earphones and dark goggles; and, finally, (10) a white noise condition. Trials were randomised and the results are shown in Figure 4.4.

In general, it was found that, whereas sensory restriction and white noise increased the duration, loudness and clarity of the

Figure 4.4: Mean ratings of duration of hallucinations of seven hallucinating patients in the study by Margo *et al.* (1981). Conditions are (1) control, no earphones; (2) reading aloud a simple prose passage; (3) listening to an interesting passage; (4) listening to a boring passage; (5) listening to pop music; (6) listening to regular electronic blips; (7) listening to speech in an unfamiliar language (Afrikaans); (8) listening to irregular electronic blips; (9) sensory restriction (dark goggles, earphones — no sound) and (10) listening to white noise. Ratings of duration were made on an eight-point scale (0 = no auditory hallucinations, 7 = continuous hallucinations) with mean baseline score shown by the dotted line. Parallel results were observed for ratings of loudness and clarity of hallucinations

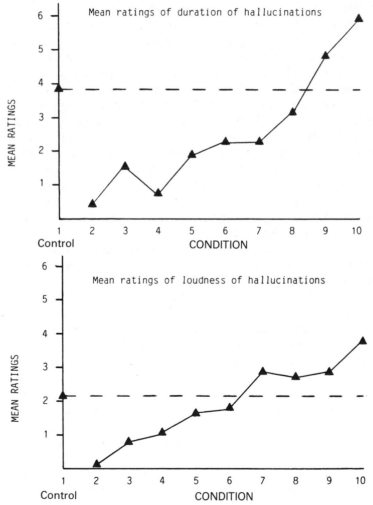

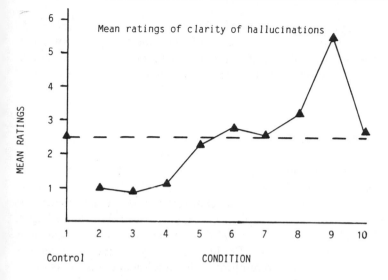

Mean ratings of clarity of hallucinations

hallucinations experienced by the subjects, the other conditions produced a reduction in hallucination. This reduction was greatest when the stimulation presented was most meaningful. As in the preceding study described above, reading seemed to be particularly effective at reducing hallucination. The finding that white noise increased the frequency of hallucination is consistent with the results obtained by Alpert (1985) in his study employing suggestion; Alpert observed that increases in hallucination were most likely to occur at moderate rather than high or low levels of white noise.

Taking these findings together with observations made during studies of sensory deprivation or release hallucinations, with the exception of the results obtained by Harris, a complex but consistent picture emerges. Low or unpatterned stimulation of moderate intensity seems to increase the probability that hallucinations will occur. Meaningful stimulation, on the other hand, seems to reduce the occurrence of hallucinations. Hallucinations are particularly likely to be inhibited when the hallucinator is required to perform some kind of verbal task such as shadowing a recorded message or reading.

These findings are consistent with recent observations made by Tarrier (1987), who asked a group of 25 schizophrenic patients suffering from auditory hallucinations and delusions to identify antecedents of their symptoms. Thirteen patients were able to do so. Not surprisingly, social isolation (reported by six patients) and, on the other hand, specific stimuli (traffic noise or the television, reported by four patients) appeared on the list of antecedents elicited.

REINFORCEMENT

A final variable that needs to be considered in the present context is reinforcement. In several case studies, the first author (Slade, 1972, 1973) noted that hallucinating patients are sometimes less disturbed following an episode of hallucination than preceding it. If this is indeed the case, it would suggest that hallucinations may serve a positive function of reducing anxiety. Reduction in anxiety might, in turn, serve to reinforce hallucination and ensure its future occurrence.

Experimental evidence in support of this hypothesis is limited. On the one hand, a number of treatment studies (described in Chapter 7) have demonstrated that operant conditioning techniques can be used for the *reduction* of hallucinations, suggesting that hallucations may sometimes be under operant control. On the other hand, Tarrier (1987), in his interview study conducted with hallucinating and deluded schizophrenics, found that 18 out of 25 of his sample reported feeling *more* disturbed after their hallucinations than beforehand. Of course, it is not necessarily the case that hallucinations must have the same emotional effect on all patients; some may feel less stressed and others feel more stressed afterwards. Nor is it the case that an increase or reduction in stress is the only consequence of hallucination that might affect their future occurrence. The functional significance of hallucinations for the hallucinator would therefore seem to be an appropriate area for future research.

SUMMARY

From the clinical and experimental evidence detailed in the present chapter it seems clear that psychotic hallucinations are a function of a number of interacting variables. These include stress, environmental stimulation, dispositional variables and, possibly, reinforcement. It seems likely that this list is not complete; in Chapter 3, for example, it was suggested that sociocultural factors might play a role in determining vulnerability to hallucination. It remains now to consider theories of the psychological and biological mechanisms of hallucination. These are the subjects of the next two chapters.

5

Psychological Theories of Hallucination

A convincing theory of hallucinations should do more than specify variables that influence their occurrence; it should describe the mechanisms — psychological or neurological — that are the substrate of the hallucination itself. In other words, it must specify a link between the variables that are known to affect the frequency of hallucination and the experience of the patient as revealed by his or her self-report.

This is a stiff requirement, for a variety of reasons outlined at the end of Chapter 1. The mediating processes that must be identified lie within the organism and can therefore only be investigated with difficulty. Indeed, for this reason the identification of such processes was widely regarded as hopeless in the era of methodological behaviourism. Fortunately, more recently techniques for the investigation of processes internal to the organism have been developed, and the models of mental processes that have been proposed as a result can serve as a source of considerable inspiration to the psychopathologist. Nevertheless, it should be remembered that the explanation of a person's conscious experience remains perhaps the most difficult task facing the psychologist. Indeed, a working theory of hallucinations would be one of only a handful of theories that have managed to relate an objective, scientific analysis of cognitive processes to phenomenological criteria.

In practice, a surprising number of models of hallucination have been proposed in relation to the dearth of experimental data available. Some of these models are psychological, some are biological, and a few involve a blend of the two approaches. (It should, of course, be remembered that a psychological analysis of a particular type of behaviour does not preclude the discovery of its substrate in the nervous system.)

The present chapter will focus on those models which are predominantly psychological in content. Historically, these models have generally emerged following the discovery of psychological phenomena which in some way appear analogous to hallucinations. For this reason, the theories that will be described tend to be speculative in nature and, in each case, it will be necessary to describe, in brief, research in normal psychology that has a bearing on their validity. Although many similarities exist between the different models, they can be broadly grouped under four main headings: conditioning theories, derived from research into classical conditioning; 'cognitive seepage' theories, mainly derived from research on sensory deprivation; imagery theories, derived from research into mental imagery; and subvocalisation theories, derived from research on inner speech.

CONDITIONING THEORIES

As noted in the previous chapter, experimental evidence showing that hallucinations may be maintained by *operant* reinforcement is lacking, although there is some evidence that hallucinations may be reduced by the use of operant procedures (see Chapter 7). In contrast, a number of authors have proposed that hallucinations may result from a history of *classical* (Pavlovian) conditioning.

Hefferline, Bruno and Camp (1972) have reviewed much of the early literature in this area. Some studies combined the use of hypnotic suggestion with classical conditioning procedures. For example, Scott (1930) exposed ten hypnotised subjects to buzzer–shock pairings and found that, on waking from trance, all continued to withdraw their fingers from the shock apparatus on hearing the buzzer alone. Furthermore, two of Scott's subjects reported feeling the shock on the test trials. More interesting studies from the present perspective are those that have employed classical conditioning alone. Seashore (1895), for example, used two procedures to elicit conditioned hallucinations. In one method, training trials consisted of a warning stimulus (the conditioned stimulus or CS) followed closely by another stimulus (the unconditioned stimulus or UCS) to which the subject was required to make a verbal or non-verbal response. Test trials, interspersed among the training trials, involved the presentation of the warning stimulus alone. In the second method a temporal conditioning procedure was used: the UCS was presented at regular intervals and the subjects were required to report each occurrence. Tests for hallucination were carried out by omitting the UCS. One advantage of these procedures was that the true nature of the experiment could be disguised; the UCS was typically a near-threshold stimulus (e.g. a tone) and the subjects were told that the purpose of the experiments was to test their discriminative abilities. Seashore succeeded in obtaining reports of the UCS on most of the trials on which it had been omitted, a result also obtained by Ellson (1941a,b) using similar procedures. Hefferline *et al.*'s (1972) own procedures varied from those of Seashore and Ellson in that they were originally designed to demonstrate conditioning to a covert (i.e. internal) stimulus. The subject was presented with a tone whenever he produced a covert thumb-twitch measured by means of an electromyograph (EMG). On hearing the tone he was required to press a key. When the tone was omitted, a covert key-press (i.e. fractional response of the muscles in the key-pressing finger) was recorded on the EMG. Given that the covert key-press could be regarded as a non-verbal report of the tone elicited by the thumb-twitch (the CS), Hefferline *et al.* argued that their subject could be said to have hallucinated the tone. Consistent with this, the subject, when questioned at the end of the experiment, reported that he had heard the tone.

A perhaps more convincing demonstration of classically conditioned hallucination has been reported more recently by Davies in a series of studies (Davies, 1974a,b, 1976; Davies, Davies and Bennett, 1982). In his earlier studies Davies was able to demonstrate weak conditioning of visual afterimages to tones in well-controlled experiments. Davies *et al.* (1982) reported more substantial conditioning using a procedure in which subjects sat in the dark, the CS was a tone, the UCS was a visual stimulus (a dimly lit equilateral triangle) designed to produce an afterimage, and the response required was a lever-press and a verbal report following the detection of a stimulus. During training, the presentation of the CS prior to the presentation of the UCS was varied up to a maximum of 180 seconds. After several sessions, subjects began to report seeing stimuli before the onset of the UCS. At first, these were described as spots or hazy patches of light; later they were described as small, black or rotating triangles; and finally they became more like the UCS so that eventually one subject reported the conditioned image as 'Normal, rather boring really, nothing to say about it.'

These results have to be considered in the light of prevailing views about human classical conditioning. Classical conditioning in animals has often been thought of as a relatively simple, automatic process, although recent animal research has indicated that quite complex associative processes may be needed to account for some of the data that have been collected (Wagner and Rescorla, 1972; Dickinson, 1980; Davey, 1981). Research with humans has indicated that human classical conditioning rarely, if ever, occurs without the subject being aware of the response he or she is expected to make (Eriksen, 1962; Brewer, 1974). For this reason it has been argued that many of the human classical conditioning data reflect the expectations of the experimental subjects and the demand characteristics of the experiments, rather than true conditioning (Wilson, 1968; Brewer, 1974; Dawson, Catania, Schell and Grings, 1979). It seems possible that the results obtained during attempts to condition hallucinations similarly reflect the subjects' expectations.

In the light of this possibility, it is interesting to compare the experiments described above with those involving suggestion (e.g. Barber and Calverley, 1964; Alpert, 1985) described in Chapters 3 and 4. In both cases, it might be argued, the subjects are led to expect a stimulus either by being told that it will occur (in the suggestion experiments) or by being repeatedly presented with the stimulus in particular circumstances (in the classical conditioning experiments). Because the stimuli are not repeatedly presented in the suggestion experiments, and because appropriate instruction appears to be an important determinant of the outcome, it is difficult to see how conditioning can be used to account for the results obtained in these studies. On the other hand, as has already been noted, the subjects' expectations, explicitly manipulated in the suggestion studies, can be evoked to account for the results of the classical conditioning studies. In the absence of convincing evidence to the contrary, then, it seems parsimonious to assume that expectancy effects and not conditioning account for the data

113

obtained in both types of study.

These considerations do not rule out the possibility that classical conditioning may play a role in hallucination, of course. A classical conditioning account would have the virtue of allowing hallucination in animals, for example. However, until firm evidence of the conditioning of hallucinations is collected, it seems that more complex processes will be required to account for the available clinical and experimental data.

SEEPAGE THEORIES

Under this heading will be considered those theories which, despite their differences, explain hallucinations in terms of some kind of 'seepage' into consciousness of mental activity that would normally remain preconscious. Of the available theories in this category, most have focused on the alleged similarities between the experiences of hallucinating individuals and the experiences of normal subjects subjected to conditions of sensory deprivation. One of the most carefully considered attempts to work out a theory of this sort has been made by West (1962, 1975).

West derived his theory from the earlier speculations of the nineteenth century neurologist Hughlings Jackson who hypothesised that the neuronal discharges underlying hallucinations and other forms of insanity were the result of the elimination of disinhibitory processes, brought about by brain damage, rather than the direct products of diseased structures. Two explicit assumptions were made by West in his modification of this theory: first, that life experiences affect the brain in such a way that they leave permanent neural traces or 'engrams' that subserve the neurophysiology of memory, thought, imagination and fantasy; secondly, that the current mental and neurophysiological state of the individual is a product of the interplay of psychobiological forces that originate both outside and within the individual. More specifically, West argued that effective sensory input normally serves to organise the filtering or attentional processes that control the scanning of information by consciousness. Conscious scanning, on the other hand, is also viewed as a function of cortical arousal as regulated by the ascending reticular activating system in the brain stem. According to this model, hallucinations occur when the level

114

of sensory input is insufficient to organise the screening and scanning mechanisms but when a sufficient level of arousal remains for conscious awareness to be maintained. Under these conditions, West postulated that the neural traces or engrams of previous experiences would be released into consciousness and perceived as if originating from a source external to the organism.

West's theory allowed him to draw a parallel not only with sensory deprivation but also with sleeping and dreaming. According to his model, effective sensory input could be reduced in three ways, either by an absolute decrease or depatterning of sensory stimulation; by input overload ('jamming the circuits'); or by decreased psychological contact with the environment resulting from the operation of various mental mechanisms (e.g. dissociation). During sensory deprivation the absolute level of stimulation is decreased but arousal is maintained with the result that, according to the theory, hallucinations occur. During sleep, on the other hand, the level of stimulation is decreased, as is, for the most part, the level of arousal. However, West was able to point to evidence indicating that cyclic variations in arousal occur throughout sleep (e.g. Dement and Kleitman, 1957), allowing him to account for the release of engrams into consciousness as dreams during periods of light sleep or as hypnagogic or hypnopompic experiences during the periods of falling asleep and waking, respectively. To account for the fact that schizophrenic patients do not need to experience sensory deprivation in order to hallucinate, West proposed that the necessary reduction of effective sensory stimulation in schizophrenics results from abnormally high arousal which causes sensory 'jamming'.

West's theory therefore represents an ingenious attempt to bring together data from a number of different areas of psychological and neurobiological inquiry. Apparent support for the theory comes from the observation of 'release' hallucinations in subjects suffering from various forms of sensory impairment (see Chapters 2 and 4). Furthermore, because of West's suggestion that abnormally high internal arousal may be important in the causation of schizophrenic hallucinations, a link is established with other theories of schizophrenia which also emphasise the role of arousal (see Gjerde, 1983, for a review of the literature on schizophrenia and arousal).

West's theory seems to run into problems because it leans so

115

heavily on the sensory deprivation literature (not surprisingly, given the time at which it was proposed). As noted in the previous chapter, hallucinations during sensory deprivation are comparatively rare and seem, to some extent, to be influenced by suggestion. The most common type of sensory deceptions experienced by normal subjects during sensory deprivation are simple (Type A) phenomena, quite unlike the symptoms experienced by psychotic patients. Moreover, the literature on the effects of sensory deprivation on psychotic individuals, as much as it exists, is inconclusive.

A number of more recent versions of the seepage theory have been put forward. A version of this theory was in fact implicit in the four-factor model outlined by the first author (Slade, 1974) and described in the previous chapter. Perhaps the most recent version of the theory was proposed by Frith (1979) who argued that all schizophrenic symptons can be regarded as disorders of consciousness. Frith's account of consciousness followed that of Shallice (1972), who argued that consciousness is a limited channel capacity processor with executive functions. In other words, consciousness is viewed as a mechanism that controls unconscious mental processes but which itself has the capacity to retain only a limited amount of information. According to this theory, perception occurs by the generation of preconscious perceptual hypotheses (the brain's 'guesses' about what is being perceived) as a result of sensory stimulation. Only the most probable hypothesis normally enters consciousness, the remaining hypotheses being filtered out in the process. Usually this hypothesis will correspond to the objects in the individual's environment but sometimes the wrong hypothesis will reach consciousness, in which case the individual will be mistaken. According to Frith, hallucinations occur when preconscious hypotheses about the nature of a stimulus fail to be filtered out, so that too much information intrudes into consciousness.

It should be noted that Shallice's model of consciousness on which this theory is based is by no means universally accepted by psychologists, and the view that consciousness is some kind of 'box' into which information may flow or be prevented from flowing seems philosophically naive. Indeed, whether consciousness is a unitary phenomenon has been repeatedly questioned by both philosophers (e.g. Armstrong, 1979) and psychologists (e.g.

Lunzer, 1979). Furthermore, Frith's theory has the implication that the frequency with which a person experiences hallucinations will *increase* in conditions of high stimulation (which will elicit many unconscious hypotheses) but decrease in conditions of minimal stimulation.

Despite Harris's (1959) findings on sensory deprivation with schizophrenics, it is clear that there is no simple relationship between the amount of stimulation experienced by an individual and the individual's rate of hallucination. The literature on release hallucinations and sensory deprivation (the reservations we have expressed notwithstanding) does suggest that low levels of stimulation may precipitate hallucinations in at least some cases. On the other hand, certain kinds of structured stimulation (e.g. meaningful messages) can lead to a marked reduction of the rate of hallucination to below baseline level (Margo, Hemsley and Slade 1981). West's theory and Frith's are both weak, therefore, because they predict simple (but opposite) relationships between stimulation and hallucination. For these reasons, it seems unlikely that a cognitive seepage account will, on its own, provide a sufficient explanation of hallucinatory experiences.

IMAGERY THEORIES

The third psychological approach to be considered involves the attempt to establish a link between hallucinations and the quality of mental imagery experienced by the individual.

Richardson (1969), in an influential review of the subject, defined mental imagery as:

(1) All those quasi-sensory or quasi-perceptual experiences of which (2) we are self-consciously aware, and which (3) exist for us in the absence of those stimulus conditions that are known to produce their genuine sensory or perceptual counterparts, and which (4) may be expected to have different consequences from their sensory or perceptual counterparts.

The similarity between this definition and the working definition of hallucination outlined in Chapter 1 should be apparent. It is perhaps not surprising, therefore, that many theorists have found

117

the distinction between imagery and hallucination a difficult one, and have regarded the two types of experience as existing on a continuum.

The study of mental imagery, and individual differences in the extent to which it is experienced, has a long and varied history in psychology. Gustav Fechner in 1860 was perhaps the first to suggest that individual differences in mental imagery might be important (Fechner, 1966), closely followed by Galton (1883). Early research into mental imagery was dominated by introspection. Unfortunately, introspection proved to be an unreliable procedure, as became increasingly obvious when psychologists failed to agree about the existence or non-existence of 'imageless' thought. It was this unreliability that led Watson to banish introspection from psychology and advocate instead the study of objectively observable behaviour. Imagery became: 'A mental luxury (even if it really exists) without any functional significance whatever' (Watson, 1913).

Following the widespread acceptance of Watson's doctrine of behaviourism, comparatively little research was carried out into mental imagery until the 1960s, when interest in the area was stimulated by the growth of cognitive psychology and the findings of research into such phenomena as sensory deprivation and hallucinogenic drugs (Holt, 1964). With the return of imagery as a respectable topic of inquiry, subsequent research into individual differences in mental imagery was carried out by means of standardised questionnaires. Richardson (1969), in his review of this area, argued that the experience of imagery varied along two dimensions — vividness, as measured by an early questionnaire devised by Betts (1909) and later modernised by Richardson and others; and mental imagery control, as measured by Gordon's (1949) questionnaire, also subsequently modernised. The Betts scale consists of a number of items in different modalities which the individual is asked to imagine before rating for vividness. On the Gordon scale individuals are asked to imagine a scene (e.g. a car standing in front of a gate) and then rate how easy or difficult it is to change the image (e.g. changing the car's colour; turning the car on its roof). An important area of research relating to the phenomenology of imagery concerned the extent to which images could be put to cognitive use. For example, Ross and Lawrence (1968) found that the recall of remembered items could be enhanced by creating

Figure 5.1: Stimuli employed in studies of mental rotation by Shepard and Metzler (1971), reproduced from Kosslyn (1983). Subjects had to decide whether the upper and lower objects were identical. Response times were found to be a function of the amount of rotation necessary to mentally 'match' the objects

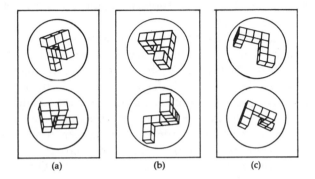

(a)   (b)   (c)

images about the items during learning. On the basis of this kind of research Pavio (1971) argued that verbal processes and imagery represent two separate types of memory and that individuals differ in the extent to which they tend to use one or the other.

In contrast, a second type of approach to the study of mental imagery placed no emphasis on first-person reports whatsoever. Research of this sort emphasised the importance of mental imagery in information processing. An example of this kind of work is the research of Brooks (1968), who attempted to test whether mental imagery and verbal processes are separate. Brooks gave his subjects a task in which they had to mentally examine a block capital letter (e.g. by picturing the letter and working around it in a clockwise direction, stating whether each corner is at the top or the bottom of the letter). When the subjects were asked to respond verbally, their performance was better than when they had to point to a 'Yes' or a 'No' on a page, implying that the visual–motor response of pointing interfered with the task whereas the verbal response did not. The reverse was true when the main task was verbal (e.g. recalling a sentence and saying or indicating which words are nouns).

A further example of this kind of research is Shepard and Metzler's (1971) study of mental rotation. Subjects were asked to look at two block diagrams (shown in Figure 5.1) and say whether

119

they were of identical objects. The time it took to respond was found to be in proportion to the amount of rotation that was necessary to mentally 'match' the objects. The important aspect of Brook's and Shepard and Metzler's studies from the present perspective is that they did not require introspection. At no point in either experiment were the subjects required to describe their experiences.

As Evans (1980) has pointed out, these two approaches are often confused. There is no logical reason why individuals good at the Shepard and Metzler task should report particularly vivid mental imagery, for example. Indeed, a persistent criticism of the phenomenological measures of mental imagery is that they correlate poorly with each other or with behavioural measures of spatial ability (Sheehan and Neisser, 1969; White, Sheehan and Ashton, 1977). In practice, most if not all theorising and research on the possible relationship between imagery and hallucination has been phenomenological in nature and the results have consequently been unclear. Early theorists simply speculated that hallucinations might consist of exaggerated mental imagery (e.g. Seitz and Molholm, 1947). Two comparatively recent theories that elaborate on this approach have been proposed by Mintz and Alpert (1972) and by Horowitz (1975).

Mintz and Alpert argued that hallucinating patients suffer from both abnormally vivid mental imagery and poor 'reality testing' (the skill of distinguishing between the 'real' and the 'imaginary'). As described in the previous chapter, Mintz and Alpert attempted to test this theory, measuring vividness of mental imagery by using the 'White Christmas' auditory suggestion task first used by Barber and Calverley (see Chapter 3). Hallucinating patients were found to be significantly more likely to state that they heard the record or that they both heard it and believed that it had been played than the control subjects (non-hallucinating schizophrenics and normals). This result has recently been replicated by the present authors (Young, Bentall, Slade and Dewey, 1987) in two experiments, one comparing students who scored low and high on the Launay–Slade scale and one comparing hallucinating and non-hallucinating psychiatric patients (see previous chapter). It will be recalled that Mintz and Alpert also attempted to measure reality testing independently of imagery vividness by asking their subjects to listen to voices against a white noise background. The correlation between the subjects' accuracy and their confidence in their judgements was less in the case of hallucinators than in the case of the other groups. (Reality testing will be dealt with in more detail in Chapter 8.)

Horowitz's theory, which is more speculative than Mintz and Alpert's, represents something of a compromise between the 'release' theory of hallucination and the image approach in that it proposes the existence of three kinds of mental representation — enactive, image and lexical. According to the model, hallucinatory experiences occur when the image representational system is accentuated relative to the other two. (As Place, 1980, has pointed out, Horowitz's model was constructed with visual hallucinations as a primary consideration, and it is not clear to what extent auditory and particularly verbal hallucinations can occur without the involvement of the hypothesised lexical system.) Horowitz argued that the image system is served by both internal and external (perceptual) inputs so that, as West had supposed, hallucinations would be more likely to occur under conditions of reduced external (relative to internal) input. In an additional refinement to the theory, Horowitz proposed that individuals with comparatively little experience of vivid mental imagery (i.e whose imagery is normally *poor*) would be more likely to interpret such imagery as 'real'.

As Neisser (1967) has pointed out, there are *a priori* reasons for doubting that the concept of imagery vividness can be employed to explain hallucinations, at least to the extent that vividness is equated with clarity. In particular, it seems that no simple relationship exists between the perceived clarity of an event and a person's belief that the event is real. Hallucinating patients often report that their hallucinations are very hard to discern. On the other hand, people who have ingested hallucinogenic drugs often report extremely vivid images, but do not believe that the events they are experiencing are in any sense 'real'.

Despite this commonsense consideration, the question of whether or not hallucinating patients suffer from abnormally vivid or deficient mental imagery has in fact been a source of enduring controversy since the late nineteenth century (cf. Seitz and Molholm, 1947). As the first author (Slade, 1976a) has pointed out, this has generally involved two separate questions: (a) whether or not hallucinators show a preference for one particular imagery modality as opposed to another; and (b) whether they experience mental imagery that is more vivid than that experienced by control subjects. Neither of these questions has been definitely answered by the research that has been directed towards them.

Cohen (1938) and Snyder and Cohen (1940) were the first to systematically investigate the preferred mode of imagery of hallucinating patients, using a method by which their subjects were required to produce mental images to 130 separately presented words. Cohen (1938) could find no relationship between visual or auditory imagery and visual or auditory hallucinations. He did, however, find a positive correlation between imagery and hallucinations in the kinaesthetic, tactile, and olfactory–gustatory modalities. Snyder and Cohen (1940), on the other hand, were unable to find even this much and (somewhat ahead of their time) questioned the value of imagery research with schizophrenic subjects. Furthermore, Seitz and Molholm (1947) found a negative relationship between hallucinations and preferred mode of imagery using exactly the same method, leading them to argue that schizophrenic hallucinators are relatively deficient in imagery in the modality for which they experience their symptoms. Using a structured interview, Roman and Landis (1945) tried to address the same issue and, like Snyder and Cohen, failed to find a relationship between preferred mode of imagery and hallucinations. Nevertheless, this issue has recently been revived. Heilbrun, Blum and Haas (1983), comparing auditorily hallucinating and non-hallucinating schizophrenics, required their subjects to imagine various multimodal events (e.g. clapping hands) and asked them to rate the clarity of the auditory and visual components. Heilbrun *et al.* claimed, as had Seitz and Molholm, that auditorily hallucinating patients show less preference for auditory imagery in comparison with visual imagery.

If anything, the available data on the vividness of mental imagery in hallucinating subjects is even more conflicting. As discussed above, Mintz and Alpert obtained data allegedly supporting their hypothesis that hallucinators experience abnormally vivid imagery. On closer examination, however, it is not clear whether they were measuring mental imagery vividness at all. Their subjects were asked to say whether they *believed* that the record 'White Christmas' had been played. As already noted, asking a subject to rate his belief in the existence of an experienced event is somewhat different from asking a subject to say how clearly he or she experienced that event.

Work employing traditional questionnaire measures of mental imagery vividness has not revealed a clear difference between hallucinators and non-hallucinators. Seitz and Molholm, in addition to investigating preferred mode of imagery, were able to compare the vividness of reported imagery of hallucinating subjects with that of controls, and found the hallucinators' imagery to be weaker. However, in a more recent, carefully controlled study carried out by the first author (Slade, 1976a), two question-naire measures of mental imagery were used and on one (the Betts scale) the schizophrenic patients were found overall to have more vivid imagery than controls, whereas hallucinating schizophrenic patients did not differ from non-hallucinating schizophrenics. On the second scale used (the Gordon scale of Mental Imagery Control), no difference was found between any of the three groups. These results stand in contrast to those of Brett and Starker (1977), who used their own versions of the Betts and the Gordon scales. On their version of the Betts scale (which inciden-tally contained an item that required the subjects to imagine the record 'White Christmas' and rate its *vividness*), Brett and Starker failed to find any difference between their hallucinating schizo-phrenic, non-hallucinating schizophrenic, and normal control groups. Their hallucinating subjects scored significantly lower than the rest on the Gordon scale, however. To confuse matters further, Catts, Armstrong Norcross and McConaghy (1980), again used the Betts and Gordon scales on hallucinating schizophrenics, non-hallucinating schizophrenics and normal controls and found no difference between the groups, a result that has recently been replicated by Chandiramani and Varma (1987) with patients in an Indian mental hospital. Finally, Heilbrun *et al.* (1983), who were also able to obtain a measure of vividness of mental imagery from their subjects (subjects were asked to imagine sixteen visual and fourteen auditory events and rate them for clarity on a seven-point scale), found that process schizophrenics, with or without hallucinations, reported less mental imagery than reactive schizo-phrenics.

It is difficult to know what to make of these findings, taken as a whole. They certainly lend no consistent support to a hypothesised relationship between mental imagery and hallucinations. It may be that the key to this lies in the different measures used to assess mental imagery or, more importantly, in the doubtful value of attempts to measure vividness of mental imagery in general. Some problems inherent in the phenomenological approach to mental imagery have already been mentioned. Following an influential review by Pylyshyn (1973), the status of this kind of research has repeatedly been called into question (cf. Evans, 1980; Pylyshyn, 1981; Kosslyn, 1983; Gardner, 1985). Pylyshyn's critique rested on a number of legs but included the observation that the presumed identity of mental imagery as measured by different operations rests on the 'metatheoretical' assumption that an image is best considered as some kind of picture. Pylyshyn doubted whether this ordinary notion of an image as something presented to perception (rather than as a by-product of various computational processes) could ever serve as an explanatory concept in cognitive science. This is not, of course, to deny that some images are experienced more vividly than others.

The objections raised by Pylyshyn (which apply in the main to the phenomenological rather than to the information-processing approach to imagery) are particularly relevant to the case of hallucinations. Indeed, the attempt to explain one phenomenal event in terms of another borders on circularity. In case this point should be misunderstood, it should perhaps be stressed that to question the value of vividness of mental imagery in explaining hallucinations is not to question the existence of a continuum between hallucinations and other mental events; it is the existence of this continuum that renders the attempt tautological. Nor is this argument to reject the value of mental imagery research for the study of hallucinations altogether. The information approach to imagery might possibly render valuable data (it would be interesting to measure how good visual hallucinators are on the Shepard and Meltzer mental rotation task, for example). However, at the time of writing, no such studies have been carried out.

In the meantime, it would seem that what remains of value from the Mintz and Alpert theory is the idea that hallucinators are poor reality testers. Unfortunately, aside from attempting to quantify reality testing by comparing the accuracy and confidence of perceptual judgements, Mintz and Alpert were unable to define this skill in any detail, or devise other means of assessing it.

A rather different approach to the measurement of reality

testing was proposed by the first author. This involved the use of the Verbal Transformation Effect (VTE) discovered by Warren and his colleagues (Warren and Gregory, 1958; Warren, 1968). The effect is elicited by playing a tape-loop on which the same word, phrase, sentence, musical note or rhythm is repeated at a fairly fast rate. The normal response is to hear phonetically related changes in the stimulus at regular intervals. In an initial study by the first author (Slade, 1976c) patients with a history of auditory hallucination were found not to differ from matched controls in terms of the frequency with which they experienced transformations but did differ in terms of their quality: they tended to hear more bizarre words and phrases than the controls. In a subsequent unpublished study (Place, 1980) with more chronically hallucinated patients the commonly reported abnormality was *not* to experience the illusion; the patients, unlike normal subjects, reported that they heard the same word repeatedly. However, an attempt to replicate these findings by Catts *et al.* (1980) was only partially successful. Although hallucinators again reported the illusions less often than the non-hallucinators, the results failed to reach significance. Finally, in a more recent study using the VTE with normal subjects, Bullen, Hemsley and Dixon (1987) found a positive correlation between the number of different words experienced on the task and LSHS scores.

The idea that hallucinators may be deficient in the skill of distinguishing between real events (external stimulation) and imaginary events (internally generated stimuli) is clearly of some importance. This view is implicit, for example, in Sarbin's (1967) conceptual analysis of hallucination and in the work of Heilbrun and his colleagues outlined in the previous chapter. What would appear to be lacking is an analysis of the components of this skill. More recent research which sheds light on this problem will be described in Chapter 8.

HALLUCINATIONS AND INNER SPEECH

The fourth group of theories that need to be considered in this chapter are those which propose a relationship between auditory hallucinations and inner speech or subvocalisation. Roughly speaking, by 'inner speech' is meant verbal thought or thinking in

125

words. Other terms that have been used to describe this phenomenon are 'private speech', 'egocentric speech', 'internalised
speech' and 'verbal self-regulation' (see Zivin, 1979, for a full
explanation of these terms and a historical account of the theories
to which they apply). Subvocalisation is a term that is used to
describe the covert activity of speech muscles that, it has often
been argued, accompanies verbal thought.

The idea that thought consists of some kind of inner speech has
enjoyed a long and chequered career that pre-dates the emergence
of psychology as an experimental science. (It was, for example,
held by the philosopher Thomas Hobbes.) After the turn of the
century, the theory was enthusiastically embraced by early experimental psychologists who saw in it a potential solution to one of
the most enduring problems in psychology — the nature of human
thought. Thus, Pavlov, in his later work, used the concept of inner
speech to account for the apparent difference between human and
animal intelligence, arguing that humans not only possess the 'first
signalling system of reality' common to animals (the neurological
mechanisms underlying conditioning) but also possess a uniquely
human 'second signalling system', consisting of words. Similarly,
Watson (1913, 1924) used the idea of inner speech and subvocalisation to incorporate thought into his programme of behaviour:

> The behaviourist advances the view that what the psychologists
> have hitherto called thought is in short nothing but talking to
> ourselves. (Watson, 1924)

It is fair to say that the role of speech in thought has remained
controversial since Watson's day and that no consensus on this
issue has yet been achieved. Jenkins (1969) considered three
hypothetical relationships between thought and language: (a)
thought is dependent on language; (b) thought *is* language; and (c)
language is dependent on thought. Jenkins concluded that, in all
likelihood, all of these were true. In the space available here it is
impossible to consider the evidence pertaining to this debate in any
detail, but before going on to look at the current evidence on
subvocalisation in general, and linking subvocalisation to auditory
hallucinations in particular, it is perhaps worth considering some of
the issues involved.

One source of information about the relationship between

speech and thought has been the study of child development. Piaget (1926) observed that young children often speak without any apparent concern for who, if anyone, is listening. Piaget described this kind of speech as 'egocentric' and argued that it occurs as a consequence of the child's inability to take into account the needs of the listener. Vygotsky (1962), on the other hand, maintained that this kind of speech is self-directed and is a transitional stage in the development of inner speech. Thus, according to Vygotsky, children first learn to speak overtly and follow instructions from adults, then go through a stage of instructing themselves overtly, before finally private speech and social speech become differentiated and private speech becomes completely internalised. In this manner, Vygotsky argued, language transforms the primitive, non-verbal thought of the child into the inner speech of the adult. Vygotsky's theory was later elaborated by Luria (1960) who, in a series of experimental studies, attempted to show that children below the age of four years are incapable of controlling their own motor behaviour by means of self-instruction. Systematic research has yielded at least partial support for Vygotsky's theory. Thus, observational studies have generally demonstrated that the private speech of younger children does have a regulatory function, but that this kind of speech is largely absent (i.e. internalised) in the case of older children (see Fuson, 1979 for a review). Early attempts to replicate Luria's experiments have produced less consistent results, although this is at least partially because researchers have misunderstood his methodology (Wozniak, 1972). More recent research, using somewhat different methodologies, has tended to support Luria's position (e.g. Bentall, Lowe and Beasty, 1985; Bentall and Lowe, 1987).

A second source of information about the relation of language to thought has emerged from the study of speech deficits. Deaf children have been a particular source of interest in this respect. In an important series of studies, Furth (1966) claimed that deaf children are capable of performing a range of intellectual tasks without the use of speech. However, Furth's work has been criticised because he may have underestimated the linguistic abilities of his subjects, and because many of his most severely handicapped subjects were probably fluent in sign language, which is a genuine linguistic form. Moreover, many of the tasks used by Furth may not have been appropriate as they required the kinds of simple

127

discrimination that animals are capable of (Cohen, 1976). A more carefully controlled study of the abilities of deaf children was carried out by Conrad (1979) who found a relationship between the use of inner speech (as assessed by a verbal memory task) and intelligence, but who supposed that intelligence helped the deaf child develop internal speech despite limited linguistic input, implying that intelligence leads to inner speech, rather than vice versa. Studies of aphasic patients (who have speech deficits as a result of brain damage) have not clarified the issue. Zangwill (1969), for example, has provided impressive evidence suggesting that even the most severely handicapped aphasics may retain considerable intellectual skills (as measured by non-verbal intelligence tests).

One way in which some researchers have attempted to assess the role of language in thought is by means of measuring the subvocalisations which many theorists (Watson and Vygotsky included) have supposed to accompany inner speech. Early attempts to do this, using a variety of crude devices (including rubber bulbs placed on the tongue, attached to pulleys), have been described by McGuigan (1978). For example, in one often cited study by Thorson (1925) no relationship was found between thought and subvocalisation as measured by the movement of a lever operated by a suction cup attached to the tongue. The measurement of subvocal speech was revolutionised by the invention of the electromyograph (EMG), a device which measures the electrical activity of muscles from electrodes placed on the skin, and which is hundreds of times more sensitive than its forerunners. However, despite the sensitivity of the EMG, interpretation of the data obtained using this device can be difficult. Raised EMG activity may be detected from the chin, lips and tongue during problem solving but it is important to establish whether or not this reflects genuine inner speech, rather than a mere increase in overall arousal.

One approach to solving this problem has been to compare speech muscle EMG with the EMG obtained from control muscles (e.g. the chest) during the performance of a variety of tasks. Using this method, increased speech muscle activity has been demonstrated in adults performing such diverse tasks as imagining speech (Jacobson, 1932), silent reading (Faaborg-Andersen and Edfelt, 1958) and memorising (Garrity, 1977a) and during the formation of counterarguments to disagreeable propositions (Cacioppo and Petty, 1981).

Further evidence that increases in speech muscle EMG reflect genuine subvocalisation comes from anatomical studies demonstrating that the muscles involved in normal speech and those implicated in apparent inner speech (as measured by EMG) are the same (Faaborg-Andersen, 1965) and from studies which have compared the EMG traces of subjects' speech with the traces produced when they are asked to think the same words to themselves (e.g. Sokolov, 1969, 1972). A final, more exacting test, which has put speech muscle activity under even greater scrutiny, has been devised by Locke and Fehr (1970), who asked subjects to remember lists of words containing either labial or non-labial phonemes (e.g. 'bomber' vs. 'chancey'). Locke and Fehr found that, as predicted, EMG activity increases more during the memorisation of the labial phonemes.

Taken as a whole, then, the evidence that inner speech is often accompanied by subvocalisation is convincing. Indeed, the EMG has proved to be a valuable research tool. Thus, Max (1937) and McGuigan (1971) have been able to show that deaf children who are fluent in sign language show raised hand and finger muscle activity during problem solving. Moreover, the limited data collected with children as subjects indicate that the amplitude of EMG activity during problem solving declines with age roughly in accordance with Vygotsky's theory (McGuigan and Bailey, 1969). (See Cacioppo and Petty, 1981, Garrity, 1977a, 1977b, and McGuigan, 1978, for more complete reviews of the results of EMG research.) Given these kinds of results, a link between subvocalisation, as measured by EMG, and auditory hallucinations appears plausible.

In a series of studies, Gould (1948, 1949, 1950) was able to show that verbal hallucinations are accompanied by subvocalisation. In Gould's 1948 study, passive EMGs were taken of a hundred psychiatric patients and a hundred controls. Raised lip and chin EMG activity was detected in 83 per cent of hallucinators but only 10 per cent of definitely non-hallucinating patients. In Gould's second study, rapid subvocal speech was recorded directly from one female hallucinating patient, using a sensitive microphone and amplifier. Finally, Gould (1950), in a number of further case studies, was able to demonstrate that raised lip and chin EMG activity actually correlated with the onset of hallucinatory activity.

Despite the apparent crudity of Gould's methods, his results have been replicated by others. McGuigan (1966) demonstrated raised lip EMG activity (compared with the activity of a control muscle) concurrent with hallucinations in a schizophrenic patient. In a more sophisticated study with nine patients, Inouye and Shimizu (1970) found a correlation between the duration of raised EMG activity and the subjects' self-reports of the duration of their hallucinations, as well as a correlation between the perceived loudness of the hallucinations and the amplitude of the EMG. Furthermore, Inouye and Shimizu were able to examine the latency between the increase in EMG activity and the reported onset of hallucinations, thus showing that the increase in speech muscle activity slightly preceded hallucinatory reports. More recently still, Green and Preston (1981) were able to record whispers concurrent with hallucinations in a male schizophrenic patient hallucinating a female voice. Moreover, auditory feedback (i.e. amplifying and playing the voice back to the patient) led to an increase in the loudness of the subvocal speech until it was virtually at normal level and the conversation between the patient and his voice could be clearly heard. While it is not obvious why auditory feedback should have this effect, the results of this study clearly support the view that auditory hallucinations occur simultaneously with subvocal speech.

If inner speech, as reflected in subvocal activity, is the basis of auditory hallucinations, then blocking or otherwise employing the capacity of the inner speech mechanisms should lead to a reduction in hallucinations. The extent to which this should happen is likely to depend upon the complexity of the verbal task used. (Available evidence suggests that giving a relatively simple task that occupies the speech musculature in a mechanical way, e.g. repeating the word 'the' over and over, has only a modest impact on performance of verbal reasoning tasks; see Sokolov, 1972; Eysenck, 1986) As should be apparent from Chapter 4, the available evidence in fact supports this prediction. For example, Slade (1974), working with two hallucinating subjects, found that a shadowing task could be used to reduce hallucination, and that the extent of the reduction was a function of the information content of the message being shadowed. Margo *et al.* (1981) found that a simple reading task was more effective at reducing auditory hallucination than simply listening to a recorded message (although listening alone produced a marked reduction). These findings are consistent with clinical observation. Hammeke *et al.* (1983), in their study of two elderly hearing-impaired persons suffering from auditory release hallucinations, found that the hallucinations could be inhibited by humming or singing. Not surprisingly, this finding has been exploited in the treatment of hallucinations (e.g. Erickson and Gustafson, 1968; James, 1983; see Chapter 7).

Based on this kind of data, a number of different theories of auditory hallucination have been proposed. Johnson (1978), describing auditory hallucinations as hallucinated inner speech, argued that a disorder of the inner speech mechanisms (which he considered to be a cardinal feature of schizophrenic cognition) might lead to the misattribution of verbal thought to an external source. He further argued that this process is reinforced by its emotional consequences for the schizophrenic. Thus, according to Johnson, 'The new and mysterious land of hallucination seduces the patient's curiosity and interest, leading to a predominance, both relatively and absolutely, of the inner hallucinatory life', and 'The person hallucinates because he enjoys what is heard, and the good voices have interesting things to say.' Johnson's hypothesis seems unlikely given the association between anxiety and hallucination observed for many psychotic individuals (see previous chapter). Moreover, despite lengthy consideration of the neural pathways possibly serving inner speech, Johnson was unable to formulate a coherent account of the inner speech defect said to be linked to hallucination.

An even more speculative account of auditory hallucinations was proposed by Jaynes (1979), who argued that human consciousness results from the perception or belief that cognitive processes occur in a subjective inner 'mind space'. According to Jaynes, the ancient Greeks living at the time of the *Iliad* were not conscious in this sense and therefore experienced their own inner speech, specifically inner speech from the right, non-dominant hemisphere, as hallucinations or voices of the Gods. (The main evidence for this, apparently, is that the *Iliad* contains no reference to mental states or volition.) According to Jaynes, the schizophrenic hallucinator is in much the same position as the characters in the *Iliad*, and Jaynes further suggested that this is a result of poor neurological communication between the two cerebral hemispheres. Green (1978a) proposed a somewhat similar account, arguing that, because of poor interhemispheric transfer of information, the dominant side of the schizophrenic's brain is unaware that the non-dominant side is speaking. (This theory will be considered in more detail in the next chapter.)

Yet another theory linking auditory hallucinations to inner speech has been proposed by Burns, Heiby and Tharp (1983) who made use of Skinner's (1957) theory of verbal behaviour. Although Burns *et al.*'s account is fairly complex, its core feature is an observed similarity between hallucinations and experiences generated by Skinner's (1936) 'verbal summator', a device that plays a vague pattern of speech sounds and which, in most people, produces an illusion of hearing voices. According to Burns *et al.*, auditory hallucinations may result from the mishearing of environmental and physiological stimuli which in turn may lead to long chains of unedited subvocal activity. It is interesting to note in this context that Skinner's verbal summator effect is quite similar to Warren's (1968) Verbal Transformation Effect (VTE). Furthermore, although expressed in a different language, Burns *et al.*'s theory is not dissimilar to Frith's cognitive seepage account described earlier in the chapter. If this theory is correct, it would be expected that hallucinating subjects would be more susceptible to the VTE than non-hallucinating subjects. However, as already described above, the available evidence on the relationship between hallucinations and response to the VTE is inconsistent (Slade, 1976c; Catts *et al.*, 1980; Place, 1980; Bullen *et al.*, 1987).

The most recent account of the relationship between subvocalisation and hallucination has been proposed by Hoffman (1986), who equated subvocalisation with verbal imagery. Hoffman's analysis was based on the more general hypothesis that schizophrenics suffer from a disorder of 'discourse planning' (Hoffman, Kirstein, Stopek and Cicchetti, 1982; Hoffman and Sledge, 1984). On this view, a 'discourse plan' is an abstract cognitive representation of the intention behind what will be said which is sensitive to the goals and beliefs of the speaker (Deese, 1978). Without this kind of plan, it is claimed, a speaker would be unable to use multiple sentences or clauses in a co-ordinated fashion in order to express a coherent message. Hypothesising that disorganised schizophrenic speech results from a disorder of this process,

Hoffman (1986) further proposed that such a disorder would make schizophrenics prone to producing 'unintended' subvocalisations. Hoffman argued that hallucinators might wrongly infer that such unintended subvocalisations originate from an external source and would therefore experience them as auditory hallucinations.

Hoffman predicted that there should be a statistical association between disordered schizophrenic speech and hallucination. In an attempt to test this prediction, Hoffman and his colleagues studied the conversational speech of 39 schizophrenics, 24 manic patients, and 40 normals (Andreasen, Grove and Hoffman, 1984; Hoffman, Stopek and Andreasen, 1986). Twenty-six of the schizophrenics and three of the manics suffered from auditory hallucinations. Because of the low number of manics suffering hallucinations, Hoffman excluded them from his analysis. A statistically significant relationship was found between absense or presence of hallucinations and disordered discourse in the schizophrenic group, the hallucinators exhibiting a greater severity of language disturbance.

The present authors and others have criticised Hoffman's account on the grounds of the evidence he presented to support his case (Bentall and Slade, 1986; Posey, 1986; Rund, 1986; Schwartz, 1986). The assumption behind the theory would seem to be that schizophrenia is a unitary condition and that the symptoms of schizophrenia must therefore have a common underlying cause. The evidence for this assumption is doubtful (Bentall, 1986; Bentall, Jackson and Pilgrim, 1987, see Chapter 2). It was this assumption that allowed Hoffman to exclude his manic subjects from his analysis. As fully three-quarters of his manic subjects were described as suffering from disordered discourse (as opposed to only two-thirds of the schizophrenic sample), it seems unlikely that a statistically significant association between disordered discourse and hallucinations would have been discovered had the manics been included. Indeed, it might be argued that the fact that so many manics can suffer from disordered discourse without hallucinating is sufficient to seriously jeopardise the credibility of the theory, although Hoffman has countered this claim by arguing that the underlying disorder of discourse planning in mania is different from that observed in schizophrenia. A further problem for Hoffman's account is presented by the kinds of hallucination experienced by normal individuals (presumably in the absence of any kind of thought disorder) described in Chapter 3 (Posey, 1986). Looked at in this light, Hoffman's theory would seem to be a case study in the perils of carrying out research on syndromes rather than symptoms.

Of course, it is not clear that the feeling of unintendedness necessarily results from a disorder of discourse planning. As noted in Chapter 1, hallucinators often feel that their experiences are beyond their control, and Hoffman's hypothesis that the feeling of unintendedness may lead to a non-self inference may still have value, whatever the ultimate truth about the association between hallucinations and thought disorder. The possible role of inference in hallucination will be discussed in detail in Chapter 8.

Like the other theories described in this section, Hoffman's account suffers from the further problem that it only seems to explain auditory hallucinations. Hallucinations, however, may occur in other modalities. A further difficulty noted by Zivin (1986) also applies to subvocalisation theories in general. Discussing Hoffman's equating of subvocalisation with verbal imagery, Zivin observed that the existing literature on normal cognition (particularly Soviet and American research on inner speech) tends to view subvocalisation as an exclusively motor phenomenon. Indeed, Salame and Baddeley (1982), in a study of speech processes in short-term (working) memory, argued that they could identify two separate inner speech components, an articulatory loop (roughly equivalent to subvocalisation) and a primary acoustic store (roughly equivalent to verbal imagery). As evidence for this distinction, Baddeley and Lewis (1981) found that the kind of articulatory suppression (saying 'the, the, the, ...') which has been found to moderately impair performance on verbal reasoning tasks had no impact on their subjects' ability to make quite complex phonemic discriminations (deciding whether visually presented nonsense words sound like real words). A task described by Eysenck (1986) which the reader might like to try quite nicely demonstrates this observation: all that is required is to read the preceding paragraph while repeating a simple word (e.g. 'the') over and over. Most people find that they can quite easily imagine the sound of the words they are reading despite this kind of articulatory suppression. It seems likely that any further attempt to explain auditory hallucinations purely in terms of inner speech production processes will have to take account of distinctions of this kind.

CONCLUSIONS

In this chapter four main types of psychological explanation of hallucination have been examined. The evidence presented in favour of a classical conditioning model of hallucination seems more readily explicable in terms of suggestibility. Seepage theories such as West's and Frith's can account for much of the data outlined in Chapter 4 but fail on two counts. First, they rest on a naive model of consciousness. Secondly, they suppose an over-simplistic relationship between environmental stimulation and hallucination. Indeed, West's theory and Frith's theory make conflicting predictions about the relationship between stimulation and hallucination, neither of which is supported by close examination of the data.

Mental imagery theories fall down because they are either circular or unsupported by the available evidence. Indeed, these theories seem to be based on a view of mental imagery that is no longer accepted by cognitive psychologists. It is possible that these theories could be restated in terms of modern thinking on the subject of imagery, in which case they would be open to testing. It would be interesting to examine how visual hallucinators perform on mental rotation tasks, for example.

Finally, subvocalisation theories enjoy at least some empirical support from electromyographic studies. Unfortunately, a general limitation of these theories is that they can only explain hallucinations in the auditory modality. Moreover, although it seems that auditory hallucinations are accompanied by subvocalisation, it is not clear why this should be so. Hoffman's suggestion that hallucinators mistakenly infer that their subvocalisations originate from an external source is particularly interesting in this respect, but his account of why such a false inference should occur is unconvincing. However, the idea that hallucinations result from an inferential error or errors is one which will be returned to at a later stage in the book.

6

Biological Theories of Hallucination

In the last chapter four types of psychological theory of hallucination were examined. Not surprisingly, given that hallucinations have generally been viewed as evidence of mental disorder, a range of biological theories of hallucination have also been proposed. It is these theories that will be examined in the present chapter.

Like most of the psychological theories of hallucination, the biological theories are generally speculative and phenomenon-driven. This is particularly the case with respect to those biochemical models which have been proposed following observations of the effects of particular drugs which either cause hallucinations (in the case of the so called 'psychedelic drugs') or prevent them from occurring (in the case of the phenothiazines). Other theories have been proposed simply by extension of already formulated models of schizophrenia. This is particularly true of the genetic approach to hallucination which will be examined first.

GENETIC THEORIES

Since the early work of Franz Kallman (1938) it has usually been assumed that schizophrenia is a condition that is at least partially determined by genetic endowment (Gottesman and Shields, 1982). Indeed, the existence of a genetic component to schizophrenia has been widely cited as evidence for the existence of a schizophrenia disease entity by those who have wished to defend traditional methods of psychiatric classification (e.g. Clare, 1976; Wing, 1978). Thus, Kety (1974) has argued that 'If schizophrenia

is a myth, it is myth with a strong genetic component.' As hallucinations, when unaccompanied by cerebral pathology, are usually
regarded as first-rank symptoms of schizophrenia, one implication
of this genetic view of schizophrenia would seem to be that
hallucinations have a genetic component, or at least that traits
associated with hallucination are under partial genetic control.
There are a number of possible objections to this argument,
however.

First, as noted in Chapter 2, serious doubts exist about the
validity of a unitary schizophrenia disease entity (Sarbin and
Manusco, 1980; Bentall, 1986; Bentall, Jackson and Pilgrim,
1988). If these doubts are at all justified, it is difficult to see how
the available genetic evidence can have much relevance. Indeed, it
may be argued that the equivocal nature of the genetic data on
schizophrenia (see below) is a result of the fact that genetic
methodology has been applied to a concept lacking in both
reliability and validity.

The second objection concerns the quality of the empirical
research into the genetics of schizophrenia. Although most
theorists, while conceding the existence of some methodological
weaknesses in the genetic research, hold that the data is convincing
overall (e.g. Gottesman and Shields, 1982; Murray and Reveley,
1986), a number of recent authors have questioned the validity of
these conclusions on the basis of extensive reviews of the literature.

The work of Franz Kallman continues to be widely cited in this
respect (Marshall, 1984). Like most of the early work on the
inheritance of schizophrenia, Kallman's research involved the
study of twins. Twins are important for genetic investigations
because they can be either monozygotic (MZ, identical) or
dizygotic (DZ, non-identical or fraternal). As MZ twins share the
same genetic endowment they should be highly concordant for any
traits that have a large genetic component. The observed concordance rate should be less in the case of DZ twins (who have no
greater genetic similarity than ordinary sibs) and even less in the
case of more distant relatives. Finally, of course, the concordance
rate for inherited traits should be at chance level for pairs of
completely unrelated individuals. (See Gottesman and Shields,
1982, for a more detailed exposition of the logic of twin research.)
This is precisely the result that Kallman claimed for his pioneer-
ing twin studies, and similar results have also been claimed by

137

subsequent researchers (Gottesman and Shields, 1982).

In fact, Kallman's work has been known to be unreliable for some years, mainly because of the poor way in which the data were reported, the looseness of the diagnostic procedures employed, because zygosity (whether the twins were identical or fraternal) was not determined independently of psychiatric diagnosis, and because of his commitment to eugenic measures which may have led him to bias his results (Jackson, 1960; Marshall, 1984; Rose, Kamin and Lewontin, 1984). Later research with twins has often been better controlled than Kallman's, and the concordance rates observed have been for the most part considerably lower than those obtained by Kallman (Gottesman and Shields, 1982). For example, in a particularly well carried out study by Fisher (1973), it was found that five out of 21 (24 per cent) MZ twin pairs and four out of 41 (10 per cent) DZ twin pairs were concordant for schizophrenia. None the less, even in the case of such methodologically sound twin studies, problems still arise. As Marshall and Pettit (1985) have demonstrated, the apparent results of twin research have been dependent on the particular methods used to calculate concordance (see Gottesman and Shields 1982, for a description of the different methods). Thus, by using a proband-wise method, instead of a pairwise method Gottesman and Shields were able to increase Fisher's MZ and DZ concordance rates to 56 per cent and 27 per cent, respectively. Another problem concerns the use of age corrections to take into account the possibility that a twin non-concordant for schizophrenia might develop the illness after the completion of a study. One commonly used correction, the abridged Weinberg method, involves doubling the concordance rates observed for those twin pairs within the age band for which there is maximum risk of schizophrenic break-down, usually considered to extend from 20 to 40 years of age. (Fisher's results were not age corrected as her subjects were all elderly at the time of her analysis.) A final objection to twin research concerns its ability to separate out environmental and genetic effects; twins are raised in similar environments and MZ twins are particularly likely to be treated alike. To test for this possibility, Rose *et al.* (1984) looked at studies in which the concordance rates for both DZ twins and ordinary sibs have been calculated. DZ twins are no more genetically identical than brothers and sisters and therefore, if the genetic theory of schizophrenia is correct, they should be no more concordant for schizophrenia than sibs in general. Rose *et al.* found that the concordance rates reported for DZ twins were generally higher than those reported for sibs.

Given the weaknesses inherent in twin research, genetic theorists have searched for new ways of establishing a hereditary component to schizophrenia. A particularly important approach involves the study of individuals who have been born of schizophrenic parents but who have been adopted at an early age. The most important series of such studies has been carried out by Danish and American researchers in Denmark (where psychiatric and adoption records are particularly good) and has involved the investigation of the adopted-away offspring of schizophrenic parents (Rosenthal, Wender, Kety, Welner and Schulsinger, 1971; Haier, Rosenthal and Wender, 1978) or, conversely, the biological and adopting relatives of adopted children who have become schizophrenic (Kety, Rosenthal, Wender, Schulsinger and Jacobsen, 1975) in comparison with appropriate controls. Although the results of these studies have been widely accepted as evidence of the inheritance of schizophrenia, the data collected prove to be more equivocal on close analysis. Lidz, Blatt and Cook (1981) found that, in the studies of the adopted-away children of schizophrenics, manic depressives and patients of uncertain diagnosis had been included in the sample of index parents; there had been a failure to replicate early positive results in a later extended series; and (as noted in Chapter 3) significant results had only been achieved by using the broad concept of 'schizophrenia spectrum disorder' (a diagnosis given to 44 per cent of the offspring of the manic depressives and to no less than 17–25 per cent of the offspring of the control parents). When these factors were allowed for, Lidz *et al.* were unable to find any significant difference in the prevalence of schizophrenia between the two groups of offspring.

Lidz and Blatt (1983) and Rose *et al.* (1984) subsequently found similar methodological flaws in the research dealing with the biological and adopting relatives of adoptees who had become schizophrenic. When Rose *et al.* obtained the raw data from the authors of these studies they found a selective adoption effect: the adopting relatives of the children who became schizophrenic were more likely to have a history of schizophrenia than the adopting relatives of the control children, suggesting, if anything, that environmental factors are important in the genesis of schizo-phrenia.

The equivocal results obtained from both twin and adoption studies should come as no surprise, given the equivocal status of the schizophrenia diagnosis. Although, on balance, it is undoub-tedly unwise to rule out the role of heredity in psychotic break-down (the better carried-out genetic studies such as Fisher's do at least suggest some effect), the use of scientifically questionable diagnostic categories may well have contributed to the obscuring of such effects. Indeed, it must be added that exactly the same considerations apply to much of the research designed to detect environmental determinants of schizophrenic breakdowns (e.g. investigations into patterns of communication in the families of schizophrenics) which has yielded similarly ambiguous results (Bentall *et al.*, 1988).

Of course, whereas it may not make sense to ask whether schizophrenia is inherited, it may make sense to ask whether there are genetic components to particular pyschotic symptoms, for example hallucinations. Indeed, this strategy is consistent with the symptom-orientated approach to psychopathology that has been advocated throughout this book. Research that has attempted to identify separate genetic components of hypothesised subtypes of schizophrenia (e.g. simple, hebephrenic, catatonic or paranoid), which might be potentially informative in this respect, has gener-ally failed to yield theoretically interesting discoveries (Gottesman and Shields, 1982). Research into the inheritance of particular symptoms is almost non-existent, although this strategy has recently been advocated by some theorists (e.g. Berenbaum, Oltmanns and Gottesman, 1985).

Berenbaum *et al.* attempted to study the inheritance of thought disorder, using the twin method. A series of schizophrenic patients and their twins (17 identical, 14 fraternal same sex, 12 fraternal opposite sex) were rated for thought disorder using a formal assessment schedule. Overall, no evidence for the inheritance of thought disorder was detected. However, when scores on the assessment schedule were factor analysed, two interpretable factors emerged: a verbosity factor (relating to pressure of speech and other similar characteristics) and a speech discontinuity factor (relating to derailment, incoherence and *non sequiturs*). There was some evidence that verbosity was influenced by non-genetic familial factors as high concordance rates were observed on this factor for both MZ and DZ twins.

The only study which has directly attempted to identify genetic determinants specific to hallucination was reported by Rosenthal and Quinn (1977), who investigated the hallucinatory experiences of four genetically identical (MZ) women (the 'Genain quadruplets') who were concordant for schizophrenia. (According to Rosenthal and Quinn, the probability of identical quadruplets being schizophrenic by chance is approximately one in every one and a half billion births.) At the time of their report, the quadruplets were in their mid-forties and had been known to the authors for more than 20 years, during which time both auditory and visual hallucinations had been prominent symptoms. On the basis of their observations, Rosenthal and Quinn concluded that all four girls were concordant for the occurrence of hallucinations and 'It is therefore likely that this sympton in this set of monozygous quadruplets is related closely or directly to their schizophrenic genotype.' A careful reading of Rosenthal and Quinn's data suggests several reasons for caution about this conclusion.

First, there was some doubt about the status of one of the four women, Myra Genain, who had never been observed hallucinating by the authors. Although the Genains' mother reported that Myra had hallucinated during a period of crisis when she was 24 years old, the examining psychiatrist reported no such symptoms at the time. Indeed, it is notable that, of the four women, Myra was the only one who had never been hospitalised (although she had taken phenothiazines during 'shaky' periods) and at the time of the report was happily married with two sons and communicating only rarely with the investigators.

A second reason for questioning Rosenthal and Quinn's conclusions concerns the possible role of the environment in precipitating the psychopathology of three Genains who were undoubtedly ill. Their father was 'somewhat unstable', 'drank to excess', and, 'at frequent intervals he would be threatening, sometimes behaving as though he were paranoid'. It seems likely that he molested at least some of the quadruplets as, according to Rosenthal and Quinn, 'He chose Nora as his favourite, at times fondling her breasts and being intrusive when she was in the bathroom.' The less than satisfactory family atmosphere can also be inferred from the following:

Iris and Hester engaged in mutual masturbation and the parents, horrified, agreed with an attending physician to have both girls circumcised and their hands tied to their beds for thirty nights. Nora and Myra were not allowed to visit their sisters and 'couldn't understand the whole situation'. Three of the girls completed high school; Hester did not. Her parents kept her at home in her senior year and she cried a great deal.

In fact, given these observations, it seems quite remarkable that the investigators did not seriously consider the role of the family structure in the development of the Genains' psychiatric problems.

Finally, the role of the investigators in the bleak and unhappy lives of the Genains bears some consideration. Rosenthal and Quinn reported that they had a special relationship with the Genains, 'visiting them at home twice a year, spending a few days with them each visit, taking them out to dinners and brunches, talking with them, discussing their thoughts, problems, current circumstances and activities, symptoms, acquaintances, etc.' As the investigators' interest in the four unfortunates depended, presumably, on their presentation of interesting psychiatric material, it is impossible to rule out (without implying any dishonesty on behalf of the Genains) the possibility that the data were distorted by its consequences for the family. With these reservations in mind it seems impossible to conclude anything about the inheritance of hallucinations on the basis of the Genain evidence.

A more recent study by Kendler and Hays (1982), while not directly focusing on the inheritance of hallucinations, provides more reliable evidence that is relevant to the issue. In a novel attempt to identify the specific role of genetic influences in schizophrenia, Kendler and Hays identified two separate groups of schizophrenics: a group of 30 subjects with first-degree relatives also suffering from schizophrenia ('familial schizophrenics') and a group of 83 subjects without close relatives suffering from schizophrenia ('non-familial schizophrenics'). Assuming that inheritance played a larger role in the schizophrenic breakdowns of the former group, Kendler and Hays hoped to identify the specific contribution of genes to psychopathology by comparing the two groups for symptoms. No differences were found in abnormal affect, delusions or hallucinations. However, the group of familial schizophrenics were more often thought disordered (56.7 per cent against 18.1 per cent). This finding would seem to imply that there is an inherited predisposition to thought disorder but not to hallucination. At first sight the former of these two conclusions seems to directly contradict the findings of Berenbaum *et al.* (1985) but the data could alternatively be interpreted as evidence that thought disorder is a phenomenon determined by family environment or perhaps even learned from a thought-disordered family member.

To summarise: there is little evidence that hallucinations or the predisposition to hallucinate is inherited, other than the equivocal evidence for the inheritance of schizophrenia in general. However, this lack of evidence may merely reflect the absence of appropriate well controlled studies. The possible contribution of genetics to hallucinations is an obvious area for future investigations.

NEUROPSYCHOLOGICAL THEORIES

Neuropsychological theorising about hallucinations is easier to find than hard data. Thus some authors have implicated the brain stem in hallucination because of its apparent role in regulating arousal, wakefulness and dreaming. Others have hypothesised that the disinhibition of cortical areas subserving perception or reality testing may be responsible. More recently, some authors have pointed to the organisation of language processes in the brain in attempts to account for hallucinations in the auditory modality.

The brain stem has been implicated in some theories of hallucination principally because of its role in the regulation of wakefulness and because of the apparent similarity between dreaming and hallucinating (Scheibel and Scheibel, 1962; West, 1962, 1975; Hartmann, 1975; Winters, 1975). Thus, Hartmann (1975) has argued that 'The dream meets the definition of hallucination in every respect and most of us, according to a large body of physiological data, spend from one to two hours dreaming every night.'

It will be recalled that West, whose theory was outlined in the previous chapter, also regarded dreaming and hallucinations as closely related, if not identical. According to West, dreams or hallucinations occur when a combination of arousal and low external stimulation allows the release of engrams into consciousness.

143

Winters (1975), in contrast to West, has hypothesised a rather different role for arousal in this respect, arguing from animal data (mostly collected from cats) that hallucinations are associated with a partial functional disorganisation of the reticular units controlling arousal and the modulation of sensory information. According to Winters, drugs affecting the nervous system first induce a state of increasing central nervous excitation, followed by central nervous system depression. On the basis of his animal observations Winters proposed that different types of hallucinatory experience are associated with different points along the continuum of CNS excitation. At moderate levels of excitation, marked by a periodic 2.5 Hz hypersynchronised EEG pattern interspersed with periods of desynchrony, visual hallucinations of the kind elicited by LSD occur. Winters argued that the periods of EEG desynchrony reflect a return to the non-hallucinatory state and the human subject's consequent awareness that he or she is hallucinating. On this view, higher states of CNS excitation are associated with hallucinations which are only remembered later (because of the lack of periods of desynchrony) or even epileptic seizures and accompanying hallucinatory auras. Winters argued that the observed hypersynchronous EEG is associated with a partial functional disorganisation of the reticular system, which then fails to adequately modulate incoming sensory information, hence the resulting hallucinations. Two general problems with this account were acknowledged by Winters. First, the evidence supporting it consists entirely of data obtained from the implanted cat preparation (although there is at least some consistent EEG data from human subjects given psychotomimetic drugs; Heath and Mickle, 1960). Secondly, Winter's own animal data suggest that it is lack of modulation of the visual system which is most often associated with EEG hypersynchrony. The extent to which the theory might be applicable to psychotic hallucinations is therefore questionable, although Winters argued that psychotic patients may under-report visual hallucinations because they find them relatively undisturbing.

In yet a further interpretation of the relationship between hallucinations and arousal, Hartmann (1975) argued that hallucinatory or hallucination-like states (such as dreams, vivid images) are so ubiquitous that the correct question to ask is not, why do hallucinations occur at all? but, what prevents hallucinations occurring during wakefulness? Hartmann viewed the tendency to hallucinate as resulting from the balance of two types of process: positive processes tending to elicit hallucinations (psychological needs, psychodynamic conflicts, high emotional arousal) and inhibitory processes (sensory input controlling conscious scanning, reality testing, interactive feedback from the 'real' world). According to Hartmann, brain-stem activation of the cortex in the absence of inhibitory factors (for example, during dreaming or psychotic states) will therefore result in hallucination.

There is not much to choose between these accounts on the basis of the available data. An apparent link between hallucination and dreaming might be supported by evidence that sleep deprivation leads to hallucination. Early sleep researchers in fact reported such an association (e.g. Berger and Oswald, 1962), although subsequent investigators have tended to argue that such hallucinations are rare and transient and may, in any case, reflect pre-existing psychopathology (Meddis, 1982). It is clear from the data described in Chapter 4 that hallucinations tend to occur during periods of high autonomic arousal. It is also true that a number of authors have hypothesised, mostly on the basis of animal data or from the study of patients with known reticular damage, that reticular disorder might account for the kinds of attentional deficits often observed in psychotic patients (Mirsky, 1978). Consistent with this hypothesis, Fisman (1975) found neuropathology of the brain stem in six out of eight schizophrenic brains examined at autopsy, although Hankoff and Peress (1981) found only one example of brain-stem pathology in a similar series of eight brains; significantly the brain in question had belonged to a patient with a long history of alcohol abuse. Even if the limited evidence for brain-stem pathology in schizophrenic patients is accepted, there is no direct evidence linking such pathology to hallucinations. It may be that future investigations of brain-stem abnormalities in hallucinating patients will shed more light on this issue.

In contrast to theories which have attempted to explain hallucinations in terms of disorders of the brain mechanisms controlling arousal, more recent theories have tended to focus on the asymmetrical properties of the brain. In right-handed individuals the neurological mechanisms subsuming speech are usually located in the left (dominant) cerebral hemisphere whereas the

145

right (non-dominant) hemisphere has linguistic skills limited, a most, to speech comprehension. In left-handed people, on the other hand, the speech mechanisms are sometimes lateralised to the right, sometimes to the left and sometimes bilaterally.

A link between schizophrenic symptoms and left hemisphere dysfunction was proposed by Flor-Henry (1969, 1986) on the basis that psychotic-like symptoms are often observed in epileptic states related to left temporal lobe lesions (see Chapter 2). Similarly, Alpert and Martz (1977), while reviewing research indicating that psychotic-like symptoms are most often associated with bilateral temporal lobe epilepsy, noted that the hypothesis of a specifically left hemisphere involvement in schizophrenia is attractive because all schizophrenic symptoms seem to involve a disturbance of typically left hemisphere functions (speech, speech perception and verbal reasoning). This would be consistent with Johnson's (1978) proposal that a disorder of inner speech mechanisms is implicated in auditory hallucinations. Although numerous studies have produced data indicating apparent left hemisphere abnormalities in a proportion of schizophrenic patients (using measures such as the EEG, CT scans, regional cerebral blood flow lateralisation of autonomic activity; see Seidman, 1984, for a review of this literature), few studies have provided empirical support for a specific relationship between hallucination and left-hemisphere dysfunction. Bazhin, Wasserman and Tonkonogii (1975) found that hallucinating schizophrenics exhibited an increased right ear (i.e. left hemisphere) threshold for tone perception during periods of hallucination. More recently, McKay, Golden and Scott (1981), in perhaps the only systematic investigation of the neuropsychological characteristics of hallucinators, gave the Luria–Nebraska battery of neuropsychological tests to 10 auditory hallucinating, 10 visual hallucinating and 20 non-hallucinating psychiatric patients. Evidence of some left frontal lobe impairment was detected for the group suffering from auditory hallucinations, but not for either the visual hallucinators or the non-hallucinators. Three further studies providing data consistent with the role of the left hemisphere have been cited by Flor-Henry (1986). In a CT scan study of a large number of schizophrenics by Takahashi, Inabe and Inanaga (1981), it was found that left temporal cortical atrophy alone was associated with hallucinations. Uchino *et al.* (1984), in a similar attempt to relate

CT scan data to florid psychotic symptoms, observed an association between auditory hallucinations and enlargement of the left sylvian fissure and the left anterior horn of the lateral ventricle. Finally, using telemetered EEG measures, Stevens and Livermore (1982) noted a significant correlation between hallucinations and suppression of left temporal alpha waves (indicating left temporal activation). Some of these results, particularly the finding of increased right tone threshold and left temporal activation during auditory hallucinations, may simply indicate that the neurological mechanisms of inner speech are active during auditory hallucinations: not a particularly surprising finding if auditory hallucinations consist of misattributed inner speech or verbal imagery. However, the anatomical abnormalities observed by CT scan, together with the neuropsychological findings of McKay *et al.* (1981), do suggest that left hemisphere abnormalities may be involved in at least some forms of auditory hallucination.

An intriguing finding that might be relevant in this respect concerns the lateralisation of hallucinations themselves. Taylor and Fleminger (1981), in a study of 44 schizophrenic patients with lateralised symptoms, found a slight but non-significant tendency for auditory hallucinations to be located on the left side. More recently, Gruber, Mangat, Balminder and Abou-Taleb (1984) found that 29 out of a series of 54 schizophrenic patients could locate the source of an auditory hallucination, approximately equal numbers attributing their voices to the left or the right ear. However, a significant association was found between mood and the location of the voices, with the more depressed patients more likely to hear their voices to the right. Gruber *et al.* suggested that this finding indicated a possible relationship between affective disturbance and right hemisphere disorder.

In contrast to those theorists who have pointed to the left hemisphere for the source of hallucinations, other authors have suggested that what may be involved is a disorder of the relationship between the two hemispheres. Jaynes (1979), in his highly speculative account of the origins of consciousness referred to in the previous chapter, argued that the historical development of conscious self-awareness was accompanied by a reorganisation of the brain such that the dominant hemisphere came to inhibit the speech-processing capabilities of the non-dominant hemisphere. One implication of this theory is that a reduction of this inhibition

147

should release right hemisphere 'voices', an explanation Jaynes proposed to account for the auditory hallucinations of schizophrenics.

A similar view of the way in which hemispheric organisation might account for auditory hallucinations was proposed by Green (1978a; Green, Glass and O'Callaghan, 1980; Green, Hallett and Hunter, 1983). Green's account followed his own research in which he obtained evidence that acute schizophrenic patients suffer from a disorder of the interhemispheric transfer of information so that, for example, tactile information presented to one hemisphere (e.g. when a subject is asked to feel the shape of an object with one hand) is unavailable to the other hemisphere (e.g. as evinced by the subject's inability to recognise the same object with the other hand; cf. Green, 1978b). Like Jaynes, Green proposed that auditory hallucinations might originate in the non-dominant hemisphere, finding expression via subvocalisation mediated through the speech motor areas of the dominant hemisphere. On the basis of evidence that schizophrenics suffer from a left ear deficit in auditory perception (Green and Kotenko, 1980), attributed to the same disorder of interhemispheric organisation, Green *et al.* (1983) further proposed that blocking the inferior ear might lead to a reduction of symptoms. In support of this idea Green offered the observation that, when testing patients on a binaural auditory perception task, the presence of auditory hallucinations sometimes appeared to covary with left ear deficits. In fact, the rationale behind such 'ear-plug' therapy is not clear, and attempts to apply it have not always met with results consistent with Green's theory (see next chapter). Moreover, Green's theory is not consistent with much of the data pertaining to left hemisphere abnormalities reviewed above. For example, Bazhin *et al.* (1975) observed *right* ear deficits in association with hallucinations rather than the left ear deficits predicted by Green; on Green's account activation of the *right* hemisphere would be expected in association with hallucinations instead of the left hemisphere activation observed by Stevens and Livermore (1982).

More generally, the hypothesis that schizophrenic patients suffer from some kind of abnormal organisation of the cerebral hemispheres has met with a great deal of enthusiasm (Seidman, 1984; Claridge, 1985), although the exact nature of the interhemispheric abnormality hypothesised to underlie schizophrenia has

148

varied from author to author. Beaumont and Diamond (1973), for example, have proposed that the two hemispheres are relatively disconnected in schizophrenia whereas Randall (1980) has suggested that the two hemispheres may be connected by too many fibres. Galin (1974) has argued that the degree of interhemispheric inhibition is increased in schizophrenia. Unfortunately, the finding of impaired interhemispheric communication in schizophrenic subjects has not been replicated by a number of researchers (Shagrass, Josiassen, Roemer, Straumans and Slepner, 1983; Sheldon and Knight, 1984; Merriam and Gardner, 1987). Indeed, a general problem that applies to all attempts to relate psychiatric symptoms to abnormalities of hemispheric asymmetry (but which is often ignored) concerns the reliability of the measures employed; a number of authors have recently pointed out that tests for asymmetry have very poor test–retest reliability, making it difficult to interpret the significance of apparently anomalous observations (Mehler, Morton and Jusczyk, 1984; Schwartz and Kirstner, 1984).

It would seem that the available neuropsychological data are not consistent enough to support any particular account of hallucinations. A cautious but perhaps realistic appraisal of the evidence on the neuropsychology of psychosis in general has been offered by Seidman (1984). On the basis of a thorough review of the available research, Seidman suggested that perhaps 20 to 35 per cent of schizophrenic patients suffer from neurological abnormalities; that these abnormalities are various and not confined to disorders of the cerebral hemispheres; and that this range of abnormalities is sufficient to call into question the idea that schizophrenia is a unitary condition admitting of a simple aetiology.

BIOCHEMICAL THEORIES

The final group of biological theories that remain to be examined are those that implicate specific neurochemical mechanisms in hallucination.

In recent years, a considerable amount has been learnt about biochemical pathways in the mammalian brain (Iversen and Iversen, 1981). Much of this information has been acquired as a result of studying the action of particular drugs or following the

149

development of new histological techniques. Although the fact that transmission of information in the nervous system occurs by chemical means has been known for many years, new chemicals are constantly being implicated as neurotransmitters (substances that carry the nervous impulse across the synaptic cleft separating different neurones). Thus, Iversen and Iversen (1981) were able to list five proven, five probable and 22 possible neurotransmitters. Biochemical theories of hallucination have generally been developed following the discovery of particular drugs that affect hallucination, each drug being hypothesised as acting by interfering (as an agonist or antagonist) with the action of a specific neurotransmitter. Thus, without attempting to be exhaustive, it is possible to classify most of the biochemical theorising on hallucination according to the drugs held to affect hallucination and the neurotransmitters through which this effect is said to be mediated. Three major types of hypothesis will be considered: those relating to the action of 'psychedelic' drugs on the neurotransmitter 5-hydroxytriptamine; those relating to the action of amphetamines on dopamine-bearing neurones; and those relating to a more recently discovered class of neurochemicals, the endogenous opiates.

(i) 5-Hydroxytriptamine (serotonin) and LSD

A neurotransmitter that has often been implicated in the causation of hallucinations is 5-hydroxytriptamine (5-HT), otherwise known as serotonin. Cell bodies containing 5-HT have been identified in the nuclei of the raphe system of the mammalian brain stem, with ascending fibres to the mesolimbic forebrain, the pontomesencephalic reticular formation, hypothalamus, lateral geniculate nuclei, amygdala, pallidum system, hippocampus, preoptic area and cortex (Iversen and Iversen, 1981; Green and Costain, 1981). 5-HT has been implicated in the causation of hallucinations mainly because of the action of hallucinogenic drugs, which are believed to affect the 5-HT system.

The most potent hallucinogen known is the d-isomer of lysergic acid diethylamide (LSD) which was synthesised by Hoffman from an alkaloid extracted from the ergot fungus in 1938. Pharmacological interest in ergot alkaloids resulted from their action on the smooth muscle, which was thought to have medical implications.

However, other naturally occurring hallucinogens have been known for some time. These include mescaline (from the peyotl cactus) and psilocybin (from the mushroom *Psilocybe mexicana*), both used by Mexican Indians, and ergot (the fungus *Claviceps purpurea*) which, when contaminating rye grain used to make bread, would cause 'St Anthony's fire', a quite common affliction in the Middle Ages in which victims became 'insane' and suffered from blackening of the body extremities.

The effects of LSD on humans have been relatively well documented. A dose of 50–500 microgrammes is sufficient to cause hallucinations. Physical effects include tachycardia, hypertension, flushing and salivation, peaking at about 3 hours after ingestion. The psychological effects, which usually last longer, include the heightened perception of sensory stimuli, a loss of boundaries between the sense modalities, distortion of the sense of time and of space perception (so that objects appear larger or smaller than in reality) and changes in mood. A person taking the drug usually retains insight into his or her experiences and does not regard them as real, although a prolonged schizophrenia-like reaction has been observed in a small number of cases (Green and Costain, 1981).

A number of investigators have attempted to explore the phenomenology of drug-induced hallucinations in some detail. The work of Heinrich Kluver (1926, 1928, 1942, 1966) is particularly important in this context. Kluver noted a number of consistencies in the effects of mescaline with respect to the kinds of visual imagery produced, either with eyes open or eyes closed. He referred to these elements as 'form constants', of which there were four main types: one described as a grating, lattice, honeycomb or chessboard design; the second resembling a cobweb; a third commonly described as a tunnel, funnel or alley; and the fourth consisting of spiral figures. Similar form constants have also been observed in the imagery associated with hypnagogic hallucinations, during insulin hypoglycaemia, during fever, under sensory deprivation, following photostimulation, and during bouts of malaria (McKellar, 1957; Siegel and Jarvik, 1975). In an attempt to quantify these phenomena, Siegel and Jarvik required trained and untrained observers to categorise their visual experiences following ingestion of a range of drugs, using a coding system devised on the basis of earlier research. With untrained observers they found clear dose-related effects with marijuana and delta-THC (the active

151

Figure 6.1: Mean percentage distributions of form, colour and movement reports for trained subjects in each six-hour dose–drug condition, from Siegel and Jarvik (1975). Form reports: R=random, L=line, C=curve, W=web, LA=lattice, T=tunnel, S=spiral, K=kaleidoscope. Colour reports: B=black, V=violet, Bl=blue, G=green, Y=yellow, O=orange, R=red, W=white. Movement reports: A=aimless, V=vertical, H=horizontal, O=oblique, E=explosive, C=concentric, R=rotational, P=pulsating

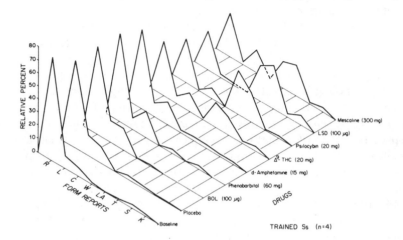

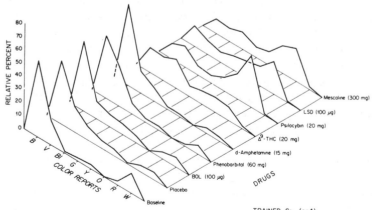

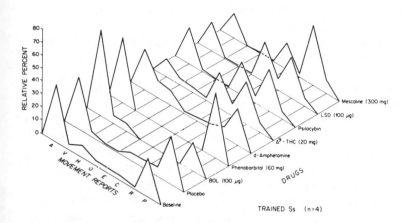

ingredient of marijuana) in respect to the form, colour and movement of the imagery produced. Extending this work, Siegel and Jarvik developed a method of training observers to describe their imagery by using specially prepared slides depicting various types of hallucinatory experience. Subjects were given LSD, BOL (bromo-lysergic acid diethylamide), psilocybin, mescaline, delta-THC, phenobarbital and *d*-amphetamine in various doses, but were not informed of the drug they were taking or the dosage they had been given. Sessions lasted for 6 hours during which the subjects were left supine in a dark, soundproofed chamber. The results are shown graphically in Figure 6.1 (taken from Siegel and Jarvik, 1975).

It is clear that BOL, phenobarbital and *d*-amphetamine had little effect on baseline imagery but that delta-THC, psilocybin, LSD and mescaline all increased the experience of complex forms, of colours at the red end of the spectrum, and of explosive, concentric, rotational and pulsating movements. Time-related effects were also observed. The shift from baseline to complex imagery typically occurred between 90 minutes and two hours after ingestion and was heralded by the appearance of lattice and tunnel forms. Subjects often reported that the imagery was like a slide show or movie located a few feet in front of their eyes. As the sessions progressed, some subjects reported that they had become part of the imagery itself. At the peak of the sessions, many subjects were unable to keep up a description of their experiences, estimating that the imagery was changing at a rate of up to ten

153

times a second (an estimate not to be taken too seriously, given the known time-distorting effects of hallucinogens).

Siegel and Jarvik noted that reports of similar imagery had been made by anthropologists who asked American natives about their use of hallucinogenic substances. However, as Wallace (1959) noted, cultural factors also seem to have an impact on the content of drug-induced hallucinations. For example, the hallucinatory experiences of Indians living in the tropical forests of South America include visions of animals and distant cities (Harner, 1973), although geometric designs of bright colours, changing shapes, tunnels and funnels are also reported (Naranjo, 1973) and are frequently painted on pottery (Reichel-Dolmatoff, 1972).

Tolerance to LSD occurs after three or four days of repeated daily doses. Moreover, LSD exhibits cross-tolerance with psilocybin and mescaline, indicating that they share a common mechanism of action (Iversen and Iversen, 1981). As Iversen and Iversen remark, 'We remain remarkably ignorant of the scientific basis for the action of any of these drugs.' However, because of its chemical similarity to 5-HT, it is thought that LSD and related substances act on the 5-HT pathways in the brain. This mode of action may be fairly complex, however. Gaddum (1953) found that LSD is a potent antagonist of the action of 5-HT on smooth muscle, suggesting that the drug might have a similar effect on 5-HT receptors in the central nervous system. Evidence supporting this view comes from radioligand binding studies in which it has been shown that the binding of H-d-LSD to sites in various parts of the brain is inhibited by 5-HT and 5-HT antagonists (Bennett and Snyder, 1975).

However, it is clear that LSD can also act as a 5-HT agonist. Thus, Aghajanian, Foote and Sheard (1970) found that, while LSD could inhibit the firing of 5-HT neurones in the raphe nuclei, it could also stimulate the firing of brain-stem neurones that receive input from 5-HT cells. To complicate matters, BOL, a derivative of LSD which remains a 5-HT antagonist, is not hallucinogenic (see above) even though it readily crosses the blood–brain barrier (Iversen and Iversen, 1981). In addition, there is evidence that, at high dosages, LSD may act via a different neurotransmitter, dopamine, for which it may be a partial agonist (Kelly and Iversen, 1975).

Animal studies provide further evidence of the mechanisms by which LSD and related substances produce hallucinations. However, some caution is necessary in this respect because of the difficulties involved in interpreting apparently hallucinatory behaviour in animals (see Chapter 1). McMillan (1973) found that mescaline depresses behaviour controlled by both positive and negative reinforcement in mammals, causing dogs and cats to become docile and tame and rats to become 'catatonic' and hypersensitive to noise. The sensory effects of LSD in animals were investigated by Evarts (1957) who recorded neural activity in the lateral geniculate bodies (LGBs — 'switching stations' in the visual pathways of the brain). Evarts found that LSD injected interarterially produces a suppression of spontaneous LGB activity. A similar result was observed by Horn and McKay (1973), who found an LSD-related loss of correlation between LGB responses to photic stimulation, indicating that LSD interferes with the transformation of sensory information. As fibres from the LGBs project on to the visual cortex, it is likely that such interference will result in perceptual disturbances.

Further evidence of the sensory effects of LSD was discovered by Fuster (1959), who observed an LSD-induced increase in reaction time and decrease in accuracy in monkeys performing on a tachistoscopically (i.e. short time exposure) presented visual discrimination task. Although Fuster argued that this effect resulted from an impairment of attention, subsequent studies (e.g. Brown and Bass, 1967) have shown that size discrimination is impaired even when ample time is given, indicating that LSD's effects are sensory. Even so, it would appear that the sensory effects of LSD vary with the kind of training given to an animal. Key (1961), for example, found that generalisation to an auditory stimulus in the cat is affected by LSD after one kind of training (the cat was shocked on presentation of a 600 Hz tone; later a 400 Hz tone was introduced unaccompanied by shock) but not following another method (both tones were presented from the beginning of the study).

A number of theories have been proposed to account for the effects of LSD and related drugs. On the basis of a detailed review of the animal literature, Bridger (1971) suggested that hallucinogens enhance the association between conditioned and unconditioned stimuli, making the two types of stimuli difficult to distinguish. This theory would be consistent with a classical

155

conditioning model of hallucination (see previous chapter).

Winters' (1975) theory linking hallucinations to central nervous system excitation has already been discussed in the previous section; on the basis of his animal data Winters argued that hallucinogenic drugs have their effect by inducing a state of nervous-system excitation and that the phenomenology of the hallucinations experienced following ingestion of drugs like LSD is therefore determined by the time course and maximum level of the excitation achieved.

Other theories have been proposed in the light of the phenomenological studies carried out with humans. Some early authors noted a similarity between drug-induced visual hallucinations and entopic phenomena (visual effects that arise from the visualisation of certain structures in the eye through the appropriate arrangement of incident light). However, Siegel and Jarvik (1975) concluded that their own experiments (carried out in darkness) showed that, at best, the potentiation of such phenomena by hallucinogens can account only for the structural templates of hallucinatory images, which must be elaborated in the central nervous system. Moreover, even this is doubtful as the similarity between entopic phenomena and form constants may be more apparent than real. Whereas Marshall (1937) and Kluver (1942) argued that retinal blood vessels and capillaries could account for form constants such as spirals, invesigators such as Wise, Dollery and Henkind (1971) have shown that the pattern and structure of such retinal vessels are not as regular and geometrical as drug-induced visual imagery. Siegel and Jarvik therefore proposed, following a number of other authors (e.g. Hebb, 1968), that drug-induced hallucinations occur as a result of the release of memory images into consciousness. This idea is clearly related to the 'seepage' models of hallucination discussed in the previous chapter. Apart from the general weaknesses inherent in this kind of account, discussed previously, it would seem that Siegel and Jarvik's theory fails to do justice to the phenomenology of drug-induced hallucinations which they themselves have been instrumental in revealing. Further research is obviously required before the exact mechanism by which the hallucinogenic drugs have their effects is revealed; however, there does appear to be at least some evidence that these drugs have a direct impact on the processing of visual information in the brain.

(ii) Dopamine and amphetamine psychosis

Perhaps the most widely held biochemical theory of schizophrenia holds that psychotic symptoms result from a disorder of the dopamine system in the brain (Green and Costain, 1981; Iversen and Iversen, 1981; Jackson, 1986). Cells using the neurotransmitter dopamine are located in the midbrain. Approximately three-quarters of the brain's dopamine is located in the nigrostriatal pathway, which projects from the substantia nigra into the medial forebrain bundle and from there to the corpus striatum (caudate nucleus and putamen) and globus pallidus. Other dopamine-carrying fibres innervate the nucleus accumbens, amygdala, olfactory tubercle, and some areas of the cortex (Iversen and Iversen, 1981). The hypothesis that a disorder of this system lies at the root of schizophrenia has been built on three main observations: (a) that repeated dosages of amphetamine, which appears to increase dopamine activity in the brain, produces a psychotic-like syndrome (including hallucinations) in normal individuals similar to that observed in patients diagnosed as paranoid schizophrenic; (b) that agents that increase dopamine activity (including amphetamine) exacerbate the symptoms of schizophrenic individuals; and (c) that chemicals that block the dopamine receptors of the brain, including the major neuroleptic drugs, are potent anti-psychotic agents (Alpert and Friedhoff, 1980; Haracz, 1982; Jackson, 1986).

Amphetamine affects arousal, and is a stimulant and an appetite suppressant. The *d*-isomer (Dexedrine) is the most potent amphetamine in this respect, although the *l*-isomer and other related compounds have stimulant effects (Iversen and Iversen, 1981). It has been known for some time that repeated ingestion of amphetamine, perhaps 50 to 100 mg every few hours over a period of several days, can produce a psychotic reaction similar to that observed in patients diagnosed as paranoid schizophrenic (Connell, 1958). For example, Beamish and Kiloh (1960) and Bell (1965) were able to identify chronic amphetamine users who had been misdiagnosed as paranoid schizophrenics; in some cases the misdiagnosis was maintained while the patients continued to take amphetamines over several years. However, this kind of observation can only provide a limited amount of information about the effects of amphetamines because it is possible that the individuals concerned had been suffering from a tendency towards psychosis, so that the drug merely triggered latent psychotic symptomatology. To test for this possibility, a number of investigators have studied the effects of amphetamine on healthy volunteers.

In perhaps the most important series of studies of this sort, Angrist and his colleagues (Angrist and Gershon, 1970; Angrist, Sathananthan, Wilk and Gershon, 1974) observed the psychotic reactions of drug abusers given amphetamine while in psychiatric hospital, and of healthy volunteers who ingested large hourly doses of amphetamine. Symptoms observed included florid paranoid delusions; excitement; belligerence; and visual, auditory, tactile and olfactory hallucinations. For example, one experimental subject,

> who had taken 465 mg of amphetamine over $22^3/_4$ hr abruptly experienced a florid paranoid psychosis. Before the experiment he had made a 'deal' with an attendant on the ward, to whom he owed several dollars. As he became psychotic, he 'heard' a gang coming on the ward to kill him (sent by the attendant). His paranoid feelings included the experimenter who he assumed had 'set up' the 'trap'. He was at times quite hostile. Explanations that his feelings were amphetamine-induced were rejected with sardonic mock agreement, i.e. 'Oh sure, ha! Is that the way its going to be?' etc. At other times he would become panicky and tearful and beg the experimenter to explain what was 'really going on'. He had visual hallucinations of gangsters, and doors opening and closing in the shadows, and visual illusions, in which papers on the bulletin board 'turned into' 'a gangster in a white coat'. He jumped at the slightest sound, assuming that it was the gang. He was so frightened that he refused to investigate the ward to prove that no one was there.

As Snyder (1973) observed, the extent to which these kinds of findings can be regarded as a complete model of psychosis is open to debate. While hallucinations are often observed following chronic amphetamine use, they tend to be visual, olfactory or tactile as often as auditory. A further problem from the present perspective concerns the degree to which the effect of amphetamine is a result of interference with the dopamine system. Jacobs and Trulson (1979) have argued that amphetamine psychosis may

158

result from the action of amphetamine on the 5-HT system; cats repeatedly injected with amphetamine exhibit behaviours similar to those often seen in animals following administration of LSD (especially limb flicks and grooming), and neurochemical analysis has demonstrated that these changes correlate well with decreases in forebrain, brain-stem and spinal-cord levels of 5-HT and its major metabolite, 5-HIAA. Consistent with the view that the effects of amphetamine are not mediated by dopamine, the time course of increased dopamine activity following amphetamine administration correlates poorly with the time of onset of amphetamine psychosis (Perlow, Chiueh, Lake and Wyatt, 1980).

The second line of evidence that has been used to support the dopamine theory of psychotic symptomatology concerns the exacerbation of symptoms in schizophrenics given amphetamines. Early studies indeed suggested that amphetamines have this effect. Janowski, El-Yousef, Davis and Sekerke (1973) and Angrist, Rotrosen and Gershon (1980) found that amphetamines or other dopamine agonists could be used to elicit the reappearance of delusions and hallucinations in recovered or partially recovered schizophrenics. The evidence in this respect is not consistent, however. For example, in a carefully controlled study Kornetsky (1976) reported no significant effect of amphetamine on the symptoms of a group of schizophrenic patients.

The final line of evidence that has been used to support the dopamine theory of psychotic symptomatology concerns the effects of neuroleptic drugs, such as the phenothiazines, which are widely used to treat patients diagnosed a schizophrenic. That these drugs are often effective at reducing florid symptoms cannot be doubted, and evidence pertaining to this issue is discussed in the next chapter. Also, there is considerable evidence that these drugs act upon the dopamine receptor, setting up a dopamine blockade (Iversen and Iversen, 1981). Unfortunately, it may be premature to conclude, on the basis of this evidence alone, that the mechanism by which neuroleptics have their therapeutic effects involves blockade of the dopamine receptor. Indeed, as Alpert and Friedhoff (1980) and Jackson (1986) have argued, there are compelling reasons for doubting that this is the case. First, the time course of dopamine blockade and the relief of symptons afforded by neuroleptic drugs do not match in the way that would be expected if neuroleptics worked by dopamine blockade. Thus, Silverstone and

Cookson (1983) found that plasma prolactin levels (which rise in relation to dopamine blockage) peak towards the end of the first week of neuroleptic administration, whereas maximum clinical improvement is usually observed in the second and third weeks of medication.

Secondly, it has been shown that response to neuroleptics can be improved in some cases by adding small doses of L-DOPA (which is metabolised to dopamine in the brain) to neuroleptic drugs (Fleming, Makar and Hunter, 1970; Inanaga, Nakazawa, Inouye, Tachibana, Oshima and Kotorii, 1975; Meltzer and Stahl, 1976), again contrary to what would be predicted on the basis of the dopamine hypothesis. Interestingly enough, Davis and Cole (1975) reported that paranoid symptoms, the most commonly occurring following chronic amphetamine use, are less amenable to neuroleptic medication than other psychotic symptoms.

On the evidence reviewed above it seems unlikely that a simple relationship holds between dopamine and psychotic symptomatology. Direct biological evidence that might be expected to provide support for the dopamine hypothesis has also been equivocal (Haracz, 1982; Jackson, 1986), although the most recently available data does suggest that dopamine abnormalities may play some role in psychotic breakdown. Thus, while increased neuroleptic binding to post-mortem brain samples from schizophrenics (indicative of dopamine receptor abnormalities) has been reported by a number of authors (Lee et al., 1978; Mackay et al., 1980; Reynolds et al., 1981) it is not clear whether these results reflect an underlying pathological process or, on the contrary, are the product of the longterm use of neuroleptic medication (which is known to affect the dopamine system). In order to resolve this problem, some investigators have attempted to measure dopamine receptor densities in the brains of patients who have not received neuroleptic medication. A sophisticated method of doing this involves measuring the binding of radioactively-labelled substances to dopamine receptors in live patients, using the technique of Positron Emission Tomography. Using this method, Wong et al. (1986) recently reported increased binding of radio-labelled haliperidol in a small group of schizophrenics who had never been medicated and who had been ill for an average of five years. Of course, given the widespread use of neuroleptic medication as the treatment of first choice for schizophrenia in most countries of the world, the possibility exists that unmedicated patients differ in some important way from medicated patients (hence their not being given medication). However, the subjects in Wong *et al.*'s study all met the DSM-III criteria for schizophrenia, suggesting that this potential pitfall had been successfully avoided. Although this evidence therefore does seem to provide strong support for the dopamine hypothesis, Wong *et al.* nonetheless argue for a cautious interpretation of their own data, pointing out that more studies are required on patients with a range of diagnoses before it can be concluded that dopamine abnormalities are causal and specific to schizophrenia.

Given these difficulties in interpreting data obtained from biochemical studies of psychiatric patients, and given the some-times inconclusive findings of research into dopamine abnorm-alities in psychotic patients, it is not surprising that some authors have argued that such abnormalities may underlie only some psychotic symptoms. Crow (1980a) has suggested that the positive and negative symptoms of schizophrenia may reflect different syndromes, with dopamine abnormalities being important in only the positive symptoms. This hypothesis has provoked considerable debate (cf. Mackay, 1980; Lewine, 1985) but it is by no means clear that positive and negative symptoms do separate neatly into the syndromes proposed by Crow or that positive symptoms are more responsive to neuroleptic medication as the theory would imply. Contrary to the theory, the patients who Kornetsky (1976) found to be hyporesponsive to the psychosis exacerbating effects of amphetamine were mainly suffering from positive symptoms. To complicate matters further, some authors have argued that dopamine abnormalities may be implicated not only in the symptoms of schizophrenic patients but also in the symptoms of patients diagnosed as manic or depressed (Swerdlow and Koob, 1987).

(iii) Endogenous opiates

The final class of biochemicals that will be considered only in passing in the present context are the recently discovered endoge-nous opiates. Terenius, Wahlstrom, Lindstrom and Widerlov (1976) reported increased endorphin levels in the cerebrospinal fluid of chronic schizophrenic patients. Following this discovery,

Gunne, Lindstrom, and Terenius (1977) reported that the opiate antagonist naloxone significantly reduced the auditory hallucinations of a group of schizophrenic patients. Subsequent studies of the effects of naloxone, reported in more detail in the next chapter, have produced contradictory results. As endorphin levels can vary with a variety of environmental factors (e.g. exercise, stimulation), it would seem premature to conclude that endophins play a role in psychotic symptomatology.

CONCLUSIONS

There is no conflict between biological and psychological models of abnormal behaviour. Whereas it is often supposed that abnormalities of the central nervous system, whether at the neuroanatomical or biochemical level, can lead to changes in behaviour, it is often forgotten that changes of behaviour caused by the environment are presumably mediated by changes in the neurological and biochemical processes of the brain (Rose, 1984). The brain and the environment are in constant interaction. It would therefore be surprising indeed if hallucinations were not accompanied by various neurological and biochemical abnormalities.

Unfortunately, despite the evidence linking a number of physiological variations and disease states to hallucination (outlined in Chapter 2), there is no clear indication of what these abnormalities might be, perhaps because the brain is a complex organ that defies easy investigation. Genetic evidence indicative of a biological predisposition towards hallucination is virtually non-existent, perhaps for the want of appropriate research. Neuropsychological models of hallucination are generally speculative, although there is some suggestion that auditory hallucinations may be related to left-hemisphere abnormalities. There is good evidence that LSD-induced hallucinations are mediated by the 5-HT system but the phenomenology of these types of experiences would seem to indicate that they do not provide a good model of psychotic hallucinations. Finally, despite the attention that has been given to dopamine as a potential mediator of psychotic symptoms, the evidence for this hypothesis is less solid on close examination, and there is no reason to link dopamine specifically to hallucinations in any case.

7

The Treatment of Hallucinations

The previous two chapters have considered psychological and biological theories that have been proposed to account for hallucinations. In the present chapter an attempt will be made to build on these theories by outlining first the drug therapies and then the psychological therapies that have been used to treat hallucinations. In addition, the coping mechanisms that sufferers themselves find most useful will be briefly considered.

DRUG THERAPIES

The use of drugs to treat hallucinations is generally predicated on the assumption that hallucinatory experiences are symptoms of one or other of a number of psychiatric syndromes (see Chapter 2) and are best dealt with accordingly. If the hallucinations are judged to be a symptom of schizophrenia, they are treated by antipsychotic medication; if they are judged to be a symptom of depression, then the treatment given is often antidepressant medication or electroconvulsive therapy (ECT); if judged to be a symptom of an organic condition such as epilepsy, the hallucinations are usually treated with anticonvulsant medication.

Since the drug and physical treatments for these conditions are generally well known and widely used, the present review will be limited to some historical developments and applications of antipsychotic medications. The interested reader is referred to standard textbooks of psychiatry (e.g. Mayer-Gross, Slater and Roth, 1975) and clinical pharmacology (e.g. Silverstone and Turner,

1982; Turner, Richens and Routledge, 1986) for more detailed information.

(i) The neuroleptics

In the early 1950s the drug chlorpromazine, one of the pheno-thiazine family of drugs, was first used clinically in France where it was found to be an effective tranquilliser without producing marked sedation. Delay and Deniker (1952), who first used the term 'neuroleptic' to describe the action of the phenothiazines, used the drug with violent and excited patients and reported that it produced a blunting of motor and emotional reactions to the environment, a reduction of anxiety and agitation without marked drowsiness or intellectual impairment, and a delayed reduction in psychotic symptoms and associated behaviour. The use of the drug spread rapidly, and positive reports of its beneficial effects appeared widely. It soon became clear that chlorpromazine had a particularly valuable role to play in the treatment of severely psychotic patients, not only for controlling violent outbursts but also because of its therapeutic effect on specific positive symptoms such as delusions and hallucinations (Harrison-Reed, 1984).

Other members of the phenothiazine group of drugs were subsequently developed and found to be useful, to varying degrees, in the treatment of psychotic symptoms. Such developments led to a collaborative, multi-hospital study in the USA of phenothiazine treatment for the schizophrenic psychoses, the results of which were reported in the mid 1960s (Goldberg, Klerman and Cole, 1965). In this study three phenothiazine drugs (chlorpromazine, fluphenazine and thioridazine) were compared with an inert placebo in terms of their effects on the symptoms and behaviour of newly admitted, acutely psychotic, schizophrenic patients. A total of 344 patients were involved in the double-blind drug trial, 270 on active drug and 74 on placebo. The general finding was that, although placebo-treated patients showed significant improvement on some symptoms, including hallucinations, the patients on active drugs improved to a significantly greater extent. In order to assess whether the phenothiazines have a specific anti-psychotic (rather than just tranquillising) action, their effectiveness was compared with that of barbiturates in a further series of trials involving several thousand patients (Klien and Davis, 1969). Whereas phenothiazines were found to be effective in the majority of these trials, phenobarbital was not found to be more effective than a placebo in any. When the effects of the drugs on specific symptoms were studied, it was found that the most improvement was observed with respect to those symptoms regarded by Bleuler (1911) as fundamental to schizophrenia, such as thought disorder, blunted affect, withdrawal and autistic behaviour. Symptom improvement was also observed for hallucinations, and paranoid and grandiose delusions, although to a lesser degree. It is generally believed that the therapeutic effects of the phenothiazines are mediated by a blockade of dopamine receptors in the limbic system, although there are at least some reasons for doubting whether such a simple account can explain much of the relevant clinical and pharmacokinetic evidence (see previous chapter).

Because of the widespread use of phenothiazines to treat psychotic states, long-acting phenothiazine preparations have been increasingly used in recent years. The major advantage of this kind of preparation is that it ensures the patient receives medication even when relatively unsupervised (e.g. when living in the community). These drugs are usually administered intramuscularly; the drug, which is suspended in oil as an ester or salt, is slowly released into the bloodstream over a period of days or weeks. Controlled trials have demonstrated the therapeutic value of this kind of preparation in the management of chronic schizophrenic patients (e.g. Hirsch, Gaind, Rohde, Stevens and Wing, 1973).

Although phenothiazines are probably the most effective antipsychotic agents, other dopamine antagonists such as the butrophenones have been used for similar purposes. Lapolla (1967), for example, reported on the positive effects achieved with haloperidol with acute and chronic schizophrenics and other psychotic patients. The most obvious effects were on motor disorders and hallucinations. Similarly, Anderson, Kuenhle and Catanzano (1976) reported on the treatment of 24 patients with acute functional psychoses using intramuscular injections of haloperidol. Substantial remission of cardinal symptoms (i.e. thought disorder, hallucinations, and delusional activity) was reported.

Despite the apparent success of the phenothiazines and related compounds, however, some caution is in order. First, over recent

165

years it has become increasingly obvious that these drugs may have serious side effects, particularly when used over a long period of time. In the short term these side effects may include neurological disorders of movement (extrapyramidal effects) resembling those observed in Parkinson's disease, including tremor, rigidity, shuffling gait, etc. Although reducing the dosage of medication can have the paradoxical effect of increasing these side effects, perhaps because of prolonged usage of neuroleptics may lead to supersensitivity of the dopamine receptor (Warner, 1985), they can often be treated successfully with anticholinergic compounds. Other side effects can include restlessness, postural hypotension, photosensitivity of the skin and jaundice (Harrison-Reed, 1984). However, the most serious side effect of all is tardive dyskinesia, characterised by involuntary tic-like movements of the face, mouth and tongue, which has been estimated to affect over 20 per cent of long-term phenothiazine users (Jeste and Wyatt, 1981). Although a wide range of chemical therapies have been used in an attempt to ameliorate this condition, none has been found to be particularly effective (Mackay and Sheppard, 1979), nor does the syndrome appear to respond to either increases or decreases of the phenothiazine medication. For all intents and purposes, then, this condition may be regarded as irreversible.

A second note of caution concerns the effectiveness of the phenothiazines and related compounds. Although early research, as detailed above, clearly demonstrated that these compounds can be highly effective in some cases, it has become increasingly obvious that not all patients respond to neuroleptic medication. Although it is difficult to make precise calculations of the proportion of patients who do benefit (because some patients will relapse irrespective of whether they are on medication), Leff and Wing (1971) estimated that, whereas up to 80 per cent of non-medicated psychotic patients may relapse over a one-year period, neuroleptic medication may reduce this rate by roughly a half. More recently, a carefully controlled trial carried out with first-admission schizophrenics at Northwick Park Hospital in the UK found that 62 per cent of patients on a placebo relapsed over a period of two years, whereas 42 per cent of patients on maintenance neuroleptic medication relapsed (Crow, Macmillan, Johnson and Johnstone, 1986; Macmillan, Crow, Johnson and Johnstone, 1986). If these figures are accurate indications of the therapeutic efficacy of the phenothiazines and related medicines, it would seem that less than half of those patients receiving such medication are likely to benefit.

There is considerable debate about which types of psychotic patients are most likely to benefit from neuroleptics. Crow (1980a, 1985) has recently proposed that the schizophrenic psychoses can be divided into two separate syndromes, the Type I syndrome consisting of florid symptoms such as hallucinations and delusions, and a Type II syndrome consisting of the defect state (withdrawal, flat affect, intellectual deterioration). Crow suggested that the Type I syndrome is caused by a disorder of the dopaminergic system (see previous chapter) and that it would therefore be most responsive to neuroleptic medication. On Crow's account, the pathology associated with the Type II syndrome is ventricular enlargement, and the syndrome is therefore unresponsive to neuroleptic medication. The implication of this hypothesis is that positive symptoms such as hallucinations should be highly influenced by dopamine antagonist medication; unfortunately the available data on this issue is unclear and open to several interpretations, and the validity of Crow's two syndromes is hotly debated (see, for example, Crow, 1980b; Mackay, 1980; and Lewine, 1985).

One variable that is known to predict whether a patient will benefit from neuroleptic medication or not is the family environment (see Chapter 4). Thus, Vaughn and Leff (1976) and subsequent researchers have found that patients who return to families judged to be low in expressed emotion (criticism, hostility or overconcern) generally have a low rate of relapse whether or not they are on medication, but that patients returning to families judged high in expressed emotion and who spend a considerable amount of time in face-to-face contact with family members have a high rate of relapse which is significantly reduced if they are on neuroleptic medication (see Figure 4.2). This finding would seem to indicate that, at the psychological level, neuroleptics achieve their therapeutic effect by protecting patients against particular types of stress.

Because there is no clear indication of which group of psychotic patients are most likely to be helped by neuroleptics, and because of the well established link, just alluded to, between benefit from phenothiazine and the family environment, a number

167

of investigators have advocated the selective and carefully monitored withholding or withdrawal of medication during the treatment of psychotic symptoms in order to assess whether relapse is likely without them (Carpenter, McGlashan and Strauss, 1977; Warner, 1985).

(ii) Benzodiazepines

While the benzodiazepines are primarily used in the treatment of anxiety-related symptoms of a neurotic type, some reports have emerged of their value in treating psychotic symptomatology. For example, Beckman and Haas (1980) reported on the effects of high doses of diazepam in schizophrenic patients. They found a particularly marked therapeutic effect on hallucinations and certain forms of delusions whereas schizo-affective symptomatology showed a poor response.

On the basis of the above kinds of report, Lingjaerde (1982) organised a multicentre double-blind trial of the benzodiazepine derivative, estazolam, to determine its effectiveness on global symptomatology and auditory hallucinations in particular. The main finding was of a superiority of active drug over placebo on both kinds of measure (i.e. global and auditory hallucination). Despite these positive reports, benzodiazepines may not come to be used widely in this area, especially given the increasing concerns being expressed about the addictive nature of these drugs (Turner *et al.*, 1986). However, it would be a pity if clinicians were to feel inhibited from trying these drugs with hallucinating patients because the long-term side effects of benzodiazapines may ultimately prove more benign than those of the neuroleptics.

(iii) Naloxone

Following an observation by Terenius, Wahlstrom, Lindstrom and Widerlov (1976) of elevated levels of endorphins (endogenous opiates) in the cerebrospinal fluid of chronic psychotic patients, and of a reduction to normal levels with clinical improvement, much interest has been centred on the therapeutic effects of the endorphin antagonist naloxone. Terenius and his colleagues (Gunne, Lindstrom and Terenius, 1977) subsequently administered 0.5 mg of naloxone intravenously to seven severe chronic schizophrenic patients in a single-blind trial, and reported that auditory hallucinations were rapidly abolished in four of them, returning only several hours later. A single-case report by Orr and Oppenheimer (1978) described the similar rapid clinical response of an auditorily hallucinated female patient. The latter authors noted that the immediacy of the clinical response is of particular interest as it 'contrasts sharply with the known effects of neuroleptic drugs, which take much longer to produce clear-cut effects on psychotic symptoms'.

Subsequent attempts to replicate these findings have yielded inconsistent results. The first three controlled studies carried out found no differences between intravenous naloxone and saline solution on psychotic symptoms, including hallucinations (Davis, Bunney, Defraites, Kleinman, van Kammen and Wyatt, 1977). By contrast, workers at Stanford University have found positive effects in both single-blind and double-blind trials in most but not all patients (Watson, Berger, Akil, Mills and Barchas, 1978; Berger, Watson, Akil and Barchas, 1981) while other studies using apparently similar procedures have found no clinically or statistically significant effects (Freeman and Fairburn, 1981; Verhoeven, van Praag and de Jong, 1981). Taking these studies as a whole, it would seem that the clinical effects of naloxone vary from the miraculous to the non-existent. Factors that may be related to such variations include dosage level (i.e. positive effects are more likely with higher dosages), patient differences and measures employed. Whatever the final resolution to the conflicting research findings, it seems unlikely that naloxone will ever become a standard treatment for psychotic patients as a result of both its cost and its relatively short half-life.

(iv) Summary of drug treatments

Phenothiazines and their derivatives were the first powerful antipsychotic drugs and remain for many clinicians the preferred treatment for schizophrenic symptoms, including hallucinations. A comparatively recent development has been the introduction of long-acting phenothiazines which are usually administered intramuscularly.

Despite the widespread preference for phenothiazines and other neuroleptics, other drugs including benzodiazapines have been tried against hallucinations with some positive results. One drug which has received particular attention has been the opiate antagonist naloxone, but the evidence concerning its effects, even in the short term, is equivocal.

Finally, it should be noted that there is a clear evidence of a powerful interaction between family stress and the efficacy of anti-schizophrenic medication. Patients from family environments in which there is a low level of expressed emotion are unlikely to benefit from neuroleptic medication. Given this finding and the serious known side effects of neuroleptic medication, an increasing number of clinicians are beginning to advocate the selective non-use of neuroleptics with psychotic patients. In these circumstances, it seems likely that the importance of psychological treatments for psychotic symptoms will be increasingly emphasised in the future.

PSYCHOLOGICAL APPROACHES

A variety of psychological treatment approaches, mainly behavioural, have been attempted with hallucinating patients whose symptoms have failed to respond to drug therapy. Some of these procedures have been developed and tested within the experimental laboratory and have already been described in previous chapters. Others have been tested within the context of the psychiatric ward. Most have involved single-case designs. These studies are summarised in Table 7.1.

(i) Operant procedures

Lindsley (1959, 1963) reported results from laboratory studies aimed at bringing 'vocal hallucinatory symptoms' under operant control. In order to do this, Lindsley studied the behaviour of 80 chronic psychotic psychiatric patients in a human operant chamber (a small, 6-foot-square experimental room containing a chair and on one wall a small plunger and delivery tray), obtaining in all more than 30000 hours of data. Lindsley began with the observation that 'If singing and whistling are ruled out, a high frequency

Table 7.1: Psychological treatment studies of hallucinated patients

Treatment study	Patients/subjects	Length of treatment (hours, days, weeks, months) and experimental design	Target procedures and behaviours	Results	Follow-up
(a) Operant procedures					
1. Lindsley (1959), 1963)	80 chronic psychotic patients	30000 hours of behavioural recording in experimental laboratory	Reinforcement of symptomatic (vocalisation rate) and non-symptomatic (plunger-pulling) behaviours	No control over vocal symptomatic behaviour	None
2. Nydegger (1972)	Single case: 20-year-old male paranoid schizophrenic	62 days; clinical study	Social reinforcement for 'responsible' talk; other symptoms: visual hallucinations, social withdrawal	Successful elimination of all four problem behaviours	2½ years FU; no relapse
3. Haynes and Geddy (1973)	Single case: 45-year-old female schizophrenic patient	35 days; clinical study	'Time-out' for inappropriate verbal behaviour (hallucinatory behaviour)	Hallucinatory behaviour decreased from 80% to 30% rate, where it stabilised	None

Table 7.1 (cont)

Treatment study	Patients/subjects	Length of treatment (hours, days, weeks, months) and experimental design	Target procedures and behaviours	Results	Follow-up
4. Anderson and Alpert (1974)	Single case: 26-year-old male chronic schizophrenic patients	49 days; repeated-measures reversal design	Token reinforcement for reductions in visual hallucinations and obsessive–compulsive behaviour. Punishment for ritualistic behaviour	Marked reduction in hallucinations during phases of contingent token reinforcement	10-month FU period: no noticeable increase in hallucination frequency
5. Davis, Wallace, Liberman and Finch (1976)	Single case; 33-year-old female chronic schizophrenic patient	284 days; repeated-measures reversal design	'Time-out' for delusional statements and hallucinatory speech	Delusions and hallucinations virtually disappeared during later period of 'time-out'	None
6. Heron and DeArmond (1978)	Single-case: 23-year-old male mentally retarded patient	128 days; A–B design	'Time-out' for hallucinatory behaviour (auditory and visual)	Reduction in hallucinations from 1 per 10 min during baseline to zero after 1 week of treatment	No hallucinatory behaviour observed during weeks 9–18

(b) Systematic desensitisation

7. Alumbaugh (1971)	Single case: 53-year-old female psychotic patient	19 days; A–B design	SD to stress situations provoking smoking and coffee drinking	Disappearance of voices after 12 sessions	1 year FU; no relapse
8. Lambley (1973)	Single case: 46-year-old male paranoid schizophrenic patient	18 sessions (over a 6-week period)	SD to emotional thoughts producing head-jerking	Development of uncomfortable thoughts: *return* of thoughts	NA
9. Cowden and Ford (1965)	Single case: 27-year-old male paranoid schizophrenic patient	18 sessions; A–B design	SD to interpersonal speaking situations	Improvement of social phobia: no return of voices	NA
10. Slade (1972)	Single case: 18-year-old male paranoid schizophrenic patient	14 sessions (over a 14-week period); A–B design	SD to stress situations involving home life and family	Reduction in frequency of voices from 15.8% to 5.95%	Further reduction to 1.98% during 5-week FU but development of depressive symptoms
11. Slade (1973)	Single case: 19-year-old male paranoid schizophrenic patient	(i) 13 sessions (ii) 10 sessions A–B design	(i) Imaginal SD to social situations (ii) SD *in vivo* to social situations	(i) No change (ii) Reduction from 11.54% to 3.85%	(ii) Further reduction to 1.91% during 5-week FU
12. Siegel (1975)	Single case: 39-year-old male chronic schizophrenic patient	15-week clinical study	SD to 'voices'	Reduction in frequency and change in quality of voice	21-month FU improvement

Table 7.1 (*cont*)

Treatment study	Patients/subjects	Length of treatment (hours, days, weeks, months) and experimental design	Target procedures and behaviours	Results	Follow-up
(c) Thought stopping					
13. Samaan (1975)	Single case: 42-year-old female with severe behaviour disturbance	6 weekly sessions; A–B design	Thought stopping for auditory and visual hallucinations	Symptoms disappeared completely during treatment	20-month FU; no relapse
14. Johnson, Gilmore and Shenoy (1983)	Single case: 30-year-old male Vietnam veteran	4 months (6 sessions); A–B design	Thought stopping for visual hallucinations and obsessional ruminations: anger induction	Thought stopping reduction from 5 to 1 per week anger induction — total extinction	11-month FU; no relapse
15. Lamontagne, Audet and Elie (1983)	Controlled trial: 20 patients assigned to two groups	4 one-hour sessions; controlled comparison	Drug alone or drug plus thought stopping (TS) for hallucinations and paranoid delusions	Hallucinations and delusions showed greater decrease during treatment in drugs + TS group (but not significant)	3- and 6-month FU no significant group differences

(d) Altered sensory input:
(i) Sensory deprivation

16. Harris (1959)	12 schizophrenic patients: uncontrolled clinical study	Brief periods of sensory deprivation (30 min to 2 h)	General symptomatic response to sensory deprivation	Hallucinations were improved during sensory deprivation but *no* generalisation to other situations	None: N/A

(iii) Counter-stimulation

17. Erickson and Gustafson (1968)	Two single cases: (1) 28-year-old male	Clinical cases 1. Several months	1. Taught to control voices by using vocal cords for other things 2. Taught to gargle	1. Able to control voices but still present	—
	(2) 43-year-old female	2. Two days		2. Voices extinguished completely	9 months FU but no relapse
18. Slade (1974)	2 male hallucinators: laboratory study	6 conditions investigated during 20s time periods	Differing levels of external input	Frequency of reported hallucinations decreased with increasing stimulation (information load)	None, N/A
19. Margo, Hemsley and Slade (1981)	7 male hallucinating schizophrenic patients: laboratory study	10 conditions investigated during 2-min time periods	Duration, loudness and clarity of voices in relation to levels of external input	Hallucinations improved with increasing information input. Verbal response also important	None; N/A

Table 7.1 (*cont*)

Treatment study	Patients/subjects	Length of treatment (hours, days, weeks, months) and experimental design	Target procedures and behaviours	Results	Follow-up
20. Alford and Turner (1976)	Single case: 32-year-old female schizophrenic patient	34 sessions: repeated-measures; reversal design	'Social disruption', 'stimulus interference' and 'electrical aversion therapy'	Counter-stimulation produced *only* *immediate* effects	—
21. Turner, Hersen and Bellak (1977)	Single case: 34-year-old female schizophrenic patient	64 weeks; repeated-measures; reversal design	'Social disruption', 'stimulus interference' and 'electrical aversion therapy'	Counter-stimulation produced *only* *immediate* effects	—
22. Feder (1982)	Single case: 21-year-old male	Several months: case report	Use of radio headphones to block voices	Immediate effects but no generalisation	—
23. Mallya and Shen (1983)	Single case: 44-year-old male	Several months: case report	Use of radio headphones to block voices	Immediate effects but no generalisation	—
(e) Self-monitoring					
24. Rutner and Bugle (1969)	Single case: 47-year-old female schizophrenic patient	(i) 3 days (ii) 13 days A–B design	(i) 'Private' recording of voices (ii) 'Public' recording of voices	(i) Reduction from 181 to 11 (ii) Reduction from 11 to zero	6 months FU; no relapse

Study	Subjects	Sessions/Design	Technique	Outcome	Follow-up
25. Reybee and Kinch (1973)	Two cases: (i) 49-year-old male schizophrenic (ii) 46-year-old male schizophrenic	(i) Not given (ii) 21 sessions (over 7 weeks) (A–B design)	(i) 'General' focusing (ii) 'Specific' focusing	(i) No change (ii) reduction in voices (1) 50% to 10% (2) 20% to 10%	No generalisation to other situations
26. Moser (1974)	Single case: 24-year-old male paranoid schizophrenic	3 sessions (6-week period) (A–B design)	Self-monitoring (daily frequency) plus covert punishment	Increase in hallucinations during self-monitoring alone; reduction and elimination with covert sensitisation	25 months FU; no relapse
27. Glaister (1985)	Single case: 46-year-old male patient	85 homework sessions over 16-month period	Concurrent recording of time, content and impact of voices	Reduction in reported voices to zero	5-year FU; no relapse
(f) Aversion therapy					
28. Bucher and Fabricatore (1970)	Single case: 47-year-old male; voices of five years' duration	10 days (A–B design)	Self-administered electric shock for voices	Hallucination frequency dropped from 5/6 per day to zero	Voices absent 25 days later *but* patient developed background voices
29. Watts and Clements (1971)	Single case:	Several sessions (A–B design)	Therapist administered white noise	Initial elimination of voices	Relapse within 2 weeks

Table 7.1 (*cont*)

Treatment study	Patients/subjects	Length of treatment (hours, days, weeks, months) and experimental design	Target procedures and behaviours	Results	Follow-up
30. Weingaertner (1971)	Controlled trial; 45 hallucinating patients with a primary diagnosis of schizophrenia	2 weeks; random allocation to one of three groups	Three groups: (a) self-shock (b) placebo shock (c) no-treatment control	All groups improved to a similar extent	None; N/A
31. Alford and Turner (1976)	Single case: 32-year-old female schizophrenic patient	34 sessions; repeated-measures; reversal design	'Electrical aversion therapy' and 'social disruption'	Only aversion therapy produced both immediate and lasting effects	1-year FU; no relapse
32. Turner, Hersen and Bellak (1977)	Single case: 33-year-old female schizophrenic patient	64 weeks; repeated-measures; reversal design	'Electrical aversion therapy', 'social disruption' and 'stimulus interference'	Only aversion therapy produced both immediate and lasting effefts	Improvement maintained at 5 and 6 months FU
33. Fonagy and Slade (1982)	Three cases: (i) 63-year-old female (ii) 28-year-old male (iii) 36-year-old female	15 weekly sessions (i) A–B–C–A–D (ii) A–C–B–A–D (iii) A–C–D–A–B	3 white noise conditions: (a) WN offset (punishment) (b) WN onset (negative reinforcement) (c) random WN	In all 3 cases, per cent time hallucinating showed a reduction. The negative reinforcement condition was the most effective	Some generalisation observed in all three cases

			Concurrent WN (WN onset)	Hallucination	Complete cessation of voices maintained at 6-month FU
34. Slade, Judkins, Clarke and Fonagy (1986)	Single case: 42-year-old female schizophrenic with 3-year history of voices	20 weekly sessions (A–B design)		Hallucination frequency reduced from 10–15 per session to zero	Complete cessation of voices maintained at 6-month FU
(g) Earplug therapy					
35. James (1983)	Two cases: (i) 39-year-old male (ii) 20-year-old female	Duration of treatment not specified	Earplug worn in one ear and then later transferred to other ear	Immediate sharp decrease in voices followed by continuing decline	(i) 3-year FU: no relapse (ii) 1 year+ FU; no relapse
36. Morley (1987)	Single case: 31-year-old male	(a) 41 sessions during 2 weeks (b) 9 days	(a) Distracting music (b) Earplug	(a) Only transient effect (b) Dramatic decrease in voices	(b) 1-month FU; no relapse No FU
38. Birchwood (1986)	Single case: 37-year-old male schizophrenic patient	6-month period A–B design	Earplug worn only in *left* ear	Reduction in hallucination frequency to approximately 50% of baseline	
(h) first person singular					
39. Greene (1978)	Two cases: (i) 20-year-old female (ii) 40-year-old female	(i) 5 sessions (ii) Several days; clinical study	Accepting personal responsibility for voices	Reduction and elimination of voices	(i) 2-year FU; no relapse (ii) —
40. Fowler (1986)	Five hallucinated psychiatric patients (3m,2f) aged 22 to 37 years	9–14 weeks	Reattribution of voices to thoughts and images	Dramatic reduction in frequency of hallucinations in 1 out of 5 patients	No FU

of vocalisation by a psychotic patient who is alone in a room almost always indicates the presence of auditory hallucinations'. He therefore defined hallucination severity as the frequency of such vocalisations. He then noted that, during a period of spontaneously increased rate of vocalisation, non-symptomatic responding (i.e. plunger-pulling for a reward) is usually decreased, indicating competition between symptomatic and non-symptomatic responding.

Lindsley attempted to manipulate both types of response (symptomatic and non-symptomatic) by means of contingent positive reinforcement with candy. He found that, when the rate of vocalisation was reinforced, manual non-symptomatic responding decreased as also did the rate of vocalisation, and that when non-symptomatic responding was reinforced, both types of response increased. Lindsley concluded from these observations that: 'The independence of the vocal psychotic symptoms from direct positive reinforcement ... appears to be due to their psychotic origin', and that 'The results of this experiment suggest that vocal psychotic symptoms are under some form of internal control that resists direct differential positive reinforcement'. However, Lindsley's conclusions need to be treated with some caution since his experimental situation and method of analysis appear to have been overly simplistic. For example, he took no account of the response of candy-eating in his recording sessions (a response seemingly directly incompatible with the vocalisation response), nor of any other kind of overt or covert behaviour which may have accompanied the vocalisation or plunger-pulling responses. In addition he failed to consider the possibility that, under conditions of contingent positive reinforcement, the observed correspondence between vocalisation rate and hallucination frequency may break down.

In contrast to Lindsley's laboratory findings, several researchers have reported more successful use of operant methods in the clinical environment. Nydegger (1972) reported on the treatment of a 20-year-old male paranoid schizophrenic whose symptoms included auditory and visual hallucinations, social withdrawal and delusions. From a careful examination of these symptoms it was found that the auditory hallucinations arose when the patient was in a conflict situation which required a difficult decision on his part. The conflict situation was usually resolved by the 'voices' telling the patient what to do, thereby removing any responsibility for the decisions from the patient. Nydegger therefore opted to use verbal conditioning to deal with this problem. He instructed the patient not to refer to 'voices' but to call them 'thoughts' (i.e. assuming responsibility for them). The therapist and nursing staff then gave social approval for any speech involving personal responsibility such as talk about 'decisions' and 'thoughts'. Within two months no more hallucinations or behaviours associated with them (i.e. talking to self, listening, looking at the ceiling, etc.) were reported.

Concurrent with the treatment of the auditory hallucinations, the patient's passive and withdrawn behaviour was dealt with by a combination of assertion training and systematic desensitisation to interpersonal situations. The frequency of the patient's inter-personal contacts and assertive behaviour increased so rapidly that by the end of a few weeks it was impractical to continue recording them. His reporting of visual hallucinations also ceased at this point. Finally the patient's delusional speech was treated by verbal conditioning in a similar manner to that used with his 'voices'. By the end of the two-month treatment period all four symptoms had ceased to be reported or observed. Follow-up $2\frac{1}{2}$ years later indicated that none of them had recurred.

In another single-case study Haynes and Geddy (1973) used a 'time-out' technique with a 45-year-old schizophrenic woman who had been in hospital for 22 years. As the patient was incapable of providing a reliable self-report of her hallucinatory experiences, the investigators defined 'hallucinatory behaviour' as verbal behaviour (such as quiet talking and mumbling and disruptive yelling) which did not appear to be in response to any identifiable stimulus. After baseline measurement of this behaviour, 'time-out' was administered whenever the patient showed the hallucinatory behaviour. This involved removing the patient from her normal social environment and placing her in isolation in a small unfurnished room for 10 minutes. After 35 days of this treatment the hallucinatory behaviour dropped from an 80 per cent incidence to a 30 per cent rate, where it seemed to stabilise. No follow-up was reported.

A further single-case operant study was reported by Anderson and Alpert (1974), whose subject was a 26-year-old male schizophrenic patient who presented with virtually continuous visual hallucinations of large objects which would dart out of other people and circle the patient. These hallucinations were followed by ritualistic obsessive–compulsive behaviours which seriously interfered with the patient's daily routine (e.g. bathing, dressing, eating, etc.) and which, Anderson and Alpert hypothesised, were being reinforced by staff attention. Moreover, the patient's movements around the hospital were seriously impaired because opening and closing doors elicited unusually large numbers of hallucinations. Using both behavioural observation and self-report measures, Anderson and Alpert monitored the patient's behaviour during repeated baseline and treatment phases. During treatment, reinforcement (in the form of conversation with a female assistant and time off the ward) was made contingent on rapid completion of daily tasks and, in addition, the patient received punishment in the form of electric shocks for the ritualistic actions which interfered with his passage through doorways. This approach was found to produce a considerable improvement in the patient's ability to perform his daily tasks, accompanied by a marked reduction in hallucination frequency. No noticeable increase in hallucinations was reported by the patient during a 10-month follow-up period.

Another study in a similar vein was described by Davis, Wallis, Liberman and Finch (1976). Their patient was a 33-year-old female chronic schizophrenic who presented with the dual problems of delusional talk and hallucinatory speech (i.e. audible verbal responses to an apparently unobservable stimulus). Baseline phases were alternated with contingent time-out periods and other phases in which the patient was simply instructed about the nature of the probable contingency although time-out was not implemented (instruction alone). Only the periods of contingent time-out with *both* delusional statements and hallucinatory speech proved successful in suppressing these behaviours in their entirety. Unfortunately no follow-up was reported.

Finally to be considered under the topic of operant approaches is a case study by Heron and De Armond (1978) in which time-out was used to control hallucinatory behaviour in a mentally retarded adult. Although a simple A–B design (i.e. baseline assessment followed by simple treatment intervention) was employed, the results were none the less impressive. Following a three-day baseline phase, contingent time-out was introduced for any observed episode of either auditory or visual hallucination. The effect of this contingency was to reduce the frequency of hallucinatory behaviour from a rate of one hallucination every 10 minutes during baseline to a rate of virtually zero after one week of treatment. After approximately nine weeks, the authors considered that the behaviour had been extinguished completely.

In summary, with the exception of the laboratory studies of Lindsley (1959, 1963), who failed to achieve operant control over his operationalised definition of hallucinatory behaviour, operant methods have been found to be effective in a series of individual clinical case studies. In all five single-case studies reported, reinforcement and time-out procedures have proved efficacious in reducing or eliminating altogether observed hallucinatory behaviour. Such methods clearly have a role to play with some chronically hallucinated patients.

(ii) Systematic desensitisation

Alumbaugh (1971) treated a 53-year-old woman who had been in hospital for 20 years suffering from auditory hallucinations and withdrawal. The patient reported that the 'voices' were almost continual, only being disrupted by social contacts, and that smoking and excessive coffee drinking (which she considered immoral) brought about their onset. Alumbaugh accordingly desensitised the patient to stressful situations in which she felt the desire to smoke. Over 12 sessions this led to a reduction in her smoking and concurrently to a gradual decline and finally disappearance of her auditory hallucinations. The ward staff noted a parallel increase in the patient's social and work activities during the treatment period, enabling them to transfer the patient to a sheltered workshop in the community. A follow-up interview one year later revealed that the patient was working well and was still free of hallucinations.

Lambley (1973) criticised Alumbaugh's systematic desensitisation, mainly on the grounds of the superficiality of his behavioural analysis. In support of this criticism Lambley described the case of a 46-year-old male patient whom he had treated by means of systematic desensitisation. This patient had a previous history of auditory hallucinations which had been absent for at least two years at the time that treatment was undertaken. The patient's principal symptom was an inability to keep his head still, which stemmed from a feeling that some force was endeavouring to 'pull his head off backwards'. Exploratory discussions with the patient revealed that his disability became worse when he had extreme emotional thoughts, such as those of 'loving' or 'hating'. Lambley therefore treated the patient with a course of 18 desensitisation sessions using a graded hierarchy of emotive words. This led to a gradual lessening of the head-jerking disability, allowing the patient to be discharged. Evaluation interviews with the patient revealed that the auditory hallucinations had returned during the treatment period, together with the development of 'uncomfortable emotional thoughts' of a psychosexual nature, which the patient had previously been able to control.

Lambley's case was obviously more complicated than Alumbaugh's. However, it is not clear whether the voices recurred because the removal of the behaviour disorder (i.e. head-jerking) served to 'unmask' the patient's hallucinations (the explanation proposed by Lambley) or whether it was because the systematic desensitisation treatment was not sufficiently extensive or intensive to cover all the sources of stress relevant to the patient's symptoms. The fact that the patient developed uncontrollable emotional thoughts during the treatment periods suggests that the latter explanation may be the correct one.

In a somewhat similar case study, Cowden and Ford (1965) desensitised a 27-year-old male paranoid schizophrenic patient to interpersonal speaking situations. The patient also had a history of auditory hallucinations which had ceased prior to the commencement of treatment. A successful outcome in terms of the patient's social phobia was *not* accompanied by any recurrence of the hallucinations. In other words, the kind of symptom substitution, which Lambley suggested was likely to result from this kind of treatment, did not occur.

Some years ago the first author published two individual case reports in which young, male, acute hallucinators were treated with systematic desensitisation (Slade, 1972, 1973). In the first case study, involving an outpatient, a detailed behavioural analysis suggested that the patient's voices were triggered during periods of increased tension and general emotional arousal. Further enquiry revealed that the tension and arousal occurred when the patient was at home, particularly in the presence of his father, or when he was thinking about the family but in another place. A hierarchy of anxiety-provoking situations was elicited, the patient was taught progressive muscular relaxation, and imaginal systematic desensitisation was carried out. The treatment led to a reduction in reported hallucinatory occurrences from approximately 16 per cent during a baseline period to approximately 6 per cent during desensitisation. During a five-week follow-up period the frequency of hallucinations reported was still lower at less than 2 per cent. Unfortunately, after the completion of the study the patient was readmitted to hospital with a depressive disorder. However, he remained totally free of auditory hallucinations and symptoms of depersonalisation or derealisation.

In the second case study, involving an inpatient (Slade, 1973), a similar detailed behavioural analysis suggested that the patient's voices were also triggered by stress. However, in this case the stressful stimuli involved general interpersonal and social situations rather than being specific to the family. The patient's voices were monitored by the author while an independent therapist conducted first, an imaginal desensitisation programme (which had no effect), followed by an *in vivo* programme. The patient's self-reported frequency of hallucination dropped from 11.54 per cent during baseline to less than 4 per cent during the latter phase of the *in vivo* programme. During a five-week follow-up period the frequency of reported voices was again under 2 per cent. However, unlike the first patient above, the patient did not become depressed following the treatment.

Finally, in this section, a case report by Siegel (1975) must be considered. Siegel suggested that, in cases of hallucination, systematic desensitisation may be useful for slightly different purposes than those already described. The author described the case of a 39-year-old male outpatient with a diagnosis of chronic undifferentiated schizophrenia. This patient had been disturbed by voices for the past eight years and it was the anxiety engendered as a result which was the major problem, particularly when the voices told the patient to jump out of a high window at bedtime. Siegel taught the patient relaxation exercises and then desensitised him to anxiety generated by the voices. The upshot was that, while the patient still continued to hallucinate, he ceased to be disturbed by the voices, which changed in quality from hostile to friendly. The improvement was maintained during a 21-month follow-up period.

On balance, it would seem that systematic desensitisation does appear to have a contribution to make in the treatment of some cases of hallucination. However, therapists do need to carry out a detailed behavioural analysis before embarking on this kind of approach, and to be clear in their own minds what they are trying to achieve with a particular patient.

(iii) Thought stopping

There have been several accounts of the use of thought-stopping procedures in the treatment of persistent hallucinations. Samaan (1975) described the case of a 42-year-old woman who suffered from multiple severe behavioural disturbance that had not responded to drug therapy or traditional psychotherapy. The author treated her obsessional fear of knives by means of flooding and her hallucinations by means of the thought-stopping procedure described by Wolpe (1973). This involved instructing the patient to raise the index finger of her right hand every time she experienced hallucinatory thoughts or frightening images and to lower her finger when they disappeared. When the patient raised her finger the therapist apparently, 'rubbed her hand and forearm and yelled repeatedly "Stop it, stop it", with increasing loudness until her finger went down.' (Clearly there are parallels between this procedure and the aversive techniques to be described below.) The patient was given a tape-recording of the therapist yelling 'Stop it', which she took home for use during the early part of treatment. Later she transferred this method of control to her own vocal control over the symptoms. After six weeks the hallucinatory experiences were extinguished completely and were still absent at a 20-month follow-up.

In another study Johnson, Gilmore and Shenoy (1983) described the case of a 30-year-old Vietnam veteran with a long history of recurrent visual hallucinations and obsessional ruminations. While serving in Vietnam the patient had shot and killed a Viet-Cong soldier who was attempting to stab him with a knife. The hallucinations consisted of this soldier's bloodied face and had begun nine years prior to the patient presenting for treatment. The frequency and intensity of the hallucinations had increased considerably over this period so that the patient was having an average of five such experiences per week at the time of treatment. Following nine weeks of baseline recording, Johnson *et al.* began the thought-stopping procedure described by Rimm and Masters (1974). This involves four stages, the first being the therapist's interruption of the patient's overt thoughts (i.e. external overt control), the last being the patient's covert interruption of his own covert thoughts (i.e. internal covert control). The patient was instructed to practise the thought-stopping procedure at home at least three times a day. Over a four-month period (involving only five therapy sessions) the frequency of hallucination reduced to only one hallucination per week. The hallucinations that remained, however, continued to be vivid and intense. The authors therefore introduced an additional therapeutic procedure involving anger induction. One session of this proved sufficient to eliminate the hallucinations completely. No further instances of hallucination were reported at an 11-month follow-up.

The third report of the use of thought stopping to treat halluci-nations was made by Lamontagne, Audet and Elie (1983), who conducted a controlled trial of chlorpromazine alone versus chlor-promazine plus four sessions of thought stopping. Twenty patients with DSM–III diagnoses of paranoid schizophrenia were randomly assigned to one or other treatment group. The daily frequencies of paranoid thoughts and hallucinations were carefully monitored and represented the target behaviours. In the first thought-stopping session, the therapist shouted 'Stop' every time the patient raised the index finger of his or her right hand to indicate when a persecutory thought came to mind or that he or she heard 'voices'. During the second session, the patient took responsibility for shouting the word 'Stop'. Then, during the third session, the patient was instructed to say 'Stop' softly to himself/herself before being taught in the final session to do this subvocally. Following treatment all patients received follow-up assessments at one month, three months and six months. The main finding was that the group receiving thought stopping in addition to chlorproma-zine showed greater improvement on most measures although, with respect to the two target behaviours, only the difference in improvement in paranoid thoughts was statistically significant. In their discussion Lamontagne *et al.* suggested that they might have achieved more impressive results if they had selected less chronic psychotic patients and given them eight 30-minute sessions rather than four 1-hour sessions. They also suggested that the use of other verbal stimuli should be investigated in relation to thought-stopping treatments. This suggestion arose as a result of an observation made by one of their patients, who found that shouting 'Stop' was completely useless but that shouting 'Go to hell' not only stopped his voices but also his persecutory thoughts. Perhaps hallucinations and delusions are more responsive to some types of instruction than others!

Finally in this section, a single-case study reported by Allen, Halperin and Friend (1985) should be considered. Following a suggestion by Rachman (1981), Allen *et al.* argued that thought-stopping procedures would tend to reduce the duration of auditory hallucinations but not their frequency. They therefore hypothesised that a combination of thought stopping and diversion tactics (designed to reduce the probability of the hallucinations occurring) would yield maximum symptom relief. A 29-year-old inpatient with a diagnosis of schizophrenia was required to increase her level of activity by attending occupational therapy classes (diversion) while at the same time learning a thought-stopping procedure similar to that employed by Lamontagne *et al.* (see above). Generally, the two approaches had the predicted effects: the occurrence of the voices decreased in the activity sessions and the patient was able to use the thought-stopping procedure successfully in the therapy sessions. However, there was no clear evidence that these effects generalised to other areas of the patient's life. This may have been because, on the patient's own admission, she rarely used the thought-stopping procedure outside the therapeutic setting, even though she knew that it produced the desired effect.

In sum, as appears to be the case with operant procedures and systematic desensitisation, thought stopping seems to have potential for the treatment of at least some cases of hallucination. However, ingenuity and flexibility would seem to be required in applying this approach to individual patients.

(iv) Reduction of sensory input

Clinicians and researchers have sought to interfere with hallucinations by manipulating the level of current environmental stimulation. As will be recalled from the review of the relevant literature in Chapter 4, the relationship between hallucination and environmental stimulation is in fact quite complex. Harris (1959) studied the effects of brief periods of sensory deprivation on the auditory hallucinations of 12 schizophrenic patients and reported beneficial results which unfortunately did not generalise to the ward environment. On the face of it, this is a surprising result as the balance of the available evidence suggests that hallucinations are more rather than less likely to occur in conditions of sensory poverty (see Chapter 4). However, the poor experimental design, the lack of clear measures and the short periods of sensory deprivation employed prevent firm conclusions from being drawn from Harris's data. Moreover, subsequent attempts to use sensory deprivation with schizophrenic patients have yielded conflicting results.

(v) Counter-stimulation

Given the available evidence on the relationship between stimulation and hallucination, procedures in which individuals are subjected to increased meaningful stimulation, especially self-generated stimulation, would seem to hold more promise for the treatment of hallucinations. Two experimental studies carried out by the first author and described in detail in Chapter 4 provide support for this idea. Slade (1974) required two hallucinating patients to shadow material presented at varying rates; the rate at which the subjects reported hearing voices decreased as an orderly function of the rate at which the material was presented to them. In a subsequent study, Margo, Hemsley and Slade (1981) required seven hallucinators to listen to various types of stimulus material presented through headphones and found that the more meaningful the material the less likely the subjects were to hallucinate. In both studies, reading aloud was also found to be a particularly effective way of reducing hallucination.

Erickson and Gustafson (1968) described the clinical use of various counter-stimulation techniques with hallucinating patients. Following the observation that 'When patients hallucinate, they are responding to internal stimuli — that is to say, they are interacting with themselves', the authors set about teaching patients to use their vocal chords for something else. The alternative behaviours found useful in this respect included 'humming' and 'gargling'. Two case studies were described in which these procedures proved effective in initially blocking and then eliminating the patients' voices altogether.

A more recent report by James (1983) described the treatment of two patients with counter-stimulation in conjunction with earplug therapy (see below) with similar results. The patients were required to point to and name objects in the room whenever they heard voices. The successful outcome was attributed to the counter-stimulation rather than the earplugs.

An important question with respect to counter-stimulation techniques concerns the extent to which the results produced are long-lasting. In the experimental studies carried out by the first author, no reduction in hallucination was observed outside the laboratory situation whereas the case studies of Erickson and Gustafson and those of James seem to indicate that relatively permanent improvements might sometimes be achieved. Two single-case studies by Turner and his associates (Alford and Turner, 1976; Turner, Hersen and Bellack, 1977) addressed this issue. In the first study a 32-year-old female with an eight-year history of auditory hallucinations was subjected to two experimental treatments, which were preceded and followed by baseline periods. The first treatment involved an interference/counter-stimulation condition in which the patient was freely engaged in non-symptom-related conversation. The investigators labelled this condition 'social disruption'. The second treatment involved contingent electrical aversion therapy. The authors noted that both treatments had the effect of suppressing hallucinations during treatment sessions but that only the effects of electrical aversion generalised to the baseline periods.

In their second investigation Turner *et al.* studied the effects of two interference conditions and electrical aversion therapy with a 33-year-old female with an 11–year history of voices. One of the interference conditions was the same 'social disruption' procedure used previously, and the other was termed 'stimulus interference'. The latter entailed the ringing of a bell whenever the patient signalled the onset of her voices. The authors found that, as before, the interference conditions virtually eliminated hallucination reports during sessions but that the effects did not generalise to baseline periods. By contrast the authors argued that the effects of the aversion procedure were lasting.

Although the above two studies suggest that counter-stimulation procedures may have only transient effects whereas aversion therapy may have durable ones, the data are not as overwhelmingly conclusive as this, for several reasons. First, in both of the Turner studies the 'interference' intervention preceded the 'aversion' one. It is possible therefore that there may have been an order effect favouring the latter intervention. Secondly, in the case of the later report the number of unbroken sessions of electrical aversion was virtually double that of the 'interference' conditions. This could also have favoured the aversion condition in terms of durability of effects. Finally, it would appear that Erickson and Gustafson attempted to teach their patients counter-stimulation as a skill which they could use to suppress hallucinations whenever they experienced them. The success of counter-stimulation procedures may therefore depend upon the extent to which patients are able to generalise their use to all situations.

Whether or not the effects of counter-stimulation are lasting or only immediate, they do appear to have a role in the clinical management of some patients with persistent auditory hallucinations. Feder (1982) reported the case of a 21-year-old male with a three-year history of intermittent 'voices'. These 'voices' became very much worse when the patient started a new job with a landscaping company which entailed his operating large, gasoline-powered lawn mowers (perhaps because of the loud and relatively unpatterned noise produced by the engines). He was advised to purchase and wear a set of stereo headphones with a built-in battery-operated AM–FM radio. The patient wore the headphones at work and reported a complete elimination of his voices while mowing lawns. However, he continued to hear the voices intermittently when not wearing the headphones. In a similar report, Mallya and Shen (1983) described the case of a 44-year-old male with a 12-year history of auditory hallucinations who obtained immediate relief from his voices by means of a set of headphones and a Sony Walkman. Again the patient continued to hallucinate when he was not wearing the apparatus.

(vi) Self-monitoring

Rutner and Bugle (1969) reported the treatment of the hallucinatory voices of a 47-year-old schizophrenic woman who had been hospitalised for 13 years. The patient privately recorded the occurrence of her voices on a chart for three days. This led to a reduction in hallucination frequency from 181 on the first day to 11 occurrences on the third. From the fourth day onwards the patient continued to record her voices on the chart which was now displayed publicly. This enabled ward staff and other patients to give her praise and attention whenever she recorded a reduction in hallucination frequency. After a further 13 days the latter had dropped to zero and no recurrence of her voices was reported during a six-month follow-up period. Concomitant with the elimination of the patient's auditory hallucinations, she showed a general improvement in her mood, appearance, and social relationships with staff and other patients.

A similar kind of technique was used by Reybee and Kinch (1973) who referred to their method as 'focusing'. They attempted to treat two male chronic schizophrenic patients who had been in hospital for 15 years and 13 years, respectively, continuous auditory hallucinations being their main complaint. Reybee and Kinch began with a 'general focusing' phase which involved the patients' retrospectively self-rating the frequency of their 'voices' at various intervals during the day. This produced no change in hallucination frequency. A 'specific focusing' phase followed where, during three sessions a week, the patients sat in front of an event recorder and signalled the commencement, duration and termination of their 'voices' by pressing a button. In this way the patients were provided with immediate visual and tactile feedback about their voices. During the seven weeks of 'specific focusing', one patient showed a steady decrease of hallucinations during the sessions from a 50 per cent rate of occurrence to a 10 per cent plateau. The other patient showed a similar decrease from a 20 per cent to a 10 per cent rate. Unfortunately, the effects did not generalise to the ward setting.

In another single-case study, reported by Moser (1974), a 24-year-old male paranoid schizophrenic was first asked to record privately the daily frequency of his hallucinations for two weeks. Over this period of time his reported frequency of auditory hallucinations showed a marked increase from 7 to 23 per day. Following this the patient was instructed to imagine a vivid, nauseous scene whenever he began experiencing an auditory or visual hallucination (i.e. a covert sensitisation procedure). His records showed that both his auditory and visual hallucinations dropped to zero over the subsequent two-week period and were still absent after a month. Over two years later, reports from the patient's parole officer indicated that there had been no return of symptoms and that the patient was functioning well.

A final study which must be considered in the present context has been reported by Glaister (1985), who used a technique he described as 'satiation' to treat a 46-year-old man suffering from persistent auditory hallucinations. The rationale for Glaister's method was similar to that described by Siegel (1975) with respect to systematic desensitisation (see above). Arguing that the hallucinations (which mainly consisted of exhortations to self-injury) were being maintained by the anxiety that they generated, Glaister set about exposing his patient to them as often as possible in order to reduce this anxiety. In practice this involved 85 half-hour periods of self-monitoring in which the patient had to take a written record of his voices and rate their 'demandingness'. The treatment was carried out over a 16-month period, during which time the frequency of the patient's hallucinations fell from 23 per hour to virtually zero. This improvement was maintained at five-year follow-up. Although it might be thought that 85 sessions amounts to a very lengthy (and thus expensive) period of therapy, it should be noted that most of these sessions were conducted by the patient alone as part of his homework; only 24 sessions involved the presence of the therapist.

Careful scrutiny of the above reports suggests that the nature and form of the self-observation/self-monitoring procedure used is of crucial importance. 'Retrospective monitoring' and simple 'daily-frequency counting' either have no effect (Reybee and Kinch) or can lead to an increase in reported frequency (Moser). The first author has similarly observed the absence of positive effect with patients asked to record retrospectively the occurrence or non-occurrence of their voices (Slade, 1972, 1973). On the other hand, concurrent monitoring of hallucinatory episodes which is ensured either through the use of an event recorder (Reybee and Kinch) or written records (Glaister) has been found to decrease the frequency of hallucinatory experiences.

(vii) Aversion therapy

Bucher and Fabricatore (1970) treated a 47-year-old male patient who had suffered from auditory hallucinations for about five years by means of aversion therapy. They gave the patient a shock box (explaining that it was 'a technique derived from scientific experimentation') and instructed him to carry it everywhere and shock himself immediately the voices began and until they ceased. From a baseline of five or six occurrences per day the patient's hallucinations dropped to zero after ten days and were still absent 25 days later. The patient was subsequently discharged and later reported the development of 'background voices' which were quite unlike the original ones. They were not affected by the use of the shock box.

In another single-case study, Watts and Clements (1971) reported initial success in eliminating auditory hallucinations in a male schizophrenic using a combination of self-monitoring (i.e. getting the patient to monitor his voices aloud) and white noise as the aversive stimulus. The 'voices', however, reappeared within a fortnight after treatment had been discontinued.

Weingaertner (1971) carried out a controlled trial in order to establish whether punishment is specifically effective in the suppression of auditory hallucinations. Auditory hallucinated patients were assigned to one of three groups: (a) a shock group; (b) a pseudo-shock group; and (c) a non-treatment control group. The two experimental groups were given shock boxes and told to press the button when they heard their 'voices'. For the first group, button pressing caused a shock to be delivered, and for the pseudo-shock group the circuit had been disconnected, resulting in no shock. While all three groups evidenced a decrease in their hallucination frequency, the shock group did not improve significantly more than the other two groups. The author concluded that 'placebo' was the primary agent of change, attributing the positive therapeutic effects to the patients' expectation of improvement.

A rather more positive conclusion was reached by Turner and colleagues in the two single-case studies already described in the section on 'counter-stimulation' (i.e. Alford and Turner, 1976; Turner et al., 1977). Their relevant finding was that, while 'interference' conditions (i.e. either engaging in social conversation or hearing a bell ringing) have immediate but no lasting effects, contingent electrical aversion therapy produced 'more lasting results ... that tended to remain fairly stable when the aversive stimulus was removed'. However, as previously noted there were other uncontrolled factors which could conceivably have influenced the validity of this comparison.

Finally, in this section, the involvement of the first author and colleagues in clinical research using white noise aversion therapy should be reported. This work has been conducted in a laboratory situation in which patients are asked to indicate the presence of their 'voices' by depressing a response key strapped to the right arm of the patient's chair. Patients wear headphones through which approximately 80 decibels of white noise can be presented according to the desired schedule. In one study (Fonagy and Slade, 1982) three white noise schedules were compared in three hallucinating patients. The 'punishment' condition involved the presentation of white noise immediately following the reported cessation of hallucinations (white noise at voice offset); the 'negative reinforcement' condition involved the presentation of white noise immediately following the reported commencement of hallucinations (white noise at voice onset); while the third condition involved non-contingent, random white noise, of comparable durations. All three patients improved, although reported reductions in hallucinations were more marked in the first two cases than in the third. The condition involving *concurrent* presentation of white noise (white noise at voice onset — the negative-reinforcement condition) appeared to be the most effective.

In a further study (Slade, Judkins, Clark and Fonagy, 1986), a 42-year-old female with a three-year history of voices (which had not responded to medication) was given an extended course of treatment involving *concurrent* white noise. Initially the patient heard six different voices, five male and one female, with a wide variety of both abusive and supportive contents. During two baseline recording sessions of fifteen minutes each, the patient reported 10 and 15 'voices' respectively (with a mean duration of 12.5 and 5.3 seconds). The third session involved 30 minutes of contingent white noise, followed by subsequent sessions involving 15-minute periods of baseline measurement and white noise treatment. During sessions 4 to 21 the frequency of hallucination fell to one per baseline period. During session 21 the patient reported that her 'voices' had totally ceased *outside of* the laboratory sessions.

195

Treatment was therefore discontinued and the patient remained free of her voices at six-month follow-up.

Several interesting observations were made on this patient during the treatment period. The first was that, concomitant with a reduction in hallucination frequency, the patient reported a reduction in the number of voices and the variety of their content such that during sessions 17 to 21 the patient only reported one male voice with the stereotyped content. 'You don't hear no more voices.' The second arose from the fact that measures of respiration rate were taken continuously throughout baseline and treatment sessions. Measures of respiration rate during the 60 seconds prior to hallucination reports were noted, broken down into 10-second intervals. During the two baseline periods an initial increase in respiration rate was observed, followed by a sudden deceleration immediately preceding hallucination onset. During treatment sessions involving a reduction of hallucination frequency, the timing of deceleration of respiration rate became increasingly earlier, whereas during the several relapse sessions it came close to hallucination onset. If it is assumed that respiration rate deceleration is a form of anticipatory response, and there are reasonable grounds for doing so (Lacey, 1967), then it follows that the contingent white noise may have been effective by helping the hallucinated patient to *anticipate* (and bring under voluntary control) the hallucination experience.

In summary, aversion therapy (both white noise and electrical) appears to provide a useful adjunct in the treatment of hallucinations. However, the mechanism underlying the therapeutic effect of this kind of treatment is open to more than one explanation. This is a point which will be returned to later.

(viii) Earplug therapy

The use of unilateral earplugs to control auditory hallucinations was first suggested by Paul Green (1978). This suggestion was made on the basis of Green's theory of defective interhemispheric transfer and integration in schizophrenia (Green, 1978b; Green, Glass and O'Callaghan, 1980), discussed in the previous chapter. This suggestion was taken up by James (1983) who carried out two single-case treatment studies, already discussed above in the context of counter-stimulation. In both cases the wearing of an earplug in one ear had an immediate and dramatic impact on reported hallucination frequency. However, in both cases transfer of the earplug to the other ear had a continuing impact on the patients' voices. For this reason, the author ascribed the positive therapeutic effect to the additional instruction to 'point and name' alternative objects in the environment whenever the voices occurred.

In another single-case study, Morley (1987) compared first the effects of three kinds of distracting speech and then the effects of earplug therapy. The subject was a 31-year-old male with complaints of auditory hallucinations, depression and general anxiety. Over a two-week period he was asked to listen to three sets of distracting music and to rate the amount of time spent hallucinating, together with the clarity and vividness of his hallucinations.

Only a transient effect on auditory hallucinations was observed. The patient was then instructed to wear an earplug. Initially it was placed in the left ear (as recommended by Green) and had no effect. It was then switched to the right ear and there was an immediate drop in the clarity of voices. After one week the location of voices had switched sides and the earplug was therefore switched back to the left ear. This resulted in an immediate cessation of all voices. The plug was discontinued after a further two days at the patient's request. At one-month follow-up he had had no recurrence of his voices.

Another single-case study of earplug therapy was reported by Done, Frith and Owens (1986). In this study, a 42-year-old male chronic schizophrenic was treated using an A–B–A–C design. The three conditions investigated were: (a) right earplug only (condition A); (b) left earplug only (condition C); and (c) no earplug at all (condition B). It was found that the right earplug condition produced a significantly greater effect on most of the measures compared with the other two conditions. This was contrary to prediction from Green's theory. Because of this finding, the authors hypothesised that the earplugs affected the patient's attributions about his voices; as he heard his voices in his right ear the presence of the plug in that ear may have created a dissonant state.

Finally, Birchwood (1986) reported a single-case study using an earplug with results that at first appear more consistent with

Green's theory. His subject, a 37-year-old male schizophrenic patient, recorded an average of more than 300 episodes of auditory hallucination per day during a 28-day baseline period. He experienced a 46 per cent reduction in the frequency of his hallucinations during the week after he began to wear an earplug in his left ear. However, there was a subsequent slow increase in the frequency of his hallucinations until this was apparently checked by the use of the naming procedure previously employed by James. During a subsequent four-day period in which the patient was asked to remove the plug but continue using the naming procedure, there was an increase in his frequency of hallucination until use of the earplug was resumed. The patient was still wearing the earplug 160 days after first using it, and was reporting hallucinations at about half the baseline rate. Unfortunately, Birchwood did not assess the effects of wearing the earplug in the right ear so, despite the results, the study does not provide particular support for Green's theory.

In summary, earplug therapy does appear to have had a dramatic impact on auditory hallucinations in the few patients with whom it has been tried. However, in none of the five cases reported does the effect seem to be clearly explicable in terms of Green's original theory.

(ix) First-person-singular therapy

The basic requirement of this form of therapy was described in the reports of Erickson and Gustafson (1968) and Nydegger (1972). However, the explicit rationale for the treatment strategem is associated with the name of Robert Greene (1978). Greene argued that 'Regardless of orientation, a key factor in auditory hallucinations is the message of maximum external control and minimum personal responsibility.' Moreover he suggested that this amounted to a form of 'conceptual avoidance'. Greene therefore proposed that in order to overcome hallucinatory experiences patients need to be educated about the nature of such experiences: specifically that they are internally generated and involve 'talking to one's self'. Patients are thus encouraged to adopt the 'first-person singular' and refer to their voices as 'talking to myself'. Greene (1978) reported the successful use of this therapeutic strategy with two female patients, both of whom reported the termination of their voices once they had fully accepted and implemented the 'first-person-singular' labelling approach.

As yet there have been no independent reports from other workers on the effectiveness of this particular method. However, an approach which is at least theoretically consistent with Greene's method has recently been described by Fowler (1986), who used a form of reattribution therapy with five persistently hallucinating psychiatric patients. The patients were encouraged to bring on and dismiss their hallucinations in the hope that this would lead them to reattribute the voices to themselves rather than to an external source. Distraction techniques of the sort described above under the heading of counter-stimulation were also used to some degree. A dramatic reduction in the frequency of hallucinations experienced by the patients was recorded for only one subject. The remaining subjects derived little benefit from the procedure.

(x) Psychological treatments: Some general considerations

It will be clear from the above review of nine kinds of psychological treatment that apparently very different and even seemingly incompatible treatments (e.g. systematic desensitisation and aversion therapy) can bring about a decrease in hallucinatory activity. This begs the question of how these nine different treatment procedures work. One possibility is that they each have their effects at a different level of the hallucinatory mechanism. Another possibility is that they share a common therapeutic effect. For example, the most likely single factor would be the placebo response (i.e. positive expectations of change). There are, however, several studies which suggest that the latter is not a tenable explanation for *all* the observed effects (e.g. Alford and Turner, 1976; Turner *et al.*, 1977; Fonagy and Slade, 1982; etc). A careful examination of the data outlined above suggests that their success might be explicable in terms of *three* processes, namely: (a) focusing; (b) anxiety reduction; and (c) distraction or counter-stimulation.

Focusing

In the section on self-monitoring it was concluded that concurrent

199

monitoring of hallucinatory episodes which is ensured either through the use of an event recorder or through a requirement on the part of the patient to make a contingent response might be the crucial variable responsible for improvement. The same hypothesis also seems to be able to account for the beneficial effects of a number of other procedures. One of these is aversion therapy. Whatever form it takes (electrical or white noise), aversion therapy provides a powerful requirement on the patient to attend to and focus on hallucinatory experiences and the circumstances surrounding such experiences. A similar argument holds for thought-stopping techniques as described earlier. A clear commonality is that both of these methods serve to *focus* the patient's attention on their voices.

A similar 'attention-focusing' process seems to be involved in first-person-singular therapy. The patient is asked to attend very carefully to his or her voices and to label these voices as 'talking to myself'. Earplug therapy, the results of which do not fit with Paul Green's (the originator's) theory, could possibly be explained in terms of the principle of attention-focusing as well. Indeed, this would be consistent with Done *et al.*'s account of their experience with this technique. The apparent efficacy of focusing is particularly interesting in the light of Heilbrun's hypothesis about the role of disattention in hallucinations (see Chapter 4), and suggests that avoiding attending to hallucinatory experiences may, in the long run, have the effect of maintaining them.

Anxiety reduction

One of the types of intervention outlined above was systematic desensitisation, of which six treatment examples were described. The apparent success of this treatment cannot easily be accounted for in terms of the principle of 'focusing' of attention. It is therefore suggested that procedures which have a specific anxiety-reduction effect may operate differently from those that serve to focus attention on hallucinations. This hypothesis is consistent with the available evidence linking hallucinations to increases in arousal (see Chapter 4).

Distraction or counter-stimulation

A third, and possibly distinctive, feature of some treatment programmes has been distraction or counter-stimulation. A variety

Table 7.2: Coping strategies reported by 40 chronic schizophrenic patients with persistent auditory hallucinations. From Falloon and Talbot (1981)

Type of strategy	N	%
1. *Behaviour change*		
(a) Postural (sit, lie down, stand, walk, run)	25	63
(b) Specific activity:		
(i) Work (including household)	11	28
(ii) Leisure (hobbies, music, reading TV)	29	73
(c) Interpersonal contact:		
(i) Initiate contact	19	48
(ii) Withdraw from contact	2	5
(d) Drug taking:		
(i) Prescribed medication (extra dose)	11	28
(ii) Non-prescribed medication (alcohol, analgesics, illicit drugs)	10	25
(e) Suicidal behaviour	11	28
2. *Physiological arousal*		
(a) Reduction:		
(i) Relax or sleep	29	73
(ii) Decrease sensory input (block ears, close eyes)	6	15
(b) Increase:		
(i) Physical exercise	22	55
(ii) Stimulating music/loud noise	5	13
3. *Cognitive strategies*		
(a) Reduced attention to 'voices' (ignore, block thoughts, distracting thoughts)	29	73
(b) Suppression of 'voices' (tell to keep quiet, go away)	6	15
(c) Reason/debate with 'voices'	13	33
(d) Accept 'voices' (listen attentively, repeat content, accept guidance)	14	35

of laboratory and clinical strategies that specifically emphasise distraction were described above. On the whole, these procedures seem to produce complete suppression of voices when present, often followed by total relapse in their absence. It would seem that methods which lead only to a short-term or concurrent suppression of voices are unlikely to be clinically useful unless they lead patients to develop stable strategies which they can use continually to suppress their symptoms. This is exactly what may have happened in those successful studies that utilised counter-stimulation or operant methods. It is possible that these methods led to the development of stable, incompatible behaviours which then acted as a permanent distraction from hallucinatory activity, or which were incompatible with hallucination.

PATIENT COPING MECHANISMS

The previous two sections have been concerned with the methods used by psychiatrists, clinicians and behavioural scientists to help patients who are tormented by their hallucinations. However, it is clear that professionals are not the only people attempting to help patients; patients also attempt to help themselves. In many of the scientific papers reviewed in the last section on psychological treatments, there are references to the patients' own observations concerning the efficacy of various procedures. It is not inconceivable therefore that something might be learnt from a study of patients' own coping strategies.

There have been at least two systematic surveys of patients' self-reported coping strategies. The first was by Falloon and Talbot (1981), who interviewed 40 consecutive outpatients meeting the Research Diagnostic Criteria (RDC) for schizophrenia (Spitzer, Endicott and Robins, 1975). Each patient was interviewed by an experienced psychiatrist who sought to explore the coping mechanisms the patient used to reduce the interference of his or her auditory hallucinations. The various strategies reported and the percentage of patients using them are shown in Table 7.2

The authors of the study classified the reported coping strategies into three main groups, namely: (a) behaviour changes; (b) changes in physiological arousal; and (c) cognitive strategies. Many of the coping strategies reported by the patients have their parallel in the psychological treatments described in the previous section. However, there are also notable exceptions and differences.

Of the three therapeutic treatment processes (i.e. focusing, anxiety reduction and distraction) suggested as underlying the nine psychological treatments reviewed in the previous section, only two are well represented in the coping strategies reported. *Anxiety reduction* was reported as a coping strategy by 73 per cent of the sample in the form of 'relaxation or sleep'. The use of *distraction* (or counter-stimulation) was also reported as a coping strategy in a number of forms such as postural change (63 per cent); leisure activities (73 per cent); interpersonal contact (48 per cent); physical exercise (55 per cent); and reduced attention to voices (73 per cent). However, the third and final process, *focusing*, was reported by only a small proportion of patients, in two forms: reasoning or debating with the voices (33 per cent) and accepting the voices — listening attentively, repeating their content, and accepting their guidance (35 per cent).

The second study to be considered in this context was carried out by Tarrier (1987), who used a similar approach to elicit coping strategies from 25 patients, suffering from auditory hallucinations and coherently expressed delusions, who were living in the community and receiving phenothiazine medication. The strategies employed included distraction or attention switching, thought stopping, self-instruction, increasing or decreasing activity, increasing external stimulation (mainly by playing music), and strategies apparently aimed at reducing arousal. Again, focusing seemed to be relatively poorly represented among these. When questioned about the effectiveness of their strategies, the majority of the patients reported at least some symptom relief; this was particularly the case with patients who employed more than one strategy.

On the basis of the results of these two studies, then, it would seem that many of the coping strategies reported by persistent hallucinators resemble the psychological treatment procedures previously described. However, few patients seem to have discovered for themselves what amounts to perhaps the most efficacious of methods: focusing. This should not be too surprising as focusing involves attending to a form of experience which many patients find distressing (see Chapter 4). However, this finding suggests a potentially important role that clinicians might play in the counselling and management of persistent hallucinators.

8

Towards an Integrative Model

In the preceding chapters of this book the available evidence concerning the functional determinants and cognitive mechanisms of hallucination has been reviewed in some depth. The purpose of the present chapter is to provide an integration of this data into a general model which may have heuristic value for future research into hallucinations. The model, which has been proposed by the second author (Bentall 1988) differd from the original model proposed by the first (Slade, 1976a) in terms of the cognitive mechanisms hypothesised to underlie hallucination, and in the addition of a fifth variable affecting hallucinations: *expectancy*. The model has been constructed particularly with psychotic hallucinations in mind but is almost certainly applicable to the kinds of normal hallucination described in Chapter 3. Caution may be required when extending the model to some hallucinatory states (particularly drug-induced hallucinations) which appear to be phenomenologically different from psychotic experiences (see Chapters 2 and 6).

It is worth briefly recalling some of the psychological models of hallucination outlined in Chapter 5. Despite the undoubted strengths of the individual theories, each demonstrated a number of weaknesses. Theories inspired by research into sensory deprivation were unable to account for the apparently complex relationship between external stimulation and hallucination, and made certain assumptions about the nature of human consciousness which, on close inspection, do not seem warranted. Theories that have emphasised mental imagery have generally failed to yield convincing and reliable evidence of imagery differences between hallucinators and non-hallucinators. Moreover, without qualification in terms of some operational measure of the cognitive mechanisms underlying mental imagery, the proposition that hallucinators experience peculiarly vivid mental imagery may well turn out to be tautologous. Finally, theories that emphasise the importance of subvocalisation, though grounded in reliable data, do not provide an explanation of why the hallucinator should mistake his or her own inner speech for voices and, in any case, cannot account for hallucinations in non-auditory modalities.

In addition to those problems peculiar to the individual theories outlined in Chapter 5, there are more general problems which none of the theories attempts to address. For example, in Chapter 3 we saw that there is at least some evidence of cultural and historical variation in the type and prevalence of hallucinatory experience. Evidence that some otherwise 'normal' people, even in Western cultures, show remarkable readiness to report hallucinations on instruction was also presented. An integrative account of hallucinations should explain these kinds of findings in addition to those findings obtained from severely disturbed psychiatric patients.

These difficulties should not be taken to indicate that no progress has been made in the understanding of hallucinations, or that the prospects for an integrative account are remote. Whereas each of the theories has its weaknesses, each has its strengths in terms of data that support it or phenomena that it seems particularly suited to address. Moreover, there is one fundamental assumption about the nature of hallucinations that all the theories have in common: that *hallucinators mistake their own, internal, mental or private events for external or publicly observable events.* Indeed, taking the ordinary language words 'real' and 'imaginary' to describe public and private events respectively, it is true by definition that the act of hallucination involves mistaking the 'imaginary' for the 'real'. (Of course, in the metaphysical sense, private or mental events are just as real as any other naturally occurring phenomena.) But to mistake the imaginary for the real presupposes that, ordinarily, it is possible to tell them apart. What is missing from existing accounts of hallucination, then, is an explanation of how, under normal circumstances, most people can tell the difference between imagined events (i.e. experiences generated by themselves, occurring within their skin) and events in the external world. It is only by first understanding the mechanisms involved in this type of judgement that the circumstances under which these mechanisms fail will be understood.

SOME CONCEPTUAL ISSUES

The term 'reality testing' has generally been used to describe the skill of discriminating between internal, mental events and events occurring in the public domain and perceived through the sense organs. Unfortunately, this term may be misleading if it implies a conscious attempt to test whether a perceived event is real or imaginary against various criteria. For this reason, the term *reality discrimination* will be used from this point onwards. In the next few pages an attempt will be made to say something about the nature of this skill and how it relates to hallucination.

It is easy to assume the ability to distinguish between the real and the imaginary is innate or *a priori*. However, as Descartes realised when he attempted to discover the foundations of empirical knowledge, a few moments' reflection will reveal examples in which our own judgement in this respect is sorely deficient. Vivid dreams and hallucinations are both examples of errors of this sort, and they so troubled Descartes that he came to doubt whether certain knowledge of the physical world was possible (Williams, 1971).

It was partly in an attempt to remedy the excesses of Descartes that the philosopher Ludwig Wittgenstein (1953) addressed the question of how people learn to have knowledge of and speak about their own private experiences. Whereas a child may learn to use words that describe public events by having their correct usage demonstrated (e.g. by being told, 'This is a table', by seeing others use the word) or by being corrected for improper usage (e.g. 'No, that's not an orange, it's an apple'), Wittgenstein pointed out that this could not be the case for events (including mental events) which can only be perceived by one person. For example, no one can point to a headache and say, 'There it is; *that's* what a pain is', and if a person were to use the word 'pleasure' to describe the private consequences of an apparently aversive event it is difficult to see how anyone could argue with him or her.

It is, of course, obvious that people are able to describe private events with some consistency, and Wittgenstein (and also the behaviourist B.F. Skinner, 1945, who made the same observations independently of Wittgenstein) considered how this might be possible. Wittgenstein concluded that, with the exception of descriptions of experience which amount to no more than unconditioned responses (e.g. yelps of pain), words used to describe private events must be tied to public stimuli. For example, a child might observe an adult use the term 'shooting pain' to describe the private result of a particular injury. Later, on receiving a similar injury in similar circumstances, it would not be surprising if the child described his or her own experience in a similar fashion. (See Bloor, 1983, and Skinner, 1945, for further examples of how descriptions of private events might be learned.) It is notable that many commonly used descriptions of private events make reference to public stimuli: a 'sharp' pain is the sort of pain that might be felt as a result of being injured by a sharp object; a 'crucifying' pain is one which is so severe that we would expect it to be the sort of pain felt on crucifixion. This analysis of the language of private events has become known as 'the private language argument' because it carries the claim that a language referring exclusively to private events is a logical impossibility. The private language argument has at least two important implications for psychologists. First, it is apparent that knowledge of mental processes must be to some degree inferential: the meaning of an experience is inferred on the basis of any (usually public) information available. The second implication of the private language argument is of particular importance to the study of hallucinations and other forms of mental disorder: it seems clear that people may sometimes make *wrong* inferences about their own mental events.

Social psychologists interested in the attribution of causality have tended to take these arguments seriously. For example, a number of investigators have demonstrated that a person's description of his or her own emotional state can be heavily influenced by contextual cues (Schacter and Singer, 1962; Pennebaker, 1980). Moreover, it seems that individuals often infer the causes of what they do on the basis of observations of their own behaviour and the context in which it occurs (Nisbett and Valins, 1972), with the result that their accounts of their own mental strategies may be seriously inaccurate when compared with their performance on actual tasks (Nisbett and Wilson, 1978). Abnormal psychology is particularly rich with examples of circumstances in which people

207

may 'mislabel' their own behaviour or emotional state. For example, this kind of process seems to be involved in 'mass hysteria', in which individuals under stress misattribute their feelings of arousal to illness (Pennebaker, 1983); in phobias, in which there may be a 'desynchrony' between physiological measures of arousal, reported fear and actual avoidance behaviour (Rachman and Hodgson, 1979); and in some chronic pain problems in which sufferers seem to base their estimates of their own pain at least partly on external cues (Fordyce, 1981).

The logic of the private language argument should apply equally to judgements about the real and the imaginary. On the basis of this kind of analysis it might be expected that: (a) individuals will base their judgements about whether an event is real or imaginary on a range of available information; and (b) judgements about the real and the imaginary will tend to be in error when the available evidence is misleading or when the individual fails to sample relevant information.

SOME EMPIRICAL DATA ON REALITY DISCRIMINATION IN NORMAL PERSONS

The term 'metacognition' has been used to denote mechanisms involved in a person's knowledge of his or her own mental processes. Considerable research has been carried out in this area in recent years, particularly by developmental psychologists who have been interested in the way that these mechanisms develop during childhood (Flavell, 1979). Reality discrimination, the ability to discriminate between public and private events, belongs to the general class of metacognitive skills.

Experimental evidence pertaining to the skill of reality discrimination has been collected from normal subjects. In particular, research has shown that reality discrimination errors can be demonstrated in normal individuals who misclassify either imaginary events as real or, conversely, real events as imaginary. (One implication of viewing reality discrimination as a skill is that people should sometimes make the opposite misattribution to that involved in hallucination, occasionally describing real events as imaginary.)

Perky (1910) was the first person to demonstrate this latter kind of error in the psychological laboratory. Subjects (trained introspectionists; the research was carried out before the advent of behaviourism) were asked to look at a blank screen and imagine an object (e.g. a banana). Unknown to them, a picture of the object was back-projected on to the screen and the brightness of the picture was slowly increased until it could clearly be seen by anyone in the room. All of Perky's 29 subjects failed to report the picture. Instead, they made statements to the effect that their visual imagery was peculiarly vivid, that the imagined object appeared at an unexpected angle, etc. In other words, the subjects appeared to believe that what they were seeing was a product of their imagination. They had been led to infer that this was the case from the demands of the experiment. Moreover, it seems likely that their beliefs about their own status might also have led them astray. As 'trained introspectionists' they would have had a high regard for their own ability to produce vivid images.

Unlikely though this result might seem, it has been replicated, particularly by Segal, who investigated the way in which a number of variables affected the 'Perky phenomenon'. Segal used undergraduate students in his experiments, with the result (not surprisingly) that the Perky phenomenon occurred less readily than for Perky's introspectionists. However, in one study Segal and Nathan (1964) found that the likelihood of the effect's occurring could be increased by giving their subjects a placebo tranquilliser. Segal and Glicksman (1967) also found that the effect occurred more readily if the subjects were lying down. Thirst, which Segal hypothesised would lead to an increase of arousal, was also found to increase the likelihood of the effect's occurring (Segal, 1968) whereas, not surprisingly, the subjects were less likely to produce the effect if they were informed of the possibility that images might be back-projected on to the screen. These results are consistent with the account of private events given above. The subjects presumably judged their experiences as more likely to be imaginary under conditions in which they were relaxed. On being given the information that their experiences could, after all, correspond to public events, their judgement became biased in the opposite direction.

In later work, Segal used signal-detection methodology to explore the Perky phenomenon further. Because signal-detection techniques have a number of implications for the study of hallucinations, it will be useful to examine this approach to research in some detail.

Signal detection methodology has been employed extensively by psychologists studying human vigilance (Green and Swetts, 1966; McNichol, 1972). In a typical signal-detection experiment subjects are asked to watch out for a stimulus presented against some kind of 'noisy' background (e.g. a voice embedded in a background hiss; a blip on a 'noisy' radar screen). After a considerable number of trials (often more than a thousand), the number of hits, false-positive detections, misses and correct rejections are calculated. The assumption made by the signal-detection theorist is that a person's decision about whether an event has occurred or not will depend on two factors: first, the amount of *noise* in the system (this might be neural noise or noise in the environment) relative to the strength of the signals being presented; and secondly, the observer's *bias* towards detecting signals. A high ratio of noise to signal will reduce the sensitivity of the system and will therefore tend to increase the number of errors occurring overall. On the other hand, bias will tend to affect the type of errors made. A person biased towards detecting signals (for example, a radar operator who believes that an enemy is about to attack) will tend to make few misses but many false-positive errors. A person who has a more conservative bias (for example, a radar operator who believes it unlikely that the enemy will attack and who is frightened of the consequences of calling a false alarm) will make few false-positive errors but will tend to miss events. (Notice how this model of perception is different from earlier models which assumed that there was a specific threshold of stimulation below which events would go undetected but above which events would almost certainly be detected accurately.) By the use of some ingenious mathematical models, signal detection theorists have found ways of estimating bias and sensitivity independently of each other from the kind of data (hits, misses, false positives and correct rejections) collected in signal-detection experiments.

Segal and Fusella (1970) applied signal-detection theory to the Perky phenomenon in a series of experiments in which subjects were asked to look into a 'ganzfeldt' (opaque visual field) and to watch out for back-projected shapes or, alternatively, to listen out for tones presented through earphones. On some trials the subjects were asked to imagine the shapes; on others they were asked to imagine the tones. In general, the results indicated that the imagination task led to a loss of perceptual sensitivity in the modality of the task but not in the other modality. In other words, imagining shapes impaired the subjects' ability to detect the shapes but not their ability to detect tones, and vice versa. This was entirely to be expected because, in terms of signal-detection theory, the instruction to imagine a stimulus amounts to an instruction to increase internal noise (cognitive activity) in the relevant modality. It is also consistent with the findings of Brooks (1968) described in Chapter 5. Unfortunately, because of the nature of the experiment (requiring many detection trials) the subjects had to be informed of the possibility of actual auditory or visual stimuli being presented, and variables likely to affect bias (e.g. placebo tranquillisers, posture) were not manipulated. However, on the basis of his signal-detection studies Segal was confident that the Perky phenomenon was not simply an attentional effect (in which case the instructions to imagine would have affected sensitivity in all modalities) but that the imagination task had actually reduced the subjects' ability to discriminate the real from the imaginary.

More recent evidence of reality discrimination failures in normal individuals has been obtained by Johnson and Raye (1981) and their associates, who used an entirely different paradigm to investigate the tendency of individuals to classify some imaginary events as real, the same kind of attributional error as that apparently involved in hallucination. Johnson and Raye were particularly interested in the way in which people sometimes confuse memories of real events with memories of thoughts (as, for example, when an academic researcher believes that he or she has originated an idea which he or she in fact heard from somebody else). Although they called the skill of distinguishing between memories of real events and memories of imaginary events 'reality monitoring', it is clearly closely related to reality discrimination as Johnson and Raye explicitly acknowledged.

In a series of studies, Johnson, Raye and others required subjects to discriminate between memories of self-generated items and memories of items presented by the experimenters. In their simplest paradigm, Johnson, Taylor and Raye (1977) asked subjects to learn a series of extremely simple paired associates, constructed from tables of cue–category norms (tables of the most common responses made when subjects are asked to provide a

Figure 8.1: Subjects' estimates of the number of times they had been presented with remembered items as a function of number of presentations (2, 5 or 8) and number of recalls (2, 5 and 8). From Johnson *et al.* (1977). See text for explanation

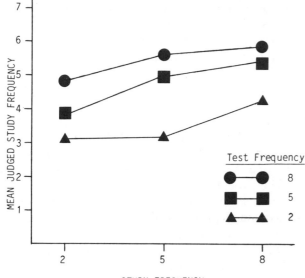

specific example of a given category, e.g. 'vehicle–car'). The number of presentations and the number of recall trials of the paired associates were independently varied so that, for example, some pairs were presented often but recalled rarely whereas others were presented on few occasions but recalled many times. At the end of the experiment, the subjects were given a surprise test in which they were asked to judge how often they had seen each of the associates. Johnson *et al.* hypothesised that subjects would confuse their recall of the items with the presentation of the items by the experimenter so that, the more often the items had been recalled, the more often the subjects would guess that they had been presented. This is precisely what happened (see Figure 8.2). Johnson and her associates called this phenomenon the 'increased frequency of external events' (IFE) effect.

In further experiments, Johnson *et al.* discovered that the IFE effect was greater when the subjects recalled the items overtly rather than covertly (e.g. by just stating whether they could

212

remember the associates). Moreover, the subjects were generally better at identifying the origin of items when they were made to discriminate between internally and externally generated events than when they were made to discriminate between two sets of externally generated items (Raye and Johnson, 1980). The implication of these findings is that memories of events and memories of thoughts are usually sufficiently different to make discrimination between them comparatively easy when compared with the difficulty involved in distinguishing between events belonging to the same class. However, as in the Perky phenomenon, sensory information seems to be an important determinant of the accuracy with which reality monitoring can occur. Overtly recalled and spoken items were more likely to be confused with presented items than covertly recalled items. In an additional test of the role of sensory information in reality monitoring, Johnson, Raye, Wang and Taylor (1979) found that, for picture items, good imagers (i.e. individuals who could describe imagined items in great detail) were more likely to show the IFE effect than poor imagers.

In a further series of investigations, Johnson, Raye, Foley and Foley (1981) found that subjects were better able to discriminate between self-generated and externally generated items when the self-generated items were harder to generate (the subjects were required to generate their own associates of varying complexity to some items). This finding suggested that one of the cues that people often use when distinguishing the real from the imaginary is 'cognitive effort'. Thinking and imagining requires some effort so that people regard experiences associated with such effort as the product of their own minds. (This result is particularly interesting in the light of Hoffman's (1986) hypothesis that hallucinations occur when mental events are unintended: see Chapter 5.)

Finally, Foley, Johnson and Raye (1983) have attempted to study the developmental course of reality monitoring and have found that, whereas six-year-olds are as capable as 17-year-olds at discriminating between memories of self-generated items and memories of words presented by others, they are slightly poorer than 17-year-olds at discriminating between memories of thoughts and memories of self-generated thoughts spoken aloud. This result is particularly interesting in the light of evidence that other meta-cognitive skills tend to develop after the age of five years (Flavell, 1979) and in the light of research that suggests that children first

213

learn to instruct themselves overtly before internalising inner speech (Vygotsky, 1962; Zivin, 1979; see also the section on subvocalisation in Chapter 5). This finding also has implications for the study of hallucinations in young children: if the ability to discriminate between the real and the imaginary is normally relatively poor in young children, it may be that the concept of hallucination is only applicable to individuals above a certain age (see Chapter 2 for evidence that hallucinations rarely occur in very young children).

To summarise, evidence gained from the experimental study of reality discrimination and reality monitoring in normal individuals supports the view that inferential processes are implicated in the skill of distinguishing between real and imaginary events.

HALLUCINATIONS CONSIDERED AS A FAILURE OF REALITY DISCRIMINATION

The central hypothesis of the present chapter is that hallucinations result from a dramatic failure of the skill of reality discrimination, leading the hallucinating individual to repeatedly misattribute his or her self-generated private events to a source external to him- or herself. This analysis has a number of advantages.

First, as Heilbrun (1980), the present authors (Bentall and Slade, 1985b, 1986) and Hoffman (1986) have previously argued, theories of hallucination should draw attention to the role of judgement in discriminating between the real and the imaginary. Most theories of hallucination to date have tended to focus on the sensory properties of private experiences without questioning the way in which that information is used by the individual to classify events as self-generated or originating from an external source. This failure to consider the role of judgement may account for some of the contradictory results obtained, particularly in respect of mental imagery. While it is entirely possible that the sensory properties of particular private experiences (e.g. if they happen to be especially vivid) may mislead a person into describing those events as externally caused, it is not clear that this is a necessary or sufficient condition for hallucination. Other types of information might be responsible for the individual being misled. Alternatively, the error might lie not in the information that is available *but in the*

inferences that the person makes on the basis of that information.
(These possibilities will be discussed in further detail below.)

A further advantage of the reality-discrimination hypothesis is
that it explains many of the phenomena associated with hallucination
which have been described in previous chapters.

1. It accounts for the observation of subvocal activity during
   auditory hallucinations (Gould, 1948, 1949, 1950; McGuigan,
   1966; Inouye and Shimizu, 1970; Green and Preston, 1981).
   Such activity is a normal concomitant of inner speech or verbal
   thought (Garrity, 1977a; McGuigan, 1978; Cacioppo and
   Petty, 1981; see Chapter 5) and so its presence concurrent
   with hallucination is not surprising (although this finding does
   not imply, as some authors have suggested, that some kind of
   defect of inner speech *causes* hallucination). On these grounds
   it might be expected that visual hallucinations would be
   accompanied by the psychophysiological concomitants of
   visual imagery. In a recent case study, Schatzman (1980)
   arranged for 'Ruth', a young woman suffering from visual
   hallucinations, to undergo psychophysiological testing. By
   calling up her 'apparition' (which was to some extent under
   voluntary control), Ruth was able to block visual evoked
   potentials which were otherwise elicited by a strong light
   source. On the other hand, when an electroretinogram was
   taken, no changes in retinal activity were associated with the
   hallucinations. (These results are also interesting in the light of
   the continuing controversy about the relationship between
   visual imagery and perception; see Kosslyn, 1983, and
   Chapter 5.)
2. It accounts for the observed effect of concurrent verbal tasks,
   which inhibit normal inner speech (Sokolov, 1972) and bring
   auditory hallucinations to an abrupt (though probably tempor-
   ary) halt (see Chapters 5 and 7). It might also be expected that
   a visual–perceptual task would inhibit visual hallucinations as
   such tasks have been shown to block normal visual imagery
   (Brooks, 1967). This possibility has yet to be tested experimentally.
3. It explains why hallucinations are sometimes experienced by
   otherwise normal individuals (Sidgewick *et al.*, 1894; West,
   1948; McKellar, 1968) as reality discrimination is presumably

215

a complex skill which may be manifest to varying degrees of accuracy in different circumstances. As already detailed in this chapter, experimental evidence indicates that reality discrimination failures sometimes occur in ordinary individuals (Segal, 1970; Johnson and Raye, 1981).

4. The argument that reality discrimination may manifest itself to varying degrees of accuracy also lends support for the view that hallucinations exist on a continuum with non-hallucinatory mental states (Strauss, 1969; Launay and Slade, 1981; Bentall and Slade, 1985a; Young, Bentall, Slade and Dewey, 1986; see Chapter 3).

So far, most of the evidence outlined pertaining to the reality-discrimination model has been circumstantial. However, direct evidence supporting the model is available from a number of studies.

Mintz and Alpert's (1972) study using Barber and Calverley's 'White Christmas' test replicated by the present authors (Young, Bentall, Slade and Dewey, 1987) will be recalled from Chapter 5. Although Mintz and Alpert interpreted their findings as indicating that hallucinators suffer from peculiarly vivid mental imagery, this hypothesis has not been substantiated by subsequent research using mental imagery questionnaires (although these may not be good measures of imagery vividness, see Chapter 5). An alternative way of interpreting Mintz and Alpert's results is to suppose that the hallucinators were more willing to describe their self-generated experiences as 'real' and to attribute them to an external source (a reality discrimination failure).

It will be recalled that reality discrimination can be considered from the point of view of signal detection theory. Overall inaccuracy in discriminating between the real and the imaginary amounts to poor sensitivity in signal detection terms. Poor sensitivity might result from a lot of internal noise (e.g. particularly vivid mental imagery), from external noise (e.g. white noise stimulation) or from sensory loss (e.g. blindness, deafness, sensory deprivation). On the other hand, it is possible that the hallucinator is just as perceptually sensitive as the non-hallucinator, but that he or she has a weaker criterion for deciding that an experience corresponds to a real event — a greater bias towards detecting signals.

216

Collicutt and Hemsley (1981) attempted to assess whether hallucinators differed from non-hallucinators in respect to internally generated noise, using a procedure in which subjects were asked to judge the diffference between the loudness of different pairs of tones. One of the earliest discovered empirical laws in psychology — Weber's law — states that the minimum difference that can be discriminated between unequal stimuli is proportional to their absolute magnitude (e.g. it is more difficult to tell the difference between weights of 30 pounds and 31 pounds than it is to tell the difference between weights of 1 pound and 2 pounds although the absolute weight difference is the same in both cases). Weber's law does not hold for very low values, because internal or 'neural' noise swamps out all stimulation. By estimating the point at which this occurred during their auditory task, Collicut and Hemsley were able to devise a measure of internal noise in the auditory modality. No difference was found between the groups, a result which was unexpected as the investigators had hypothesised that the hallucinators would be suffering from a perceptual disorder which would manifest itself in high internal noise. Because they could find no evidence of such high internal noise, Collicutt and Hemsley argued that hallucinators could only have greater bias towards classifying their experiences as 'real'. In other words, the only remaining possibility seemed to be that hallucinations resulted from a defect of judgement, rather than perception.

The present authors attempted to find evidence consistent with this hypothesis using signal detection methodology (Bentall and Slade, 1985b). In one experiment, subjects scoring high or low on the Launay–Slade scale were selected from over a hundred male undergraduate subjects who had filled in the scale as part of a previous study (Bentall and Slade, 1985a). Both groups of subjects were given an auditory signal detection task consisting of 200 trials in which they were asked to identify a verbal stumulus (the word 'Who' because it was considered that the signal, like many hallucinations, should make reference to the subject) against a white noise background. The stimulus was presented on a randomly selected 50 per cent of the trials; on the remaining trials only white noise was presented. For each trial, the subjects were required to respond using a five-point scale on which a score of 1 indicated that they were certain that the stimulus had not been presented, a score of 2 indicated that they believed that the stimulus had probably not been presented, a score of 3 indicated that they were completely uncertain, a score of 4 indicated that they believed that the stimulus had probably been presented, and a score of 5 indicated that they were certain that they had perceived the stimulus. This method, known as the rating scale method (McNichol, 1972), allows measures of perceptual sensitivity and bias to be calculated on the basis of a relatively small number of trials.

Figure 8.2 shows the results obtained from the experiment. It can be seen that high Launay–Slade scorers differed from low scorers in bias but not in sensitivity. Specifically, the high scorers were more ready to believe that a signal had been presented than the low scorers. In a second experiment, the results of which are also shown in Figure 8.2, a similar procedure was used with groups of hallucinating and non-hallucinating patients who all had a diagnosis of schizophrenia. (The procedure had to be modified because of the difficulties of keeping disturbed patients involved in a relatively boring task; more instructions and practice were given but the number of test trials was reduced to 100.) Again, the hallucinators and non-hallucinators did not differ in sensitivity but differed in bias in the expected direction. (As the procedure used with the psychiatric subjects differed from that employed with the undergraduates, the scores for the two measures cannot be directly compared so that the strikingly similar mean values obtained for bias in the two experiments is probably not theoretically significant.)

These results are consistent with those of Collicutt and Hemsley; the observed differences in bias indicate that, in conditions of uncertainty, hallucinators and individuals predisposed to hallucination are more inclined than non-hallucinators to judge a perceived event as real. The failure to find a difference in sensitivity between the groups is also interesting in the light of Segal and Fusella's (1970) finding that the generation of mental images causes a reduction of sensitivity in the modality concerned.

The recent study by Jakes and Hemsley (1986), described in Chapter 4 under the heading of suggestibility, should be considered in this context. It will be recalled that Jakes and Hemsley asked normal subjects differing in Launay–Slade scores to watch a television screen and report anything they saw. The screen in fact

Figure 8.2: Results for signal sensitivity and bias for high and low Launay–Slade scoring students and hallucinating and non-hallucinating psychiatric patients. From Bentall and Slade (1985b). See text for explanation

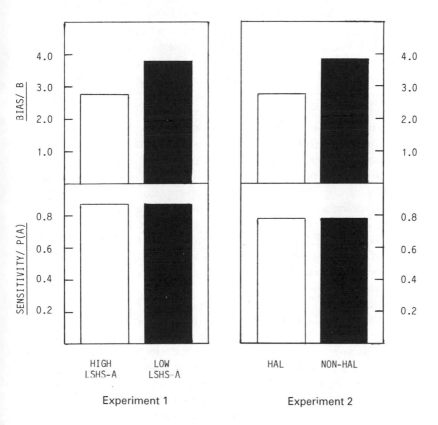

showed nothing but visual noise (a random dot display). The number of reports of meaningful stimuli (Type B reports) corre-lated with Launay–Slade scores whereas this was not the case for reports of simple stimuli (Type A reports). As no stimuli were actually presented on the screen, this finding could not be the result of low perceptual sensitivity and could therefore only reflect a greater bias towards believing that perceived events are real.

If hallucinators show a defect of the metacognitive skill of reality discrimination, it might also be expected that they would show a deficit in the related metacognitive skill of reality monitoring (discriminating between memories of thoughts and memories of events). Although this possibility has not been tested directly, the study by Heilbrun (1980) also described in Chapter 4 has some bearing on the issue. Heilbrun recorded the opinions of hallucinating and non-hallucinating psychiatric patients on a variety of topics. When asked to identify their own verbatim opinions from a multiple-choice list at a later date, the hallucinators proved less able to do so than the non-hallucinators, a result suggestive of a reality-monitoring deficit. Heilbrun interpreted his findings as indicating that hallucinators are less familiar with the characteristics of their own thoughts than non-hallucinators, and therefore more likely to attribute them to an external source.

One final line of evidence supporting the view that hallucinations result from an error of judgement emerges from those studies of cognitive factors predisposing individuals to hallucination described in Chapter 4. It will be recalled that measures taken in four separate studies (Mintz and Alpert, 1972; Schneider and Wilson, 1983; Heilbrun, Blum and Haas, 1983; Alpert, 1985) all indicated that hallucinators tend to make rapid, over-confident judgements about their perceptions, indicating that they are less tolerant of ambiguous perceptual information than non-hallucinators.

The evidence outlined in this section can therefore be summarised as follows: hallucinators make over-rapid perceptual judgements and are more willing than non-hallucinators to believe that a perceived event is real. It is not surprising, therefore, that they tend to mistake their own cognitive processes (inner speech or verbal imagery in the case of auditory hallucinations; visual imagery in the case of visual hallucinations) for events in the external world.

FIVE FACTORS AFFECTING HALLUCINATION

A comprehensive theory of hallucination must explain not only the mechanisms involved in reality discrimination but also why reality discrimination tends to fail under certain circumstances. In the original four-factor theory outlined by the first author (Slade, 1976a) the variables of stress-induced arousal, predisposing factors, environmental stimulation and reinforcement were hypothesised to affect the likelihood that a person would hallucinate in any particular situation. The likely effects of these variables, together with a fifth variable, *expectancy*, on the reality testing mechanisms outlined above will now be considered.

(i) Stress-induced arousal

There is ample evidence that stress-induced arousal increases the probability that a person will hallucinate. There is also evidence that at least one group of hallucinators, those diagnosed as schizophrenic, are particularly vulnerable to stress associated with face-to-face contact with hostile or overinvolved family members. Research on the effect of arousal on information processing suggests that abnormally high arousal levels bias the individual's information search towards readily accessible forms of information (Eysenck, 1976), increase the selection of information pertaining to physical characteristics of stimuli and decrease the processing of semantic information (Schwartz, 1975). It is to be expected that this more superficial style of information processing will decrease the efficiency of reality discrimination by limiting the ability of the subject to access and use appropriate cognitive cues.

(ii) Predisposing factors

Cognitive deficits that predispose individuals to hallucination have already been discussed in the context of reality discrimination above, and therefore need not be considered in detail here; in general, any trait or deficit that leads an individual to make over-rapid judgements about the sources of his or her perceptions, that deprives the individual of relevant information, or that provides the individual with misleading reality discrimination cues, is likely to lead to hallucination. The apparent relationship between neuroticism and hallucination (Chapter 4) should also not be surprising because this trait may reflect vulnerability to stress-induced arousal.

In the present context it should be noted that there may be many reasons why reality discrimination fails, and different types of hallucination may reflect the breakdown of different types of reality-discrimination skill. For example, it seems unlikely that an inability to locate sounds in space, identified by Heilbrun *et al.* (1983) as a deficit in some schizophrenic hallucinators, will be implicated in pseudo-hallucinations in which the individual correctly locates his or her voice inside his or her own head (Heilbrun and his associates did not test for this possibility). On the other hand, it is reasonable to suppose that a deficit in the ability to use cues about cognitive effort (an important component of reality monitoring identified by Johnson and Raye, 1981) may be implicated in pseudo-hallucinations as the voices seem to the percipient to appear in the mind unbidden. Clearly, the mapping of particular reality discrimination deficits on to different types of hallucination is likely to be a fruitful avenue of future research.

(iii) Environmental stimulation

The reality testing model explains the apparently contradictory effects of perceptual attenuation (for example, when progressive deafness leads to 'release hallucinations', see Chapter 2) and unpatterned environmental noise (see Chapter 4), which both lead to increases in the rate of hallucination. The judgement about whether an event is real or imaginary is likely to be most difficult when the sensory properties of internal and external events are most similar, and it is therefore under these conditions that the hallucinator's bias towards attributing an ambiguous event to an external source is likely to become most evident. In the terminology of signal detection theory, this is most likely to happen when the signal to noise ratio is poor (for example, when self-generated experiences are relatively vivid compared with impoverished environmental stimulation, or when information from the environment is swamped by unpatterned stimulation). On the other hand, despite his or her reality-testing deficits, the hallucinator is likely to have little trouble discriminating between imaginary and real events when the real events occur against a noise-free background.

(iv) Reinforcement

Case-study data indicate that some patients experience a reduction

222

of arousal following hallucination. On the other hand, some patients report being *more* disturbed rather than less following their hallucinations. Either consequence is likely to lead to further hallucination as a reduction of arousal is likely to reinforce the over-rapid and biased judgement that lies at the root of the hallucinator's reality-discrimination deficit, whereas an increase in arousal is likely to elicit further hallucinations (see above). It would seem that the wise hallucinator is best advised to develop a studied indifference to his experiences.

It may be that a broader concept of reinforcement is required to understand the positive consequences that hallucinations can have for the hallucinator. The possible functions of hallucinations have not been considered so far in this book because of the dearth of relevant data. However, it is notable that Freud (1924), extending his theory of dreams, suggested that hallucinations may express wishes which are unacceptable to the conscious mind of the patient. Unfortunately, there have been no empirical studies which address this issue, although Forgus and DeWolfe (1969) found that hallucinators required to remember brief stories more readily recalled themes relating to their hallucinations than neutral themes, suggesting that the contents of their hallucinations reflect dominant psychological concerns. Clinical experience certainly suggests that hallucinations often express ideas and intentions which seem to have been disowned by the patient, as the example of Brian, described in Chapter 1, seems to indicate. It is by no means impossible that some reality discrimination failures should be reinforced by their psychological consequences for the patient in this way. This possibility would seem worthy of future research.

(v) Expectancy

It is hypothesised above that reality discrimination, like other metacognitive processes, is affected by contextual cues. The implication is that information presented to a person, which will affect his or her beliefs and expectations, will also affect the likelihood that he or she will class a particular event as real or imaginary. This phenomenon might be thought of as a particular form of *perceptual set*; just as a person's expectations might lead him or her to 'see' an ambiguous stimulus as either one thing or another, so too

223

particular beliefs and expectations might lead the individual to experience ambiguous events as either real or imaginary. This hypothesis makes sense of two hitherto unexplained phenomena associated with hallucination.

First, there is considerable evidence that hallucinators are more likely than non-hallucinators to be affected by contextual information relevant to the source of their perceptions. Thus, a number of studies have demonstrated that hallucinators are more easily influenced than non-hallucinators in this respect (Mintz and Alpert, 1972; Buss, Larson and Nakashima, 1983; Alpert, 1985; Jakes and Hemsley, 1986; Young, Bentall, Slade and Dewey, 1987). Given their apparent intolerance of perceptual ambiguity it is perhaps not surprising that hallucinators should respond readily to any additional information made available to them.

Secondly, this hypothesis makes sense of the observed cultural and historical differences in the prevalence and type of hallucinations reported (see Chapter 3) as, by hypothesis, information about the likelihood of a perceived event being real or imaginary will be encoded in cultural practices. (A person coming from a culture that evinces a widespread belief in the supernatural is more likely to see ghosts than someone coming from a scientific–materialist background.)

Finally, this issue raises the question of why hallucinations are often seen in association with delusions. Although it has conventionally been believed that delusions may be secondary to hallucinations (Maher, 1974; Hamilton, 1985) the role of expectancy in the causation of hallucinations suggests that hallucinations may sometimes be secondary to strongly held beliefs.

THE ROLE OF BIOLOGICAL VARIABLES

Within the reality discrimination model, biological variables may play several roles. In some cases, biological factors may directly influence psychological variables which in turn affect the likelihood of hallucination. Thus, the hallucinations of alcohol psychosis seem to be associated with high levels of arousal (Chapter 2); release hallucinations are associated with perceptual impairment leading to a poor signal-to-noise ratio in the relevant modality (Chapter 3); and drug-induced hallucinations may result from impairment of the visual pathways of the brain (Chapter 6). It is of course possible that biological factors may also influence the skill of reality discrimination more directly. Despite the dearth of relevant evidence, it seems not unlikely that cerebral disorganisation, perhaps of the left (verbally conscious) hemisphere, would lead to a reality discrimination impairment.

RESPONSE TO TREATMENT

Finally, the hypothesised processes underlying the psychological methods of treatment described in the previous chapter must be considered. Three main factors appear to be responsible for a good response to the psychological interventions which have been attempted with hallucinating individuals: attentional focusing, anxiety reduction, and distraction or counter-stimulation.

Focusing involves the patient attending to his or her hallucinatory experiences and seems to be an important component in a variety of procedures ranging from self-monitoring to Robert Greene's first-person-singular technique. The significance of this component can be explained in several ways. First, by attending to his or her hallucinations, the hallucinator may learn to identify sensory properties that mark them out as self-generated rather than externally caused. Secondly, by learning to label his or her experiences as imaginary, rather than real, the hallucinator may develop an expectancy which will make him or her less biased towards describing ambiguous events as 'real'. Focusing may also lead the hallucinator to take responsibility for his or her own thoughts (which may be difficult if they are of a hostile or unpleasant nature) rather than attributing them to another source. Finally, the act of attending may slow down the hallucinator's perceptual judgements, making them more accurate.

In contrast to focusing, anxiety-reduction techniques probably have a more simple mode of action, directly affecting one of the variables (stress-induced arousal) that tends to precipitate hallucinations.

Finally, distraction and counter-stimulation techniques seem to affect hallucinations in a variety of ways: by taking the hallucinator's mind off stressful events, by increasing the level of patterned environmental stimulation (as in Walkman therapy) and

225

by making the hallucinator make responses (particularly verbal responses in the case of auditory hallucinations) which are incompatible with hallucination.

CONCLUSIONS

In the present chapter an attempt has been made to formulate an integrative model that accounts for the data described in the rest of the book. The model is shown diagrammatically in Figure 8.3 and might be considered a reformulation of the earlier model shown in Figure 4.1. The model differs from its predecessor by proposing a mechanism of hallucination (defective reality discrimination); it also hypothesises that hallucination may be affected by a fifth variable (expectancy), and takes into account the experimental data that have become available in the ten years since the original model was described by the first author.

Central to the reformulated model is the idea that reality discrimination is a judgemental process, and that hallucinations occur when defective reality judgements are made. Evidence supporting this hypothesis was outlined from three sources: (a) philosophical analyses of mental processes; (b) studies of reality discrimination and related processes in normal individuals; and (c) direct evidence from the study of hallucinating psychiatric patients. In addition, it was shown that the model is consistent with much of the existing evidence on hallucinations (e.g. with respect to subvocalisation, suggestibility and cultural factors), some of which has not been accounted for by previous theories. Several important points about the model remain to be emphasised.

First, although the model proposes that a defective judgemental process lies at the root of hallucinations, it should not necessarily be supposed that this process is a conscious one. Hallucinators do not, typically, consciously consider whether a perceived event is real or imaginary. Nor, for that matter, do non-hallucinators. (Indeed, with respect to hallucinators the evidence seems to indicate that they spend rather less time contemplating the source of their perceptions than other people.) Reality discrimination may be no different than other perceptual phenomena in this respect. A person observing an ambiguous stimulus does not usually debate its meaning, at least not at first; he or she just expects it to be one

Figure 8.3: A cognitive model of psychotic hallucinations (after Bentall, 1988)

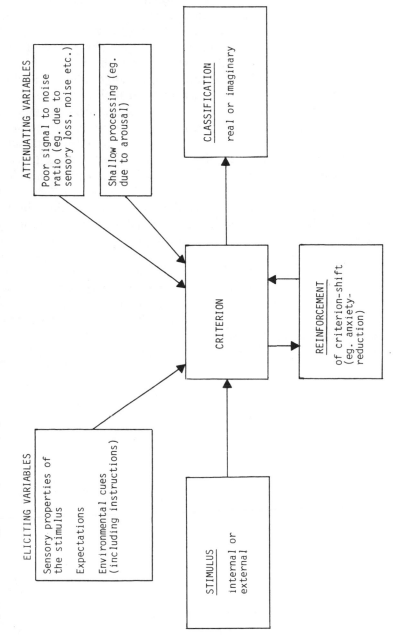

thing or another and sees it accordingly. Research into human perception indicates that extremely complex perceptual judgements are made quite automatically (Gregory, 1970; Wilding, 1982); if this were not the case, every-day looking and listening would be too effortful to allow us to get on with anything else.

For this reason, it is not surprising that hallucinators sometimes experience some dissonance between what their senses appear to be telling them and what their common sense seems to indicate must be the case, especially when they are on the way to recovery. For several weeks, Brian (see Chapter 1) struggled with the idea that his experiences were imaginary (grasped during psychotherapy with the second author) while still experiencing his voices as distressingly real.

The second point to be made about the model outlined in this chapter concerns its speculative nature. Although it appears to account for the bulk of the data on psychotic hallucinations it amounts, as always in science, to no more than a hypothesis awaiting further investigation. For this reason, it is the hope of the present authors that, whatever the model's ultimate value, it should be heuristically useful. If the model does no more than generate further research into hallucinations, it will have more than adequately served its purpose.

References

Aggernaes, A. (1972a) The experienced reality of hallucinations and other psychological phenomena: an empirical analysis. *Acta Psychiatrica Scandinavica, 48,* 220–238.

Aggernaes, A. (1972b) The difference between the experienced reality of hallucinations in young drug abusers and schizophrenic patients. *Acta Psychiatrica Scandinavica, 48,* 287–299.

Aggernaes, A., Haugsted, R., Myschetzky, A., Paikin, H. and Vitger, J. (1976) A reliable clinical technique for investigation of the experienced reality and unreality qualities connected with everyday life experiences in psychotic and non-psychotic persons. *Acta Psychiatrica Scandinavica, 53,* 241–257.

Aggernaes, A. and Myschetzky, A. (1976) Experienced reality in somatic patients more than 65 years old: a comparative study of disturbed and clear, but demented, states of consciousness. *Acta Psychiatrica Scandinavica, 54,* 225–237.

Aggernaes, A. and Nyeborg, O. (1972) The reliability of different aspects of the experienced reality of hallucinations in clear states of consciousness. *Acta Psychiatrica Scandinavica, 48,* 239–252.

Aghajanian, G.K., Foote, W.E. and Sheard, M.H. (1970) Action of psychotogenic drugs on single midbrain raphe neurons. *Journal of Pharmacology and Experimental Therapeutics, 171,* 178–187.

Alford, G.S. and Turner, S.M. (1976) Stimulus interference and conditioned inhibition of auditory hallucinations. *Journal of Behavior Therapy and Experimental Psychiatry, 7,* 155–160.

Al-Issa, I. (1977) Social and cultural aspects of hallucinations. *Psychological Bulletin, 84,* 570–587.

Al-Issa, I. (1978) Sociocultural factors in hallucinations. *International Journal of Social Psychiatry, 24,* 167–176.

Allen, T.E. and Agus, B. (1968) Hyperventilation leading to hallucinations. *American Journal of Psychiatry, 125,* 632–637.

Allen, H.A., Halperin, J. and Friend, R. (1985) Removal and diversion tactics and the control of auditory hallucinations. *Behaviour Research and Therapy, 23,* 601–605.

Alpert, M. (1985) The signs and symptoms of schizophrenia. *Comprehensive Psychiatry, 26,* 103–112.

Alpert, M. and Friedhoff, A.J. (1980) An un-dopamine hypothesis of schizophrenia. *Schizophrenia Bulletin, 6,* 387–390.

Alpert, M. and Martz, M.J. (1977) Cognitive views of schizophrenia in light of recent studies of brain asymmetry. In C. Shagrass and S. Gershon (Eds), *Psychopathology and brain dysfunction.* New York: Raven Press.

Alpert, M. and Silvers, K.N. (1970) Perceptual characteristics distinguishing auditory hallucinations in schizophrenia and acute alcoholic psychoses. *American Journal of Psychiatry, 127,* 298–302.

Alroe, G.J. and McIntyre, J.N. (1983) Visual hallucinations, the Charles Bonnet syndrome and bereavement. *Medical Journal of Australia, 2,* 674–675.

Alumbaugh, R.V. (1971) Use of behaviour modification techniques toward reduction of hallucinatory behaviour: a case study. *Psychological Record, 21,* 415–417.

American Psychiatric Association. (1980) *Diagnostic and statistical manual of mental disorders,* (DSM III) APA, Washington.

Anderson, L.T. and Alpert, M. (1974) Operant analysis of hallucination frequency in a hospitalized schizophrenic. *Journal of Behaviour Therapy and Experimental Psychiatry, 5,* 13–18.

Anderson, W.H., Kuehnle, J.C. and Catanzano, D.M. (1976) Rapid treatment of acute psychosis. *American Journal of Psychiatry, 133,* 1076–1078.

Andreasen, N.C., Grove, W. and Hoffman, R. (1984) Language abnormalities in schizophrenia. In M. Seeman and N. Menuck (Eds), *New perspectives in schizophrenia.* D.C. Heath, Lexington, Mass.

Angrist, B. and Gershon, S. (1970) The phenomenology of experimentally induced amphetamine psychosis: preliminary observations. *Biological Psychiatry, 2,* 95–107.

Angrist, B., Rotrosen, J. and Gershon, S. (1980) Responses to apomorphine, amphetamine and neuroleptics in schizophrenic subjects. *Psychopharmacology, 67,* 31–38.

Angrist, B., Sathananthan, G., Wilk, S. and Gershon, S. (1974) Amphetamine psychosis: behavioural and biochemical aspects. *Journal of Psychiatric Research, 11,* 13–23.

Armstrong, D.M. (1979) Three types of consciousness. In *CIBA Foundation symposium 69: Brain and mind.* Excerpta Medica: Amsterdam.

Armstrong, D.M. and Malcolm, N. (1984) *Consciousness and causality.* Blackwell, Oxford.

Arnold, T. (1806) *Observations on the nature, causes and preventions of insanity,* 2nd edn. Phillips, London.

Asaad, G. and Shapiro, B. (1986) Hallucinations: theoretical and clinical overview. *American Journal of Psychiatry, 143,* 1088–1097.

Atkinson, M. (1985) *Schizophrenia at home.* Croom Helm, London.

Baddeley, A.D. and Lewis, V.J. (1981) Inner active processing in reading: the inner voice, the inner ear and the inner eye. In A.M. Lesgold and C.A. Perfetti (Eds), *Interactive processes in reading,* Erlbaum, New York.

Bahzin, E.F., Wasserman, L.I. and Tonkongii, I.M. (1975) Auditory hallucinations and left temporal lobe pathology. *Neuropsychologia, 13,* 481–487.

Baillarger, M.T. (1846) De l'influence de l'etat intermédiare à la vielle et au sommeil sur la production et la marche des hallucinations, *Mem. Acad. Roy. Med., 12,* 476.

Baldwin, M. and Frost, L. (1970). Cited in W. Keup (Ed.), *Origin and mechanisms of hallucinations.* Plenum Press, New York.

Baldwin, M., Lewis, S.A. and Bach, S.A. (1959) The effects of lysergic acid after cerebral ablation. *Neurology, 9,* 469–474.

Bannister, D. (1968) The logical requirements of research into schizophrenia. *British Journal of Psychiatry, 114,* 119–121.

Barber, T.X. (1969) *Hypnosis: a scientific approach.* Van Nostrand Reinhold, New York.

Barber, T.X. (1970) Hypnosis, suggestions, and auditory–visual 'hallucinations': a critical analysis. In W. Keup (Ed.), *Origin and mechanisms of hallucinations,* Plenum Press, New York.

Barber, T.X. and Calverley, D.S. (1963) Hypnotic-like suggestibility in children and adults. *Journal of Abnormal and Social Psychology, 66,* 589–597.

Barber, T.X. and Calverley, D.S. (1964) An experimental study of 'hypnotic' (auditory and visual) hallucinations. *Journal of Abnormal and Social Psychology, 63,* 13–20.

Barraquer-Bordas, L., Pena-Casanova, J. and Pons-Iraz'abal, L. (1980) Central deafness without aphasic disorders due to bilateral temporal lesion. *Acta Neurologica Latinoamericana, 26,* 165–174.

Barron, F. (1953) An ego-strength scale which predicts response to psychotherapy. *Journal of Consulting and Clinical Psychology, 17,* 327–333.

Barrowclough, C. and Tarrier, N. (1984) Psychosocial interventions with families and their effects on the course of schizophrenia: a review. *Psychological Medicine, 14,* 629–642.

Bazhin, E.F., Wasserman, L.I. and Tonkonogii, I.M. (1975) Auditory hallucinations and left temporal lobe pathology. *Neuropsychologia, 13,* 481–487.

Beamish, P. and Kiloh, L.G. (1960) Psychoses due to amphetamine consumption, *Journal of Mental Science, 106,* 337–343.

Beaumont, J.G. and Diamond, S.J. (1973) Brain dysfunction and schizophrenia. *British Journal of Psychiatry, 123,* 661–662.

Beck, A.T. (1967) *Depression: clinical, experimental and theoretical aspects.* Harper and Row, New York.

Beckman, H. and Haas, S. (1980) High dose diazepam in schizophrenia. *Psychopharmacology, 71,* 79–82.

Belenky, G.L. (1979) Unusual visual experiences reported by subjects in the British army study of sustained operations, exercise early call. *Military Medicine, 144,* 695–696.

Bell, D.S. (1965) A comparison of amphetamine psychosis and schizophrenia. *British Journal of Psychiatry, 3,* 701–707.

Bender, G.H. (1970) The maturation process and hallucinations in children. In W. Keup (Ed.), *Origins and mechanisms of hallucinations,* Plenum Press, New York.

Benedetti, G. (1952) *Die Alkohalluzinosen.* Georg Thieme, Stuttgart.

Bennett, B.M. (1978) Vision and audition in biblical prophecy. *Parapsychology Review, 9,* 1–12.

Bennet, J.P. and Snyder, S.H. (1975) Stereospecific binding of *d*-lysergic

231

acid diethylamide (LSD) to brain membranes: relationship of serotonin receptors. *Brain Research, 94,* 523–544.

Bentall, R.P. (1985) Behaviourism, real and imaginary: a reply to Tibbets. *Mental Handicap, 13,* 119–121.

Bentall, R.P. (1986) The scientific validity of the schizophrenia diagnosis: a critical evaluation. In N. Eisenberg and D. Glasgow (Eds) *Current Issues in Clinical Psychology,* Vol. 5. Gower, Aldershot.

Bentall, R.P. (1987) The illusion of reality: A review and integration of psychological research on hallucinations. *Psychological Bulletin,* in press.

Bentall, R.P., Jackson, H.F. and Pilgrim, D. (1988) Abandoning the concept of 'schizophrenia': some implications of validity arguments for psychological research into psychotic phenomena. *British Journal of Clinical Psychology,* in press.

Bentall, R.P. and Lowe, C.F. (1987) The role of verbal behaviour in human learning: III Instructional effects in children. *Journal of the Experimental Analysis of Behaviour, 47,* 177–190.

Bentall, R.P., Lowe, C.F. and Beasty, A. (1985) The role of verbal behaviour in human learning: II Developmental differences. *Journal of the Experimental Analysis of Behaviour, 3,* 165–181.

Bentall, R.P. and Slade, P.D. (1985a) Reliability of a measure of disposition towards hallucination. *Personality and Individual Differences, 6,* 527–529.

Bentall, R.P. and Slade, P.D. (1985b) Reality testing and auditory hallucinations: a signal detection analysis. *British Journal of Clinical Psychology, 24,* 159–169.

Bentall, R.P. and Slade P.D. (1986) Verbal hallucinations, unintendedness, and the validity of the schizophrenia diagnosis. *The Behavioural and Brain Sciences, 9,* 519–520.

Bentall, R.P., Claridge, G.S. and Slade, P.D. (1988) The multidimensional nature of schizotypal traits: a factor analytic study with normal subjects. Submitted for publication.

Berenbaum, H., Oltmanns, T.F. and Gottesman, I. (1985) Formal thought disorder in schizophrenics and their twins. *Journal of Abnormal Psychology, 94,* 3–16.

Berger, P.A., Watson, S.J., Akil, H. and Barchas, J.D. (1981) The effects of naloxone in chronic schizophrenia. *American Journal of Psychiatry, 138,* 913–918.

Berger, R.J. and Oswald, I. (1962) Effects of sleep deprivation on behaviour, subsequent sleep and dreaming. *Journal of Mental Science, 108,* 457–465.

Berrios, G.E. and Brook, P. (1982) The Charles Bonnet syndrome and the problem of visual perceptual disorders in the elderly. *Age and Ageing, 11,* 17–23.

Berrios, G.E. and Brook, P. (1984) Visual hallucinations and sensory delusions in the elderly. *British Journal of Psychiatry, 144,* 662–664.

Betts, G.H. (1909) *The distribution and functions of mental imagery.*

Columbia University, New York.

Birchwood, M. (1986) Control of auditory hallucinations through occlusion of monaural auditory input. *British Journal of Psychiatry*, *149*, 104–107.

Birley, J.L.T. and Brown, G.W. (1970) Crises and life changes preceding the onset or relapse of acute schizophrenia: clinical aspects. *British Journal of Psychiatry*, *116*, 327–333.

Blashfield, K. (1984) *The classification of psychopathology: Neo-Kraepelinian and quantitative approaches*. Plenum Press, New York.

Bleuler, E. (1911) *Dementia praecox or the group of schizophrenias*. International University Press, New York (English translation 1950).

Bleuler, M. (1978) The long term course of schizophrenic psychoses. In L.C. Wynne, R.L. Cromwell and S. Matthysse (Eds), *The nature of schizophrenia*. Wiley, New York.

Bloor, D. (1983) *Wittgenstein: a social theory of knowledge*. Macmillan, London.

Bollati, A., Galli, G., Gandolfini, M. and Marini, G. (1980) Visual and auditory hallucinations (the only symptoms in a case of meningioma of the lesser sphenoidal wing). *Journal of Neurosurgical Science*, *24*, 41–44.

Borst, C.V. (Ed.) (1970) *The mind–brain identity theory*. Macmillan, London.

Bourguignon, E. (1970) Hallucinations and trance: an anthropologist's perspective. In W. Keup (Ed.), *Origin and mechanisms of hallucinations*, Plenum Press, New York.

Bowers, K.S. (1967) The effect of demands for honesty of reports of visual and auditory hallucinations. *International Journal of Clinical and Experimental Hypnosis*, *15*, 31–36.

Bowman, K.M. and Raymond, A.F. (1931) A statistical study of hallucinations in the manic-depressive psychoses. *American Journal of Psychiatry*, *88*, 299–309.

Brett, E.A. and Starker, S. (1977) Auditory imagery and hallucinations. *Journal of Nervous and Mental Disease*, *164*, 394–400.

Brewer, W.F. (1974) There is no convincing evidence of classical or operant conditioning in human adults. In W.B. Weimer and D.S. Palermo (Eds) *Cognition and the symbolic processes*. Wiley, New York.

Bridger, W.H. (1971) Psychotomimetic drugs, animal behaviour, and human psychopathology (cited in Iverson and Iverson, 1981).

Brockington, I.F., Kendell, R.E., Wainwright, R.S., Hillier, V.F. and Walker, J. (1979) The distinction between the affective psychoses and schizophrenia. *British Journal of Psychiatry*, *135*, 243–248.

Brooks, L. (1967) The suppression of visualization by reading. *Quarterly Journal of Experimental Psychology*, *19*, 289–299.

Brooks, L. (1968) Spatial and verbal components of the act of recall. *Canadian Journal of Psychology*, *22*, 349–365.

Brown, H. and Bass, W.C. (1967) Effects of drugs on visually controlled avoidance behaviour in rhesus monkeys: a psychophysical analysis. *Psychopharmacologia (Berlin)*, *11*, 142–153.

233

Brown, G.W., Birley, J.L.T. and Wing, J.K. (1972) Influence of family life on the course of schizophrenic disorders: a replication. *British Journal of Psychiatry, 121*, 241–258.

Brown, G.W. and Harris, T. (1978) *Social origins of depression: a study of psychiatric disorder in women.* Tavistock, London.

Brust, J.C.M. and Behrens, M.M. (1977) 'Release hallucinations' as the major symptoms of posterior cerebral artery occlusion: a report of two cases. *Annals of Neurology, 2*, 432–436.

Buchanan, D.C., Abram, H.S., Wells, C. and Teschan, P. (1977–78) Psychosis and pseudo dementia associated with hemodialysis. *International Journal of Psychiatry and Medicine, 8*, 85–87.

Bucher, B. and Fabricatore, J. (1970) Use of patient-administered shock to suppress hallucinations. *Behavior Therapy, 1*, 382–385.

Bullen, J.G., Hemsley, D.R. and Dixon, N.F. (1987) Inhibition, unusual perceptual experiences and psychoticism. *Personality and Individual Differences, 8*, 687–692.

Burns, C.E.S., Heilby, E.M. and Tharp, R.G. (1983) A verbal behaviour analysis of auditory hallucinations. *The Behavior Analyst, 6*, 133–143.

Buss, E.L., Larson, E.M. and Nakashima, S.R. (1983) Auditory hallucinations and schizophrenia. *Journal of Nervous and Mental Disease, 171*, 30–33.

Cacioppo, J.T. and Petty, R.E. (1981) Electromyograms as measures of extent of affectivity and information processing. *American Psychologist, 36*, 441–456.

Caine, I.M., Foulds, G.A. and Hope, K. (1967) *Manual for the hostility and direction of hostility questionnaire (HDHQ).* University of London Press, London.

Carpenter, W.T., McGlashan, T.H. and Strauss, J.S. (1977) The treatment of acute schizophrenia without drugs: an investigation of some current assumptions. *American Journal of Psychiatry, 134*, 14–20.

Catts, S.V., Armstrong, M.S., Norcross, K. and McConaghy, N. (1980) Auditory hallucinations and the verbal transformation effect. *Psychological Medicine, 10*, (1), 139–144.

Chandiramani, K. and Varma, V.K. (1987) Imagery in schizophrenic patients compared to normal controls. *British Journal of Medical Psychology, 60*, 335–341.

Chapman, L.J. and Chapman, J.P. (1980) Scales for rating psychotic and psychotic-like experiences as continua. *Schizophrenia Bulletin, 6*, 477–489.

Chapman, L.J., Chapman, J.P. and Raulin, M.L. (1976) Scales for physical and social anhedonia. *Journal of Abnormal Psychology, 85*, 374–382.

Chapman, L.J., Edell, E.W. and Chapman, J.P. (1980) Physical anhedonia, perceptual aberration and psychosis proneness. *Schizophrenia Bulletin, 6*, 639–653.

Ciompi, L. (1980) The natural history of schizophrenia in the long term. *British Journal of Psychiatry, 136*, 413–420.

Clare, A. (1976) *Psychiatry in dissent: controversial issues in thought and*

234

practice. Tavistock, London.

Claridge, G. (1985) *Origins of mental illness,* Blackwell, Oxford.

Claridge, G. and Broks, P. (1984) Schizotypy and hemisphere function: I Theoretical considerations and the measurement of schizotypy. *Personality and Individual Differences, 5,* 633–648.

Cleveland, S.E., Reitman, E.E. and Bentinck, C. (1963) Therapeutic effectiveness of sensory deprivation. *Archives of General Psychiatry, 8,* 51–56.

Cochrane, R. and Stopes-Roe, M. (1980) Factors affecting the distribution of psychological symptoms in urban areas of England. *Acta Psychiatrica Scandinavica, 61,* 445–460.

Cogan, D. (1973) Visual hallucinations as release phenomona. *Albrecht Von Graefes Arch. Klin. Esp. Opthalnod, 188,* 139–150. Cited in Hammeke, McQuillen and Cohen (1983).

Cohen, G. (1976) *The psychology of cognition.* Academic Press, London

Cohen, L.H. (1938) Imagery and its relations to schizophrenic symptoms, *Journal of Mental Science, 84,* 284–346.

Collicutt, J.R. and Hemsley, D.R. (1981) A psychophysical investigation of auditory functioning in schizophrenia. *British Journal of Clinical Psychology, 20, 199–204.*

Collomb, H. (1965) Bouffées délirantes en psychiatrie Africaine. *Psychopathologie Africaine, 1,* 167–237.

Comer, N.L., Madow, L. and Dixon, J.J. (1967) Observations of sensory deprivation in a life-threatening situation. *American Journal of Psychiatry, 124,* 164–169.

Connell, P.H. (1958) *Amphetamine psychosis.* Chapman & Hall, London.

Conrad, R. (1979) *The deaf schoolchild.* Harper & Row, London.

Cooklin, R., Sturgeon, D. and Leff, J. (1983) The relationship between auditory hallucinations and spontaneous fluctuations of skin conductance in schizophrenia. *British Journal of Psychiatry, 142,* 47–52.

Cooper, C. Sartorius, N. (1977) Cultural and temporal variations in schizophrenia: a speculation on the importance of industrialisation. *British Journal of Psychiatry, 130,* 50–55.

Cowden, R.C. and Ford, L.I. (1965) Systematic desensitisation with phobic schizophrenics. In L. Ullman and L. Krasner (Eds), *Case studies in behavior modification.* Holt, Rinehart & Winston, New York.

Cox, T. (1976) *Stress.* Macmillan, London.

Crow, T.J. (1980a) Molecular pathology of schizophrenia: more than one disease process? *British Medical Journal, 280,* 66–68.

Crow, T.J. (1980b) Positive and negative schizophrenic symptoms and the role of dopamine. *British Journal of Psychiatry, 137,* 383–386.

Crow, T.J. (1985) The two-syndrome concept: origins and current status. *Schizophrenia Bulletin, 11,* 471–486.

Crow, T.J., Macmillan, J.F., Johnson, A.L. and Johnstone, E.C. (1986) The Northwick Park studies of first episodes of schizophrenia: II A randomised controlled trial of prophylactic neuroleptic treatment. *British Journal of Psychiatry, 148,* 120–127.

REFERENCES

Damas-Mora, J., Skelton-Robinson, M. and Jenner, F.A. (1982) The Charles Bonnet syndrome in perspective. *Psychological Medicine, 12,* 251–261.

Davey, G.C.L. (1981) *Animal learning and conditioning.* Macmillan, London.

Davies, P. (1974a) Conditioned visual afterimages I. *British Journal of Psychology, 65,* 191–204.

Davies, P. (1974b) Conditioned visual afterimages II. *British Journal of Psychology, 65,* 377–393.

Davies, P. (1976) Conditioned visual afterimages III. *British Journal of Psychology, 67,* 181–189.

Davies, P., Davies, G.L. and Bennett, S. (1982) An affective paradigm for conditioning visual perception in human subjects. *Perception, 11,* 663–669.

Davis, G.C., Bunney, W.E., Defraites, E.G., Kleinman, J.E., van Kammen, D.P. and Wyatt, R.J. (1977) Intravenous naloxone administration in schizophrenia and affective illness. *Science, 197,* 74–76.

Davis, J.M. and Cole, J.O. (1975) Organic therapies and antipsychotic drugs. In A.M. Friedman, H.I. Kaplan and B. Sadock (Eds), *Comprehensive Textbook of Psychiatry* (2nd edn), Williams & Wilkins, Baltimore.

Davis, J.R., Wallace, C.J., Liberman, R.P. and Finch, B.E. (1976) The use of a brief isolation to suppress delusional and hallucinatory speech. *Journal of Behaviour Therapy and Experimental Psychiatry, 7,* 269–275.

Dawson, M.E., Catania, J.J., Schell, A.M. and Grings, W.W. (1979) Autonomic classical conditioning as a function of awareness of stimulus contingencies. *Biological Psychology, 9,* 23–40.

Deese, J. (1978) Thought into speech. *American Scientist, 66,* 314–321.

Deiker, T. and Chambers, H.E. (1978) Structure and content of hallucinations in alcohol withdrawal and functional psychosis. *Journal of Studies in Alcohol, 39,* 1831–1840.

Delay, J. and Deniker, P. (1952) *Le Congres de Psychiatrie et de Neurologie de Langue Française,* Masson et Cie, Luxembourg.

Dement, W., Halper, C., Pivik, T., Ferguson, J., Cohen, H., Henriksen, S., McGarr, K., Gonda, W., Hoyt, G., Ryan, L., Mitchell, G., Barchas, J. and Zarcone, V. (1970) Hallucinations and dreaming. In D. Hamburg (Ed.) *Perception and its disorders.* Williams & Wilkins, Baltimore.

Dement, W. and Kleitman, N. (1957) Cyclic variations in EEG during sleep and their relation to eye movements, body motility and dreams. *Electroencephalography and Clinical Neurophysiology, 9,* 673–690.

Dickinson, A. (1980) *Contemporary animal learning theory.* Cambridge University Press, Cambridge.

Diethelm, O. (1956) Report of the Payne Whitney Psychiatric Clinic, New York Hospital (cited by Al-Issa, 1978).

Dixon, N.F. (1981) *Preconscious processing,* Wiley, New York.

Dohrenwend, B.P. and Dohrenwend, B.S. (1974) Psychiatric disorders in urban settings. In S. Arietti and G. Caplan (Eds) *American handbook*

236

of psychiatry, Vol. 2, Basic Books, New York.

Done, D.J., Frith, C.D. and Owens, D.C. (1986) Reducing persistent auditory hallucinations by wearing an ear-plug. *British Journal of Clinical Psychology, 25,* 151–152.

Early, L.F. and Lifschutz, J.E. (1974) A case of stigmata. *Archives of General Psychiatry, 30,* 197–200.

Eggers, C. (1973) *Verlaufsweisen Kindlicher and prepuberaler Schizophrenien.* Springer Verlag, Berlin.

Eggers, C. (1982) Psychoses in childhood and adolescence. *Acta Paedopsychiatrica, 48,* 81–98.

Eisenberg, L. (1962) Hallucinations in children. In L.J. West (Ed.), *Hallucinations.* Grune and Stratton, New York.

Ellson, D.G. (1941a) Hallucinations produced by sensory conditioning. *Journal of Experimental Psychology, 28,* 1–20.

Ellson, D.G. (1941b) Experimental extinction of hallucination produced by sensory conditioning. *Journal of Experimental Psychology, 28,* 350–361.

Erickson, G.D. and Gustafson, G.J. (1968) Controlling auditory hallucinations, *Hospital and Community Psychiatry, 19,* 327–329.

Eriksen, C.W. (1962) *Behaviour and awareness.* Duke University Press, Durham.

Esquirol, J.E.D. (1832) Sur les illusions des sens chez les aliénes, *Archives Générales de Médicine, 2,* 5–23.

Evans, J. St.B. (1980) Thinking: experiential and information processing approaches. In G. Claxton (Ed.) Cognitive psychology: new directions. Routledge & Kegan Paul, London.

Evarts, E.V. (1957) A review of the neurophysiological effects of lysergic acid diethylamide (LSD) and other psychotomimetic agents. *Annals of the New York Academy of Science, 66,* 479–495.

Everitt, B.S., Gourlay, A.J. and Kendell, R.E. (1971) An attempt at validation of traditional psychiatric syndromes by cluster analysis. *British Journal of Psychiatry, 119,* 399–412.

Eysenck, H.J. and Eysenck, S.B.G. (1976) *Psychoticism as a dimension of personality.* Hodder & Stoughton, London.

Eysenck, H.J., Wakefield, J.A. and Friedman, A.F. (1983) Diagnosis and clinical assessment: the DSM-III. *Annual Review of Psychology, 34,* 167–193.

Eysenck, M. (1976) Arousal, learning and memory. *Psychological Bulletin, 83,* 389–404.

Eysenck, M. (1986) Working memory. In G. Cohen, M. Eysenck and M.E. LeVoi (Eds), *Memory: a cognitive approach,* Open University Press, Milton Keynes.

Eysenck, S.B, and Eysenck, H.J. (1973) The measurement of psychoticism: a study of factor stability and reliability. *British Journal of Social and Clinical Psychology, 7,* 286–294.

Faaborg-Anderson, K. (1965) Electromyography of laryngeal muscles in humans: techniques and results. In W.F. Trojan (Ed.), *Current problems in phoniatrics and logopedics, Vol. 3*, Karger, New York.

Faaborg-Anderson, K. and Edfelt, A.W. (1958) Electromyography of intrinsic and extrinsic laryngeal muscles during silent speech: correlation with reading activity. *Acta Ortolaryngologia, 49*, 478–482.

Falloon, I.R. and Talbot, R.E. (1981) Persistent auditory hallucinations: coping mechanisms and implications for management. *Psychological Medicine, 11*, 329–339.

Fay, T. (1959) Early experiences with local and generalised refrigeration of the brain. *Journal of Neurosurgery, 19*, 239–260.

Fechner, G.T. (1966) *Elements of psychophysics*, Holt, Rinehart & Winston, New York, (originally published in 1860).

Feder, R. (1982) Auditory hallucinations treated by radio headphones. *American Journal of Psychiatry, 139*, 1188–90.

Feinberg, I. (1962) A comparison of the visual hallucinations in schizophrenics with those induced by mescaline and LSD-25. In L.J. West (Ed.), *Hallucinations*, Grune & Stratton, New York and London.

Finucane, R.C. (1982) *Appearances of the dead: a cultural history of ghosts*. Junction Books, London.

Fisher, M. (1973) Genetic and environmental factors in schizophrenia: a study of schizophrenic twins and their families. *Acta Psychiatrica Scandinavica, Supplement 238*.

Fisman, M. (1975) The brain stem in psychosis. *British Journal of Psychiatry, 126*, 414–422.

Flavell, J.H. (1979) Metacognition and cognitive monitoring. *American Psychologist, 34*, 906–911.

Flavell, J.H. (1986) The development of children's knowledge about the appearance-reality distinction. *American Psychologist, 41*, 418–425.

Fleming, R., Makar, H. and Hunter, K.R. (1970) Levodopa in drug-induced extrapyramidal disorders. *Lancet, 2*, 1186.

Fletcher, S., Vardi, J., Allelov, M. and Streifler, M. (1978) Paroxysmal visual colored hallucinosis as an incipient sign in a developing C.V.A., *Archivo di Psicologia, Neurologia e Psychiatria, 39*, 502–512.

Flor-Henry, P. (1969) Psychosis and temporal lobe epilepsy. *Epilepsia, 10*, 363–395.

Flor-Henry, P. (1986) Auditory hallucinations, inner speech and the dominant hemisphere. *The Behavioral and Brain Sciences, 9*, 523–524.

Florio, V., Fuentes, J.A., Ziegler, H. and Longo, V.G. (1972) EEG and behavioural effects in animals of some amphetamine derivatives with hallucinogenic properties. *Behavioural Biology, 7*, 401–414.

Foley, M.A., Johnson, M.K. and Raye, C.L. (1983) Age-related changes in confusion between memories for thoughts and memories for speech. *Child Development, 54*, 51–60.

Fonagy, P. and Slade, P.D. (1982) Punishment vs negative reinforcement in the aversive conditioning of auditory hallucinations. *Behaviour Research and Therapy. 20*, 483–492.

Fonagy, P. and Slade, P.D. (1986) Unpublished study

Fordyce, W.E. (1981) A behavioural perspective on chronic pain. *British*

Journal of Clinical Psychology, 21, 313–320.

Forgus, R.H. and DeWolfe, A.S. (1969) Perceptual selectivity in hallucinatory schizophrenics. *Journal of Abnormal Psychology, 74,* 288–292.

Forrer, G.R. (1960) Benign auditory and visual hallucinations. *Archives of General Psychiatry, 3,* 95–98.

Foulds, G.A. and Bedford, A. (1975) Hierarchy of classes of personal illness. *Psychological Medicine, 5,* 181–192.

Foulkes, D. and Fleisher, S. (1975) Mental activity in relaxed wakefulness. *Journal of Abnormal Psychology, 84,* 66–75.

Fowler, D. (1986) A cognitive approach to hallucinations: implications for theory and therapy. Unpublished MSc thesis, University of Leeds.

Freeman, C.P. and Fairburn, C.G. (1981) Lack of effect of naloxone and schizophrenic auditory hallucinations. *Psychological Medicine, 11,* 405–407.

Freud, S. (1924) The loss of reality in neurosis and psychosis. Reprinted in A. Richards (Ed.), *Penguin Freud Library, 10,* 219–226.

Freyhan, F.A., Giannelli, S., O'Connell, R.A. and Mayo, J.A. (1971) Psychiatric complications following open heart surgery. *Comprehensive Psychiatry, 12,* 181–195.

Frieske, D.A. and Wilson, W.P. (1966) Formal qualities of hallucinations: a comparative study of the visual hallucinations in patients with schizophrenic, organic and affective psychoses. In Hock and J. Zubin (Eds), *Psychopathology of schizophrenia.* Grune & Stratton, New York.

Frith, C.D. (1979) Consciousness, information processing and schizophrenia. *British Journal of Psychiatry, 134,* 225–235.

Furth, H. (1966) *Thinking without language.* Free Press, New York.

Fuson, K.C. (1979) The development of self-regulatory speech: a review. In G. Zivin (Ed.), *The development of self-regulation through private speech.* Wiley, New York.

Fuster, J.M. (1959) Lysergic acid and its effects on visual discrimination in monkeys. *Journal of Nervous and Mental Disease, 129,* 252–256.

Gaddum, J.H. (1953) Antagonism between lysergic acid diethylamide and 5-hydroxytryptamine. *Journal of Physiology, 121,* 15.

Galin, D. (1974) Implications for psychiatry of left and right cerebral specialisation. *Archives of General Psychiatry, 31,* 572–583.

Galton, F. (1880) Statistics of mental imagery. *Mind, 5,* 300–318.

Galton, F. (1883) *Inquiries into human faculty and its development.* Macmillan, London.

Gardner, H. (1985) *The mind's new science.* Basic Books, New York.

Garralda, M.E. (1984) Psychotic children with hallucinations. *British Journal of Psychiatry, 145,* 74–77.

Garrity, L. (1977a) A review of the current status of subvocal speech research. *Memory and Cognition, 5,* 615–622.

Garrity, L. (1977b) A review of short term memory studies of covert speech in young children. *Journal of Psychology, 95,* 249–261.

Gjerde, P. (1983) Attentional capacity dysfunction and arousal in schizophrenia. *Psychological Bulletin, 93*, 57–72.

Glaister B. (1985) A case study of auditory hallucination treated by satiation. *Behaviour Research and Therapy, 23*, 213–215.

Goldberg, S.C., Klerman, G.L. and Cole, J.O. (1965) Changes in schizophrenic psychopathology and ward behaviour as a function of phenothiazine treatment. *British Journal of Psychiatry, 111*, 120–133.

Goodwin, D.W., Alderson, P. and Rosenthal, R. (1971) Clinical significance of hallucinations in psychiatric disorders. *Archives of General Psychiatry, 24*, 76–80.

Gordon, R. (1949) An investigation into some of the factors that favour the formation of stereotyped images. *British Journal of Psychology, 39*, 156–167.

Gottesman, I. and Shields, J. (1982) *Schizophrenia: the epigenetic puzzle.* Cambridge University Press, Cambridge.

Gould, L.N. (1948) Verbal hallucinations and activity of vocal musculature, *American Journal of Psychiatry, 105*, 367–372.

Gould, L.N. (1949) Auditory hallucinations and subvocal speech. *Journal of Nervous and Mental Disease, 109*, 418–427.

Gould, L.N. (1950) Verbal hallucinations as automatic speech. *American Journal of Psychiatry, 107*, 110–119.

Green, A.R. and Costain, D.W. (1981) *Pharmacology and biochemistry of psychiatric disorders.* Wiley, London.

Green, D.M. and Swetts, J.A. (1966) *Signal detection by human observers.* Wiley, New York.

Green, P. (1978a) Interhemispheric transfer in schizophrenia: recent developments. *Behavioural Psychotherapy, 6*, 105–110.

Green, P. (1978b) Defective interhemispheric transfer in schizophrenia. *Journal of Abnormal Psychology, 87*, 472–480.

Green, P., Glass, A. and O'Callaghan, M.A.J. (1980) Some implications of abnormal hemisphere interaction in schizophrenia. In J.H. Gruzelier and P. Flor-Henry (Eds), *Hemisphere asymmetries in psychopathology.* Macmillan Press, London.

Green, P., Hallett, S. and Hunter, M. (1983) Abnormal hemispheric specialisation in schizophrenics and high-risk children. In P. Flor-Henry and J. Gruzelier (Eds), *Laterality and psychopathology.* Elsevier, Amsterdam.

Green, P. and Kotenko, V. (1980) Superior speech comprehension in schizophrenics under monaural versus binaural listening conditions. *Journal of Abnormal Psychology, 89*, 399–408.

Green, P. and Preston, M. (1981) Reinforcement of vocal correlates of auditory hallucinations by auditory feedback: a case study. *British Journal of Psychiatry, 139*, 204–208.

Greene, R.J. (1978) Auditory hallucination reduction: first person singular. *Journal of Contemporary Psychotherapy, 9*, 167–170.

Gregory, D.W., Schaffner, W., Alford, R.H., Kaiser, A.R. and McGee, Z.A. (1979) Sporadic cases of Legionnaires' disease: the expanding clinical spectrum. *Annals of Internal Medicine, 90*, 518–521.

Gregory, R. (1970) *The intelligent eye.* McGraw-Hill, New York.

Gross, M.M., Halpert, E., Sabot, L. and Polizos, P. (1963) Hearing disturbances and auditory hallucinations in the acute alcoholic psychoses: I tinnitus, incidence and significance. *Journal of Nervous and Mental Disease, 137*, 455–465.

Gross, M.M., Halpert, E. and Sabot, L. (1968) Towards a revised classification of the acute alcoholic psychoses. *Journal of Nervous and Mental Disease, 145*, 500–508.

Grove, W.M. (1982) Psychometric detection of schizotypy. *Psychological Bulletin, 92*, 27–38.

Gruber, L.N., Mangat, B., Balminder, S. and Abou-Taleb, H. (1984) Laterality of auditory hallucinations in psychiatric patients. *American Journal of Psychiatry, 141*, 586–588.

Gudjonsson, G.H. (1983) A new scale of interrogative suggestibility. *Personality and Individual Differences, 5*, 303–314.

Gunne, L.M., Lindstrom, L. and Terenius, L. (1977) Naloxone-induced reversal of schizophrenic hallucinations. *Journal of Neural Transmission, 40*, 13–19.

Hachinski, V.C., Porchawka, J. and Steele, J.C. (1973) Visual symptoms in the migraine syndrome. *Neurology, 23*, 570–579.

Haier, R.J., Rosenthal, D. and Wender, P. (1978) MMPI assessment of psychopathology in the adopted-away offspring of schizophrenics. *Archives of General Psychiatry, 35*, 171–175.

Hall, R.C., Popkin, M.K. and Faillace, L.A. (1978) Physical illness presenting as a psychiatric disease. *Archives of General Psychiatry, 35*, 1315–1320.

Hall, R.C., Popkin, M.K. and Kirkpatrick, B. (1978) Tricyclic exacerbation of steroid psychosis. *Journal of Nervous and Mental Disease, 166*, 738–742.

Hamilton, M. (1984) Fish's schizophrenia. Wright, London.

Hamilton, M. (1985) Fish's clinical psychopathology. Wright, Bristol

Hammeke, T.A., McQuillen, M.P. and Cohen, B.A. (1983) Musical hallucinations associated with acquired deafness. *Journal of Neurology, Neurosurgery and Psychiatry, 46*, 570–572.

Hankoff, L.D. and Peress, N.S. (1981) Neuropathology of the brain stem in psychiatric disorders. *Biological Psychiatry, 16*, 945–952.

Haracz, J.L. (1982) The dopamine hypothesis: an overview of studies with schizophrenic patients. *Schizophrenia Bulletin, 8*, 438–469.

Hare, E.H. (1973) A short note on pseudo-hallucinations. *British Journal of Psychiatry, 122*, 469–476.

Hare, E.H. (1983) Was insanity on the increase? *British Journal of Psychiatry, 142*, 439–455.

Harner, M.J. (1973) Common themes in South American Indian yage experiences. In M.J. Harner (Ed.), *Hallucinogens and shamanism*, Oxford University Press, New York.

Harris, A. (1959) Sensory deprivation and schizophrenia. *Journal of Mental Science, 105*, 235–237.

Harrison-Reed, P.E. (1984) The use of drugs in psychiatry. In D.J. Sanger

241

and D.E. Blackman (Eds), *Aspects of psychopharmocology*. Methuen, London.

Hartmann, E. (1975) Dreams and other hallucinations: an approach to underlying mechanism. In R.K. Siegel and L.J. West (Eds), *Hallucinations: behaviour, experience and theory*. Wiley, New York.

Hawke, A.B., Strauss, J.S. and Carpenter, W.T. (1975) Diagnostic criteria and five-year outcome in schizophrenia. *Archives of General Psychiatry, 32*, 343–347.

Haynes, S.N. and Geddy, P. (1973) Suppression of psychotic hallucinations through time-out. *Behaviour Therapy, 4*, 123–127.

Heath, R.G. and Mickle, W.A. (1960) Evaluation of seven years' experience with depth electrode studies in human patients. In E.R. Ramey and D.S. O'Doherty (Eds), *Electrical studies on the unanesthetized brain*. Hoeber, New York.

Hebb, O. (1968) Concerning imagery. *Psychological Review, 75*, 466–477.

Hefferline, R.F., Bruno, L.J. and Camp, J.A. (1972) Hallucinations: an experimental approach. In F.J. McGuigan and R.A. Schoonover (Eds), *The psychophysiology of thinking: studies of covert processes*. Academic Press, New York.

Heilbrun, A.B. (1980) Impaired recognition of self-expressed thought in patients with auditory hallucinations. *Journal of Abnormal Psychology, 89*, 728–736.

Heilbrun, A.B. and Blum, N.A. (1984) Cognitive vulnerability to auditory hallucination: impaired perception of meaning. *British Journal of Psychiatry, 144*, 508–512.

Heilbrun, A.B., Blum, N. and Haas, M. (1983) Cognitive vulnerability to auditory hallucination: preferred imagery, mode and spatial location of sounds. *British Journal of Psychiatry, 143*, 294–299.

Heilbrun, A.B., Diller, R., Fleming, R. and Slade, L. (1986) Strategies of disattention and auditory hallucinations in schizophrenics. *Journal of Nervous and Mental Disease, 174*, 265–273.

Heron, D.P. and DeArmond, D. (1978) The use of time-out in controlling hallucinatory behaviour in a mentally retarded adult. *Bulletin of the Psychonomic Society, 11*, 115–116.

Hibbert, S. (1825) *Sketches of the philosophy of apparitions*. Oliver & Boyd, Edinburgh.

Hirsch, S.R., Gaind, R., Rohde, P., Stevens, B.C. and Wing, J.K. (1973) Outpatient maintenance of chronic schizophrenic patients with long-acting fluphenazine: double-blind placebo trial. *British Medical Journal, 1*, 633–637.

Hoffman, R.E. (1986) Verbal hallucinations and language production processes in schizophrenia. *The Behavioural and Brain Sciences, 9*, 503–548.

Hoffman, R.E., Kirstein, L., Stopek, S. and Cicchetti, D. (1982) Apprehending schizophrenic discourse: a structural analysis of the listener's task. *Brain and Language, 15*, 207–233.

Hoffman, R.E. and Sledge, W. (1984) A microgenetic model of paragram-

242

matisms produced by a schizophrenic speaker. *Brain and Language,* *21,* 147–173.

Hoffman, R.E., Stopek, E. and Andreasen, N.C. (1986) A discourse analysis comparing manic versus schizophrenic speech disorganisation. *Archives of General Psychiatry, 43,* 831–838.

Holden, J.M. and Itil, T. (1970) The influences of the standard prefrontal lobotomy operation on hallucinatory phenomena associated with psychotomimetic drugs. In W. Keup (Ed.), *Origins and mechanisms of hallucination,* Plenum Press, New York.

Holmboe, R. and Astrup, C. (1967) A follow-up study of 255 patients with acute schizophrenia and schizophreniform psychoses. *Acta Psychiatrica Neurologica Scandinavica,* Suppl. 115.

Holt, R.R. (1964) Imagery: the return of the ostracized. *American Psychologist, 19,* 254–264.

Hooley, J.M., Orley, J. and Teasdale, J.D. (1986) Levels of expressed emotion and relapse in depressed patients. *British Journal of Psychiatry, 148,* 642–647.

Horn, G. and McKay, J.M. (1973) Effects of lysergic acid diethylamide on the spontaneous activity and visual receptive fields of cells in the lateral geniculate nucleus of the cat. *Experimental Brain Research, 17,* 271–284.

Horowitz, M. (1975) Hallucinations: an information processing approach. In R.K. Siegel and L.V. West (Eds), *Hallucinations: behaviour, experience and theory,* Wiley, New York

Horowitz, M. and Adams, J.E. (1970) Hallucinations on brain stimulation: evidence for revision of the Penfield hypothesis. In W. Keup (Ed.), *Origins and mechanisms of hallucination.* Plenum Press, New York

Huber, G., Gross, G., Schuttler, R. and Linz, M. (1980) Longitudinal studies of schizophrenic patients. *Schizophrenia Bulletin, 6,* 592–605.

Hunter, R. (1968) Three cases of frontal meningiomas presenting psychiatrically. *British Medical Journal, 3* (5609), 9–16.

Inanaga, K., Nakazawa, Y., Inouye, K., Tachibana, H., Oshima, M. and Kotorii, T. (1975) Double-blind controlled study of *l*-dopa therapy in schizophrenia. *Folia Psychiatrica et Japonica, 29,* 123–143.

Inouye, T. and Shimizu, A. (1970) The electromyographic study of verbal hallucination. *Journal of Nervous and Mental Disease, 151,* 415–422.

Isaev, D.N. and Aleksandrova, N.V. (1983) Age and infectious psychoses in children and adolescents. *Zhurnal Nevropatologii i Psikhiatrii Imeni S.S. Korsakova, 83,* 267–271.

Ishibashi, T., Hori, H., Endo, K and Sato, T. (1964) Hallucinations produced by electrical stimulation of the temporal lobes in schizophrenic patients. *Tohuku Journal of Experimental Medicine, 82,* 124–239.

Iversen, S.D. and Iversen, L.L. (1981) *Behavioural pharmacology.* Oxford University Press, Oxford.

REFERENCES

Jablensky, A. and Sartorius, N. (1975) Culture and schizophrenia. *Psychological Medicine, 5,* 113–124.

Jackson, C.W. and Kelly, E.L. (1962) Influence of suggestion and subjects' prior knowledge in research on sensory deprivation. *Science, 135,* 211–212.

Jackson, D.D. (1960) A critique of the literature on the genetics of schizophrenia. In D.D. Jackson (Ed.), *The etiology of schizophrenia.* Basic Books, New York.

Jackson, H.F. (1986) Is there a schizotoxin?: A critique of the evidence and rationale for the major contender — dopamine. In N. Eisenberg and D. Glasgow (Eds), *Current issues in clinical psychology, Vol. 5,* Gower: Aldershot.

Jacobs, B.L. and Trulson, M.E. (1979) Dreams, hallucinations and psychosis — serotonin connection. *Trends in Neurosciences,* 276–280.

Jacobs, L., Karpik, A., Bozian, D. and Gothgen, S. (1981) Auditory-visual synaesthesia: sound-induced photisms. *Archives of Neurology, 38,* 211–216.

Jacobson, E. (1932) Electrophysiology of mental activities. *American Journal of Psychology, 64,* 677–694.

Jain, V.K. (1972) A psychiatric study of hypothyroidism. *Psychiatrica Clinica, 5,* 121–130.

Jakes, S. and Hemsley, D.R. (1986) Individual differences in reaction to brief exposure to unpatterned stimulation. *Personality and Individual Differences, 7,* 121–123.

James, D.A.E. (1983) The experimental treatment of two cases of auditory hallucinations. *British Journal of Psychiatry, 143,* 515–516.

Janowski, D.S., El-Yousef, M.K., Davis, J.M. and Serkerke, H.J. (1973) Provocation of schizophrenic symptoms by intravenous administration of methylphenidate. *Archives of General Psychiatry, 28,* 185–191.

Jansson, B. (1968) The prognostic significance of various types of hallucinations in young people. *Acta Psychiatrica Scandinavica, 44,* 401–409.

Jaspers, K. (1911) Zur Analyse der Trugwahrnehmunger (Leibhaftigkeit und Realitätsurteil). *Zeitschift für die gesamte Neurologie und Psychiatrie, 6,* 460–535.

Jaynes, J. (1979) *The origins of consciousness in the breakdown of the bicameral mind.* Penguin, Harmondsworth.

Jenkins, J.J. (1969) Language and thought. In J.F. Ross (Ed.), *Approaches to thought.* Merrill, Ohio.

Jeste, D.V. and Wyatt, R.J. (1981) Changing epidemiology of tardive dyskinesia: an overview. *American Journal of Psychiatry, 138,* 297–309.

Johnson, C.H., Gilmore, J.D. and Shenoy, R.S. (1983) Thought-stopping and anger induction in the treatment of hallucinations and obsessional ruminations. *Psychotherapy: Theory, Research and Practice, 20,* 445–448.

Johnson, F. (1978) *The anatomy of hallucination.* Nelson Hall, Chicago.

Johnson, M.K. and Raye, C.L. (1981) Reality monitoring. *Psychological Review, 88,* 67–85.

Johnson, M.K., Raye, C.L., Foley, H.J. and Foley, M.A. (1981) Cognitive operations and decision bias in reality monitoring. *American Journal of Psychology, 91*, 37–64.

Johnson, M.K., Raye, C.L., Wang, A.Y. and Taylor, T.H. (1979) Fact and fantasy: the roles of accuracy and variability in confusing imaginations with perceptual experiences. *Journal of Experimental Psychology: Human Learning and Memory, 5*, 229–240.

Johnson, M.K., Taylor, T.H. and Raye, C.L. (1977) Fact and fantasy: the effects of internally generated events on the apparent frequency of externally generated events. *Memory and Cognition, 5*, 116–122.

Johnson, R.L. and Miller, M.D. (1965) Auditory hallucinations and intellectual deficit. *Journal of Psychiatric Research, 3*, 37–41.

Johnstone, E.C., Crow, T.J., Johnson, A.L. and Macmillan, J.F. (1986) The Northwick Park study of first episodes of schizophrenia: I. Presentation of the illness and problems relating to admission. *British Journal of Psychiatry, 148*, 115–120.

Judkins, M. and Slade, P. (1981) A questionnaire study of hostility in persistent auditory hallucinators. *British Journal of Medical Psychology, 54*, 243–250.

Kallman, F.J. (1938) *The genetics of schizophrenia*, Augustin, New York.

Kandinsky, V. (1885) *Kritische und klinische Betrachtungen im Gebiete der Sinnestauschungen*. Friedlaender, Berlin

Kasanin, J. (1933) The acute schizoaffective psychoses. *American Journal of Psychiatry, 13*, 97–126.

Kelly, P.H. and Iversen, L.L. (1975) LSD as an agonist at mesolimbic dopamine receptors. *Psychopharmacologia, 45*, 221.

Kendell, R.E. (1975) *The role of diagnosis in psychiatry*. Blackwell, Oxford.

Kendell, R.E. and Brockington, I. (1980) The identification of disease entities and the relationship between schizophrenia. *British Journal of Psychiatry, 137*, 324–331.

Kendell, R.E. and Gourlay, J.A. (1970) The clinical distinction between the affective psychoses. *British Journal of Psychiatry, 117*, 261–266.

Kendler, K.S. and Hays, P. (1982) Familial and sporadic schizophrenia: a symptomatic, prognostic and EEG comparison. *American Journal of Psychiatry, 139*, 1557–1562.

Kety, S.S. (1974) From irrationality to reason. *American Journal of Psychiatry, 131*, 957–962.

Kety, S.S., Rosenthal, D., Wender, P.H. and Schulsinger, F. (1968) The types and prevalence of mental illness in the biological and adoptive families of adopted schizophrenics. In D. Rosenthal and S.S. Kety (Eds), *The transmission of schizophrenia,* Pergamon, Oxford.

Kety, S.S., Rosenthal, D., Wender, P.H., Schulsinger, F. and Jacobsen, B. (1975) Mental illness in the biological and adoptive families of adopted individuals who have become schizophrenic. In R. Fiove, D. Rosenthal and H. Brill (Eds), *Genetic research in psychiatry*. Johns Hopkins

University Press, Baltimore.

Key, B.J. (1961) The effect of drugs on discrimination and sensory generalization of auditory stimuli in cats. *Psychopharmacologia* (Berl.), *2*, 352–363.

Klien, D.F. and Davis, J.M. (1969) *Diagnosis and drug treatment of psychotic disorder.* Williams & Wilkins, Baltimore

Kluver, H. (1926) Mescal viscous and eidetic vision. *American Journal of Psychology, 37*, 502–515.

Kluver, H. (1928) *Mescal: The 'divine' plant and its psychological effects,* Kegan Paul. London.

Kluver, H. (1942) Mechanisms of hallucinations. In Q. McNemar and M. Merrill, (Eds), *Studies in personality.* McGraw-Hill, New York.

Kluver, H. (1966) *Mescal and mechanisms of hallucinations.* Chicago University Press, Chicago.

Kolvin, I., Ounsted, C., Humphrey, M. and McNay, A. (1971) Studies in the childhood psychoses: II The phenomenology of childhood psychoses. *British Journal of Psychiatry, 118*, 385–395.

Kornetsky, C. (1976) Hyporesponsivity of chronic schizophrenic patients to dextroamphetamine. *Archives of General Psychiatry, 33*, 1425–1428.

Kosslyn, S.M. (1983) *Ghosts in the mind's machine: creating and using images in the brain.* Norton, New York.

Kouretas, D. (1967) The oracle of Trophonius: a kind of shock treatment associated with sensory deprivation in Ancient Greece. *British Journal of Psychiatry, 113*, 441–446.

Krassoievitch, M., Perez-Rincon, R. and Suarez, P. (1982) Correlation between visual and auditory hallucinations in a population of Mexican schizophrenics. *Confrontation Psychiatriques, 15*, 149–162.

Kraupl-Taylor, F. (1981) On pseudo-hallucinations. *Psychological Medicine, 11*, 265–279.

Kretschmer, E. (1925) *Physique and character.* Routledge and Kegan Paul, London.

Kroll, J. and Bachrach, B. (1982) Medieval visions and contemporary hallucinations. *Psychological Medicine, 12*, 209–722.

Lacey, J.I. (1967) Somatic response patterning and stress: some revisions of activation theory. In M.H. Appley and R. Trumbull (Eds), *Psychological stress: issues in research.* Appleton-Century-Crofts, New York.

Lambley, P. (1973) Behaviour modification techniques and the treatment of psychosis: a critique of Alumbaugh. *Psychological Record, 23*, 93–97.

Lamontagne, Y., Audet, N. and Elie, R. (1983) Thought-stopping for delusions and hallucinations: a pilot study. *Behavioural Psychotherapy, 11*, 177–184.

Langner, T.S. and Michael, S.T. (1962) *Life stress and mental health: the Midtown Study.* Free Press, Glencoe, II.

Lapolla, A. (1967) Clinical efficacy of haloperidol in chronic psychotic patients. *International Journal of Neuropsychiatry*, (3) Supplement, 1, 68–77.

Launay, G. and Slade, P.D. (1981) The measurement of hallucinatory predisposition in male and female prisoners. *Personality and Individual Differences*, 2, 221–234.

Lee, T., Seeman, P., Tourtellotte, W.W., Farley, I.J. and Hornykiewicz, O. (1978) Binding of ³H-apomorphine and ³H-neuroleptics in schizophrenic brains. *Nature*, 274, 897–900.

Lefevre, A.B., Diament, A.J. and Valente, M.I. (1969) Psychological disorders in children . with neurocysticercosis. *Arquivos de Neuropsiquitria*, 27, 103–108.

Leff, J. and Vaughn, C. (1980) The interaction of life events and relatives' expressed emotion in schizophrenia and depressive neurosis. *British Journal of Psychiatry*, 136, 146–153.

Leff, J.P. and Wing, J.K. (1971) Trial of maintenance therapy in schizophrenia. *British Medical Journal*, 3, 559–604.

Leinz, H.L. (1964) *Verleichende Psychiatrie. Eine Studie über die Beziehung von Kulture Sociologie und Psychopathologie.* Wilhelm Mandrich Verlag, Vienna.

Lewine, R.R.J. (Ed.) (1985) Negative symptoms in schizophrenia. *Schizophrenia Bulletin*, 11, 361–486.

Lewinsohn, P.M. (1968) Characteristics of patients with hallucinations. *Journal of Clinical Psychology*, 23, 423.

Liddle, P. (1987) The symptoms of chronic schizophrenia: A re-examination of the positive–negative dichotomy. *British Journal of Psychiatry*, 151, 145–151.

Lidz, T. and Blatt, S. (1983) Critique of the Danish-American studies of the biological and adoptive relatives of adoptees who became schizophrenic. *American Journal of Psychiatry*, 140, 426–431.

Lidz, T., Blatt, S. and Cook, B. (1981) Critique of the Danish-American studies of adopted away offspring of schizophrenic parents. *American Journal of Psychiatry*, 138, 1063–1068.

Lindsley, O.R. (1959) Reduction in rate of vocal psychotic symptoms by differential positive reinforcement. *Journal of the Experimental Analysis of Behaviour*, 2, 269.

Lindsley, O.R. (1963) Direct measurement and functional definition of vocal hallucinatory symptoms. *Journal of Nervous and Mental Disease*, 136, 293–297.

Lingjaerde, O. (1982) Effect of the benzodiazepine derivative estazolam in patients with auditory hallucinations: a multicentre double-blind, crossover study. *Acta Psychiatrica Scandinavica*, 65, 339–354.

Linn, E.L. (1977) Verbal auditory hallucinations: mind, self and society. *Journal of Nervous and Mental Disease*, 164, 8–17.

Lipowski, Z.J. (1967) Delirium, clouding of consciousness and confusion. *Journal of Nervous and Mental Disease*, 145, 227–255.

Lipowski, Z.J. (1975) Organic brain syndromes: Overview and classification. In D.F. Benson and D. Blumer (Eds) *Psychiatric aspects of neurological disease.* Grune and Stratton, London.

Liss, J.L., Welner, A., Robins, E. and Richardson (1973) Psychiatric symptoms in white and black patients: I Record study. *Comprehensive Psychiatry, 14,* 475–481.

Lloyd, D.W. and Tsuang, M.T. (1981) A snake lady: post-concussion syndrome manifesting visual hallucinations of snakes. *Journal of Clinical Psychiatry, 42,* 246–247.

Locke, J.L. and Fehr, F.S. (1970) Subvocal rehearsal as a form of speech. *Journal of Verbal Learning and Verbal Behaviour, 9,* 495–498.

Lorr, M. (1953) Multidimensional scale for rating psychiatric patients. *Veterans Administration Technical Bulletin,* 10–507.

Lowe, G.R. (1973) The phenomenology of hallucinations as an aid to differential diagnosis. *British Journal of Psychiatry, 123,* 621–633.

Lunzer, E.A. (1979) The development of consciousness. In G. Underwood and R. Stevens (Eds), *Aspects of consciousness, Vol. 1: Psychological issues.* Macmillan: London.

Luria, A.R. (1960) *The role of speech in regulation of normal and abnormal behaviour.* Pergamon Press, Oxford.

Mackay, A.V.P. (1980) Positive and negative schizophrenic symptoms and the role of dopamine. *British Journal of Psychiatry, 137,* 379–384.

Mackay A.V.P., Bird, E.D., Iversen, L.L., Spokes, E.G., Creese, I. and Snyder, S.H. (1980) Dopaminergic abnormalities in post mortem schizophrenic brain. In F. Cattabeni, G. Racaghi, P.F. Spano and E. Costa (Eds), *Long term use of neuroleptics. Advances in biochemical psychopharmacology, Vol. 24,* Raven Press, New York.

Mackay A.V.P. and Sheppard, G.P. (1979) Pharmacotherapeutic trials in tardive dyskinesia. *British Journal of Psychiatry, 137,* 379–384.

Macmillan, J.F., Crow, T.J. Johnson, A.L. and Johnstone, E.C. (1986) The Northwick Park study of first episodes of schizophrenia: III Short-term outcome in trial entrants and trial eligible patients. *British Journal of Psychiatry, 148,* 128–133.

Maher, B. (1974) Delusional thinking and perceptual disorder. *Journal of Individual Psychology, 30,* 98–113.

Mahl, C.F., Rothenburg, A., Delgado, J.N. and Hamlin, H. (1964) Psychologic response in the human to intracerebral electrical stimulation. *Psychosomatic Medicine, 26,* 337–368.

Maletzky, B.M. (1976) The diagnosis of pathological intoxication. *Journal of Studies on Alcohol, 37,* 1215–1228.

Malitz, S., Wilkiens, B. and Essecover, H. (1962) A comparison of drug-induced hallucinations with those seen in spontaneously occurring psychoses. In L.J. West (Ed.), *Hallucinations,* Grune & Stratton, New York and London.

Mallya, A.R. and Shen, W.W. (1983) Radio in the treatment of auditory hallucinations. *American Journal of Psychiatry, 140,* 1264–1265.

Malone, G.L. and Leiman, H.I. (1983) Differential diagnosis of palinacousis in a psychiatric patient. *American Journal of Psychiatry, 140,* 1067–1068.

Margo, A., Hemsley, D.R. and Slade, P.D. (1981) The effects of varying

248

auditory input on schizophrenic hallucinations. *British Journal of Psychiatry*, *139*, 122–127.

Marshall, C.R. (1937) An enquiry into the cause of mescal visions. *Journal of Neurology and Psychopathology*, *17*, 289–304.

Marshall, J.R. (1984) The genetics of schizophrenia revisited. *Bulletin of the British Psychological Society*, *37*, 177–181.

Marshall, J.R. and Pettit, A.N. (1985) Discordant concordant rates. *Bulletin of the British Psychological Society*, *38*, 6–9.

Matchett, W.F. (1972) Repeated hallucinatory experiences as part of the mourning process among Hopi Indian women. *Psychiatry*, *35*, 185–194.

Maury, A. (1848) Des hallucinations hypnagogiques de système nerveux. *Annales Medico-Psychologiques*, *11*, 26.

Max, L.M. (1937) An experimental study of the motor theory of consciousness IV: Action current responses in the deaf during awakening, kinaesthetic imagery and abstract thinking. *Journal of Comparative Psychology*, *24*, 301–344.

May, P. and Ebaugh, F. (1953) Pathological intoxication, alcoholic hallucinosis and other reactions to alcohol. *Quarterly Journal of Studies of Alcohol*, *14*, 200.

Mayer-Gross, W., Slater, E. and Roth, M. (1975) *Clinical psychiatry*, 4th ed. Bailliere, Tindall and Cassell, London.

McCabe, M.S. (1976) Symptom differences in reactive psychoses and schizophrenia with poor prognosis. *Comprehensive Psychiatry*, *17*, (2), 301–307.

McDonald, W.S. and Oden, C.W. (1977) Aumakua: behavioural direction visions in Hawaiians. *Journal of Abnormal Psychology*, *86*, 189–194.

McGuigan, F.J. (1966) Covert oral behaviour and auditory hallucinations. *Psychophysiology*, *3*, 73–80.

McGuigan, F.J. (1971) Covert linguistic behaviour in deaf subjects during thinking. *Journal of Comparative and Physiological Psychology*, *75*, 417–420.

McGuigan, F.J. (1978) *Cognitive psychophysiology: principles of covert behaviour*. Prentice Hall, Englewood Cliffs, NJ.

McGuigan, F.J. and Bailey, S.L. (1969) Longitudinal study of covert oral behaviour during silent reading. *Perceptual and Motor Skills*, *28*, 170.

McKay, S.E., Golden, C.J. and Scott, M. (1981) Neuropsychological correlates of auditory and visual hallucinations. *International Journal of Neurosciences*, *15*, 87–94.

McKellar, P. (1957) *Imagination and thinking*. Basic Books, New York.

McKellar, P. (1968) *Experience and Behaviour*. Penguin Press, Harmondsworth.

McMillan, P.E. (1973) Drugs and punished responding: I Rate dependent effects under multiple schedules. *Journal of the Experimental Analysis of Behaviour*, *19*, 133–145.

McNamara, M.E., Heros, R.C. and Boller, F. (1982) Visual hallucinations in blindness: the Charles Bonnet syndrome. *International Journal of Neuroscience*, '*17*, 13–15.

REFERENCES

McNichol, D. (1972) *A primer of signal detection theory.* Allen & Unwin, London.
McPeake, J.D. and Spanos, N.P. (1973) The effects of the wording of rating scales on hypnotic subjects' descriptions of visual hallucinations. *American Journal of Clinical Hypnosis, 15,* 239–244.
Meddis, R. (1982) Cognitive dysfunction following loss of sleep. In A. Burton, (Ed.), *The pathology and psychology of cognition.* Methuen, London.
Meehl, P.E. (1962) Schizotaxia, schizotypia, schizophrenia. *American Psychologist, 17,* 827–838.
Mehler, J., Morton, J. and Jusczyk, P.W. (1984) On reducing language to biology. *Cognitive Neuropsychology, 1,* 83–116.
Meltzer, H.Y. and Stahl, S.M. (1976) The dopamine hypothesis of schizophrenia: a review. *Schizophrenia Bulletin, 2,* 19–76.
Merriam, A.E. and Gardner, E.B. (1987) Corpus callosum function in schizophrenia: a neuropsychological assessment of interhemispheric information processing. *Neuropsychologia, 25,* 185–193.
Meyendorf, R. (1982) Psychopatho-ophthalmology gnostic disorders and psychosis in cardiac surgery: visual disturbances after open heart surgery. *Archives Psychiatr. Nervenkr., 232,* 119–135.
Miller, E.N. and Chapman, L.J. (1983) Continued word association in hypothetically psychosis prone college students. *Journal of Abnormal Psychology, 92,* 468–478.
Miller, T.C. and Crosby, J.W. (1979) Musical hallucinations in a deaf elderly patient. *Annals of Neurology, 5,* 381–382.
Miller, M.D., Johnson, R.L. and Richmond, L.H. (1965) Auditory hallucinations and descriptive language skills. *Journal of Psychiatric Research, 3,* 43–56.
Mintz, S. and Alpert, M. (1972) Imagery vividness, reality testing, and schizophrenic hallucinations. *Journal of Abnormal Psychology, 79,* 310–316.
Mirsky, A.F. (1978) Attention: a neuropsychological perspective. In J.S. Chall and A.F. Mirsky (Eds) *Education and the brain.* Chicago University Press, Chicago.
Mize, K. (1980) Visual hallucinations following viral encephalitis: a self report. *Neuropsychologia, 18,* 193–202.
Monroe, R.R. (1978) The episodic psychoses of Vincent van Gogh. *Journal of Nervous and Mental Disease, 166,* 480–488.
Morley, S. (1987) Modification of auditory hallucinations: experimental studies of headphones and earplugs. *Behavioural Psychotherapy, 15,* 252–271.
Moser, A.J. (1974) Covert punishment of hallucinatory behaviour in a psychotic male. *Journal of Behaviour Therapy and Experimental Psychiatry, 3,* 225–227.
Mott, R.H., Iver, F.S. and Anderson, J.M. (1965) Comparative study of hallucinations. *Archives of General Psychiatry, 12,* 595–601.
Muntaner, C. and Garcia-Sevilla, L. (1985) Factorial structure of the Eysenck Personality Questionnaire in relation to other psychosis

250

proness scales. Paper presented at the 2nd Conference of the International Society for the Study of Individual Differences. St. Felieu, Spain, June 1985.

Murphy, D.B., Myers, T.I. and Smith, S. (1962) Reported visual sensations as a function of sustained sensory deprivation and social isolation. USA Leadership HRU draft research report, Presidio of Monterey (Pioneer VI).

Murphy, H.B.M., Wittkower, E.D., Fried, J. and Ellenberger, H.A. (1963) A cross cultural survey of schizophrenic symptomatology. *International Journal of Social Psychiatry*, 9, 235–249.

Murray, R.M. and Reveley, A.M. (1986) Genetic aspects of schizophrenia: an overview. In A. Kerr and P. Snaith (Eds) *Contemporary issues in schizophrenia*. Gaskell, London.

Naranjo, C. (1973) Psychological aspects of the yage experience in an experimental setting. In M.J. Harner (Ed.), *Hallucinogens and Shamanism*. Oxford University Press, New York.

Ndetei, D.M. and Singh, A. (1983) Schneider's first rank symptoms of schizophrenia in Kenyan patients. *Acta Psychiatrica Sandinavica*. 67, 148–153.

Neisser, U. (1967) *Cognitive Psychology*, Appleton-Century-Crofts, New York.

Nemeth, J. and Petrovich, M. (1967) Chlorpromazine and trifluoperazine treatment. *Diseases of the Nervous System*, 28, 812–814.

Nisbett, R. and Valins, S. (1972) Perceiving the causes of one's own behaviour. In E.E. Jones, D.E. Kanouse, H.H. Kelley, R.E. Nisbett, S. Valins and B. Weiner (Eds) *Attributes: perceiving the causes of behaviour*. General Learning Press, Morristown, NJ.

Nisbett, R. and Wilson, T.D. (1978) Telling more than we can know: verbal reports on mental processes. *Psychological Review*, 84, 231–259.

Noonan, J.P. and Ananth, J. (1977) Compulsive water drinking and water intoxication. *Comprehensive Psychiatry*, 18, 183–187.

Nydegger, R.V. (1972) The elimination of hallucinatory and delusional behavior by verbal conditioning and assertive training: a case study. *Journal of Behaviour Therapy and Experimental Psychiatry*, 3, 225–227.

Ollerenshaw, D.P. (1973) The classification of the functional psychoses. *British Journal of Psychiatry*, 122, 517–530.

Orne, M.T. and Scheibe, K.E. (1964) The contribution of non-deprivation factors in the production of sensory deprivation effects: the psychology of the panic button. *Journal of Abnormal Social Psychology*, 68, 3–12.

Ornstein, R. (1979) *The psychology of consciousness*. Penguin, Harmondsworth.

Orr, M. and Oppenheimer, C. (1978) Effects of naloxone on auditory hallucinations. *British Medical Journal*, 25, 481.

Owen, F., Cross, A.J., Crow, T.J., Longden, A., Poulter, M. and Riley, J.

REFERENCES

(1978) Incresed dopamine receptor sensitivity in schizophrenia. *Lancet,* 2, 223–225.

Pavio, A. (1971) *Imagery and verbal processes.* Rinehart & Winston, New York.

Penfield, W. and Jasper, H. (1954) *Epilepsy and the functional anatomy of the brain.* Little, Brown & Co., Boston.

Penfield, W. and Perot, P. (1963) The brain's record of auditory and visual experience: a final summary and conclusion. *Brain, 86,* 595–696.

Penfield, W. and Rasmussen, T. (1950) *The cerebral cortex of man.* Macmillan, New York.

Pennebaker, J.W. (1980) Self-perception of emotion and internal sensation. In D.M. Wegner and R.R. Vallacher (Eds), *The self in social psychology,* Oxford University Press, Oxford.

Pennebaker, J.W. (1983) *The psychology of physical symptoms.* Springer Verlag, New York.

Perky, C.W. (1910) An experimental study of imagination. *American Journal of Psychology, 21,* 422–452.

Perlow, M.J., Chiueh, C.C., Lake, R. and Wyatt, R.J. (1980) Increased dopamine and norepinephrine concentrations in primate CSF following amphetamine and phenylethylamine administration. *Brain Research, 186,* 469–473.

Persons, J.B. (1986) The advantages of studying psychological phenomena, rather than psychiatric diagnoses. *American Psychologist, 41,* 1252–1260.

Phillips, L., Broverman, I.K. and Zigler, E. (1966) Social competence and psychiatric diagnosis. *Journal of Abnormal Psychology, 71,* 209–214.

Piaget, J. (1926) *The language and thought of the child.* Routledge & Kegan Paul, London.

Piaget, J. (1974) *The child and reality.* Muller, London.

Place, M. (1980) Unpublished Master of Psychology Thesis, University of Liverpool.

Posey, T.B. (1986) Verbal hallucinations also occur in normals. *Behavioral and Brain Sciences, 9,* 530.

Posey, T.B. and Losch, M.E. (1983) Auditory hallucinations of hearing voices in 375 normal subjects. *Imagination, Cognition and Personality, 2,* 99–113.

Preuss, J. (1975) Mental disorders in the Bible and Talmud. (Trans. F. Rosner) *Israeli Annals of Psychiatry and Related Disciplines, 13,* 221–238.

Pylyshyn, Z.W. (1973) What the mind's eye tells the mind's brain: a critique of mental imagery. *Psychological Bulletin, 80,* 1–24.

Pylyshyn, Z.W. (1981) The imagery debate: analogue media versus tacit knowledge. *Psychological Review, 87,* 16–45.

Rabkin, R. (1970) Do you see things that aren't there? Construct validity of the concept of 'hallucination'. In W. Keup (Ed.), *Origin and mechanisms of hallucinations,* Plenum Press, New York.

Rabkin, J.G. (1980) Stressful life events and schizophrenia: a review of the research literature. *Psychological Bulletin, 87,* 407–425.

Rachman, S. (1981) Unwanted intrusive cognitions. *Advances in Behaviour Research and Therapy, 3,* 88–89.

Rachman, S. and Hodgson, R.J. (1979) Synchrony and desynchrony in fear and avoidance. *Behaviour Research and Therapy, 12,* 311–318.

Rasch, G. (1966) An item analysis which takes individual differences into account. *British Journal of Mathematical and Statistical Psychology, 19,* 49–57.

Ramanathan, A. (1984a) A study of interference with the activities of schizophrenics by auditory hallucinations. *Indian Journal of Psychiatry, 26,* 206–212.

Ramanathan, A. (1984b) A study of coping with auditory hallucinations in schizophrenics. *Indian Journal of Psychiatry, 26,* 229–236.

Ramanathan, A. (1986) An exploratory story on the relation between neuroticism and certain aspects of auditory hallucinations in schizophrenics. *Indian Journal of Psychiatry, 28,* 69–72.

Randall, P.L. (1980) A neuroanatomical theory on the aetiology of schizophrenia. *Medical Hypotheses, 6,* 645–658.

Raye, C.L. and Johnson, M.K. (1980) Reality monitoring versus discrimination between external sources. *Bulletin of the Psychonomic Society, 15,* 405–408.

Reed, G.F. (1979) Sensory deprivation. In G. Underwood and R. Stevens (Eds), *Aspects of consciousness, Vol. 1: Psychological issues.* Academic Press, London.

Reese, W.D. (1971) The hallucinations of widowhood. *British Medical Journal, 210,* 37–41.

Reichel-Dolmatoff, G. (1972) The cultural context of an aboriginal hallucinogen, *Banisteriopsis caapi.* In P.T. Furst (Ed.), *Flesh of the gods: the ritual use of hallucinogens.* Praeger, New York.

Reybee, J. and Kinch, B. (1973) Treatment of auditory hallucinations using focusing. Unpublished study.

Reynolds, G.P., Riederer, P., Jellinger, K. and Gabriel, E. (1981) Dopamine receptors and schizophrenia: the neuroleptic drug problem. *Neuropharmacology, 20,* 1319–1320.

Richardson, A. (1969) *Mental imagery.* Routledge & Kegan Paul, London.

Richardson, R., Karkalas, Y. and Lal, H. (1972) Application of operant procedures in treatment of hallucinations in chronic psychotics. *Advances in behaviour therapy.* Academic Press, New York.

Rimm, D. and Masters, J. (1974) *Behaviour therapy: techniques and empirical findings.* Academic Press, New York.

Robertson, M.H. (1964) Facilitating therapeutic changes in psychiatric patients by sensory deprivation methods. *Final progress report of the research foundation of the National Association for Mental Health.*

Roman, R. and Landis, C. (1945) Hallucinations and mental imagery. *Journal of Nervous and Mental Disease, 102,* 327–331.

Rose, S. (1984) Disordered molecules and diseased minds. *Journal of*

Psychiatric Research, 18, 351–360.

Rose, S., Kamin, L.J. and Lewontin, R.C. (1984) *Not in our genes.* Penguin, Harmondsworth.

Rosenthal, B. and Mele, H. (1952) The validity of hypnotically induced color hallucinations. *Journal of Abnormal and Social Psychology, 47,* 700–704.

Rosenthal, D. and Quinn, O.W. (1977) Quadruplet hallucinations: phenotypic variations of a schizophrenic genotype. *Archives of General Psychiatry, 34,* 817–827.

Rosenthal, D., Wender, P.H., Kety, S.S., Welner, J. and Schulsinger, F. (1971) The adopted away offspring of schizophrenics. *American Journal of Psychiatry, 128,* 307–311.

Ross, E.D. (1978) Musical hallucinations in deafness revisited. *Journal of the American Medical Association, 240,* 716.

Ross, E.D., Jossman, P.D., Bell, B., Sarbin, T. and Geschwind, N. (1975) Musical hallucinations and deafness. *Journal of the American Medical Association, 231,* 620–622.

Ross, J. and Lawrence, K.A. (1968) Some observations on memory artifice, *Psychonomic Science, 13,* 107–108.

Rubinstein, D. (1976) Beyond the cultural barriers: observations on emotional disorders among Cuban immigrants. *International Journal of Mental Health, 5,* 69–79.

Rund, B.V. (1986) Verbal hallucinations and information processing. *Behavioral and Brain Sciences, 9,* 531–532.

Rutner, I.T. and Bugle, C. (1969) An experimental procedure for the modification of psychotic behavior. *Journal of Consulting and Clinical Psychology, 33,* 651–653.

Salame, P. and Baddeley, A. (1982) Disruption of short-term memory by unattended speech: implications for the structure of working memory. *Journal of Verbal Learning and Verbal Behavior, 21,* 150–164.

Samaan, M. (1975) Thought-stopping and flooding in a case of hallucinations, obsessions, and homicidal–suicidal behavior. *Journal of Behaviour Therapy and Experimental Psychiatry, 6,* 65–67.

Saravay, S.M. and Pardes, H. (1967) Auditory elementary hallucinations in alcohol withdrawal psychosis. *Archives of General Psychiatry, 16,* 652–658.

Sarbin, T.R. (1967) The concept of hallucination. *Journal of Personality, 35,* 359–380.

Sarbin, T.R. and Andersen, M.L. (1963) Base-rate expectancies and perceptual alterations in hypnosis. *British Journal of Social and Clinical Psychology, 2,* 112–121.

Sarbin, T.R. and Juhasz, J.B. (1967) The historical background of the concept of hallucination. *Journal of the History of the Behavioural Sciences, 5,* 339–358.

Sarbin, T.R., Juhasz, J.B. and Todd, P. (1971) The social psychology of hallucinations. *Psychological Record, 21,* 87–93.

Sarbin, T.R. and Mansuco, J.C. (1980) *Schizophrenia: medical diagnosis or moral verdict.* Pergamon, New York.

Sartorius, N., Jablensky, A., Korten, A., Ernberg, G., Anker, M., Cooper, J.E. and Day, R. (1986) Early manifestations and first contact incidence of schizophrenia in different cultures. *Psychological Medicine, 16,* 909–928.

Schacter, S. and Singer, J.E. (1962) Cognitive, social and physiological determinants of emotional state. *Psychological Review, 69,* 379–399.

Schaefer, T. and Bernick, N. (1965) Sensory deprivation and its effects on perception. In P.H. Hock and J. Zubin (Eds), *Psychopathology of perception.* Grune & Stratton, New York.

Schatzman, M. (1980) *The story of Ruth.* Penguin, Harmondsworth.

Scheibel, M.E. and Scheibel, A.B. (1962) Hallucinations and brain stem reticular core. In L.J. West (Ed.), *Hallucinations.* Grune & Stratton, New York.

Schneider, K. (1959) *Clinical psychopathology.* Grune & Stratton, New York.

Schneider, S.J. and Wilson, C.R. (1983) Perceptual discrimination and reaction time in hallucinatory schizophrenics. *Psychiatry Research, 9,* 243–253.

Schuckit, M.A. and Winokur, G. (1971) Alcoholic hallucinosis and schizophrenia: a negative study. *British Journal of Psychiatry, 119,* 549–550.

Schwartz, S. (1975) Individual differences in cognition: some relationships between personality and memory. *Journal of Research in Personality, 9,* 217–225.

Schwartz, S. (1986) Hallucinations, rationalizations and response set. *Behavioral and Brain Sciences, 9,* 532–533.

Schwartz, S. and Kirstner, K. (1984) Can group differences be inferred from behavioral laterality indices? *Brain and Cognition, 3,* 56–71.

Scott, D.F. (1967) Alcoholic hallucinosis. An aetiological study. *British Journal of Addiction, 62,* 113–125.

Scott, H. (1930) Hypnosis and the conditioned reflex. *Journal of General Psychology, 4,* 113–130.

Scull, A. (1979) *Museums of madness.* Penguin, Harmondsworth.

Seashore, C.E. (1895) Measurements of illusions and hallucinations in normal life. *Studies of the Yale Psychology Laboratory, 3,* 1–67.

Sedman, G. (1966) A comparative study of pseudohallucinations, imagery and true hallucinations. *British Journal of Psychiatry, 112,* 9–17.

Segal, S.J. (1968) Patterns of response to thirst in an imagery task (Perky technique) as a function of cognitive style. *Journal of Personality, 36,* 574–588.

Segal, S.J. (1970) Imagery and reality: can they be distinguished? In W. Keup (Ed.), *Origin and Mechanisms of Hallucinations.* Plenum Press, New York.

Segal, S.J. and Fusella, V. (1970) Influence of imaged pictures and sounds on detection of visual and auditory signals. *Journal of Experimental Psychology, 83,* 458–464.

Segal, S.J. and Glicksman, M. (1967) Relaxation and the Perky effect: the influence of body position on judgements of imagery. *American Journal of Psychology, 80,* 257–262.

Segal, S.J. and Nathan, S. (1964) The Perky effect: incorporation of an external stimulus into an imagery experience under placebo and control conditions. *Perceptual and Motor Skills, 18,* 469–480.

Seidman, L.J. (1984) Schizophrenia and brain dysfunction: an integration of recent neurodiagnostic findings. *Psychological Bulletin, 94,* 195–238.

Seitz, P.F. and Molholm, H.B. (1947) Relation of mental imagery to hallucinations. *Archives of Neurology and Psychiatry, 57,* 469–480.

Shagrass, C., Josiassen, R.C., Roemer, R.A., Straumans, J.J. and Slepner, S.M. (1983) Failure to replicate evoked potential observations suggesting corpus callosum dysfunction in schizophrenia. *British Journal of Psychiatry, 142,* 471–476.

Shallice, T. (1972) Dual functions of consciousness. *Psychological Review, 79,* 383–393.

Sheehan, P.W. and Neisser, U. (1969) Some variables affecting the vividness of imagery in recall. *British Journal of Psychology, 60,* 47–80.

Sheldon, E.J. and Knight, R.G. (1984) Interhemispheric transmission times in schizophrenics. *British Journal of Clinical Psychology, 23,* 227–228.

Shepard, R.N. and Metzler, J. (1971) Mental rotation of three dimensional objects. *Science, 171,* 701–703.

Sidgewick, H.A. and many others (1894) Report of the census of hallucinations. *Proceedings of the Society for Psychical Research, 26,* 259–394.

Siegel, J.M. (1975) Successful systematic desensitization in a chronic schizophrenic patient. *Journal of Behaviour Therapy and Experimental Psychiatry, 6,* 345–346.

Siegel, R.K. (1984) Hostage hallucinations. Visual imagery induced by isolation and life-threatening stress. *Journal of Nervous and Mental Disease, 172,* 264–272.

Siegel, R.K., Brewster, J.M. and Jarvik, M.E. (1974) An observational study of hallucinogen-induced behaviour in unrestrained *Macaca mulatta. Psychopharmacologia, 40,* 211–223.

Siegel, R.K. and Jarvik, M.E. (1975) Drug-induced hallucinations in animals and man. In R.K. Siegel and L.J. West (Eds), *Hallucinations: behaviour, experience and theory.* Wiley, New York.

Siegel, R.K. and West, L.J. (Eds), (1975) *Hallucinations: behaviour, experience and theory.* Wiley, New York.

Silverstone, T. and Turner, P. (1982) *Drug treatment in psychiatry.* Routledge and Kegan Paul, London.

Silverstone, T. and Cookson, J. (1983) Examining the dopamine hypothesis of schizophrenia and of mania using the prolactin response to antipsychotic drugs. *Neuropharmacology, 22,* 539–541.

Skinner, B.F. (1936) The verbal summator and a method for the study of latent speech. *Journal of Psychology, 2,* 71–107.

Skinner, B.F. (1945) The operational analysis of psychological terms.

Psychological Review, 52, 270–277.

Skinner, B.F. (1957) *Verbal behaviour.* Prentice-Hall, Englewood Cliffs, NJ.

Slade, P.D. (1972) The effects of systematic desensitization on auditory hallucinations. *Behaviour, Research and Therapy, 10,* 85–91.

Slade, P.D. (1973) The psychological investigation and treatment of auditory hallucinations: a second case report. *British Journal of Medical Psychology, 46,* 293–296.

Slade, P.D. (1974) The external control of auditory hallucinations: an information theory analysis. *British Journal of Social and Clinical Psychology, 13,* 73–79.

Slade, P.D. (1976a) Towards a theory of auditory hallucinations: outline of an hypothetical four-factor model. *British Journal of Social and Clinical Psychology, 15,* 415–423.

Slade, P.D. (1976b) Hallucinations. *Psychological Medicine, 6,* 7–13.

Slade, P.D. (1976c) An investigation of psychological factors involved in the predisposition to auditory hallucinations. *Psychological Medicine, 6,* 123–132.

Slade, P.D. (1984) Sensory deprivation and clinical psychiatry. *British Journal of Hospital Medicine,* Nov., 256–260.

Slade, P.D. and Cooper, R. (1979) Some conceptual difficulties with the term 'schizophrenia': an alternative model. *British Journal of Social and Clinical Psychology, 18,* 309–317.

Slade, P.D., Judkins, M., Clark, P. and Fonagy, P. (1975) Unpublished study.

Slade, P.D., Judkins, M., Clark, P. and Fonagy, P. (1986) Unpublished study.

Slade, P.D., Judkins, M. and Fonagy, P. (1976) Unpublished study.

Small, I.F., Small, J.G. and Anderson, J.M. (1966) Clinical characteristics of hallucinations of schizophrenia. *Diseases of the Nervous System, 27,* 299–309.

Snyder, S.H. (1973) Amphetamine psychosis: a 'model' schizophrenia mediated by catecholamines. *American Journal of Psychiatry, 130,* 61–67.

Snyder, W.V. and Cohen, L.H. (1940) Validity of imagery-testing in schizophrenia. *Character and Personality, 9,* 35–43.

Sokolov, A.N. (1969) Studies of the speech mechanisms of thinking. In M. Cole and I. Maltzman (Eds), *Handbook of contemporary Soviet psychology.* Basic Books, New York.

Sokolov, A.N. (1972) *Inner speech and thought.* Plenum Press, New York.

Spanos, N.P. (1986) Hallucinations and contextually generated interpretations. *Behavioral and Brain Sciences, 9,* 533–534.

Spanos, N.P. and Barber, T.X. (1968) 'Hypnotic' experiences as inferred from subjective reports: auditory and visual hallucinations. *Journal of Experimental Research in Personality, 3,* 136–150.

Spanos, N.P., Ham, M.W. and Barber, T.X. (1973) Suggested ('hypnotic') visual hallucinations: experimental and phenomenological data. *Journal of Abnormal Psychology, 81,* 96–106.

Spitzer, R.L., Endicott, J. and Gibbon, M. (1979) Crossing the border into borderline personality and borderline schizophrenia. *Archives of General Psychiatry, 36*, 17–24.

Spitzer, R.L., Endicott, J. and Robins, E. (1975) Research diagnostic criteria. *Psychopharmacology Bulletin, 11*, 22–25.

Srole, L., Langner, T.S., Michael, S.T., Opler, M.K. and Rennie, T.A.C. (1961) *Mental health in the metropolis: The Midtown Manhattan study.* McGraw-Hill, New York.

Stern, J.A., Surphlis, W. and Koff, E. (1965) Electrodermal responsiveness as related to psychiatric diagnosis and prognosis. *Psychophysiology, 2*, 51–61.

Stevens, J.R. and Livermore, A. (1982) Telemetered EEG in schizophrenia: Spectral analysis during abnormal behaviour episodes. *Journal of Neurology, Neurosurgery and Psychiatry, 45*, 385–395.

Strauss, J.S. (1969) Hallucinations and delusions as points on continua function. *Archives of General Psychiatry, 21*, 581–586.

Strauss, J.S. and Carpenter, W.I. (1974a) The prediction of outcome in schizophrenia: II. Relationships between predictor and outcome variables. *Archives of General Psychiatry, 31*, 37–42.

Strauss, J.S. and Carpenter, W.T. (1974b) Characteristic symptoms and outcome in schizophrenia. *Archives of General Psychiatry, 30*, 429–434.

Swerdlow, N.R. and Koob, G.F. (1987) Dopamine, schizophrenia, mania and depression: Towards a unified hypothesis of cortico-striato-pallido-thalamic function. *Behavioural and Brain Sciences, 10*, 197–245.

Takahashi, R., Inabe, Y. and Inanaga, K. (1981) CT scanning and the investigation of schizophrenia. Third World Congress of Biological Psychiatry, Stockholm (cited by Flor-Henry, 1986).

Tarrier, N. (1987) An investigation of residual psychotic symptoms in discharged schizophrenic patients. *British Journal of Clinical Psychology, 26*, 141–143.

Taylor, M.A. and Abrams, R. (1975) Acute mania: clinical and genetic study of responders and nonresponders to treatments, *Archives of General Psychiatry, 32*, 863–865.

Taylor, P. and Fleminger, J.J. (1981) The lateralization of symptoms in schizophrenia, *British Journal of Medical Psychology, 54*, 59–65.

Terenius, L., Wahlstrom, A., Lindstrom, L. and Widerlov, E. (1976) Increased CSF levels of endorphins in chronic psychosis. *Neuroscience Letters, 3*, 157–162.

Thorne, D.E. (1967) Is the hypnotic trance necessary for performance of hypnotic phenomena? *Journal of Abnormal Psychology, 72*, 233–239.

Thorson, A.M. (1925) The relation of tongue movements to internal speech. *Journal of Experimental Psychology, 8*, 1–32.

Toone, B.K., Cooke, E. and Lader, M.H. (1981) Electrodermal activity in the affective disorders and schizophrenia. *Psychological Medicine, 11*, 497–508.

Turner, P., Richens, A. and Routledge, P. (1986) *Clinical Psychopharma-*

cology, 5th edn, Churchill Livingstone, Edinburgh.
Turner, S.M., Hersen, M. and Bellack, A.S. (1977) Effects of social disruption, stimulus interference, and aversive conditioning on auditory hallucinations. Behaviour Modification, 1, 249–258.

Uchino, J., Araki, K., Tominaga, Y., Niwa, H., Nakama, I., Michitsuji, S., Ischizawa, M., Ohta, Y., Nakane, Y. and Takahashi, R. (1984) Correlation between CT findings and their clinical symptoms: 2. Using discriminant analysis and chi-squared test. Folia Psychiatrica et Neurologia Japonica, 38, 179.
Underwoood, H.W. (1960) The validity of hypnotically induced visual hallucinations. Journal of Abnormal and Social Psychology, 61, 39–46.

van Praag, H.M. (1976) About the impossible concept of schizophrenia. Comprehensive Psychiatry, 17, 481–497.
Vaughn, C.E. and Leff, J.P. (1976) The influence of family and social factors on the course of psychiatric illness. British Journal of Psychiatry, 129, 125–137.
Verhoeven, W.M., van Praag, H.M. and de Jong, J.T. (1981) Use of naloxone in schizophrenic psychoses and manic syndromes. Neuropsychobiology, 7 (3), 159–168.
Victor, M. and Hope, J.M. (1953) Auditory hallucinations in alcoholism. A.M.A. Archives of Neurology and Psychiatry, 70, 659–661.
Vitols, M.M., Waters, H.G. and Keeler, M.H. (1963) Hallucinations and delusions in white and negro schizophrenics. American Journal of Psychiatry, 120, 472–476.
Vygotsky, L.S. (1962) Thought and language. MIT Press, Cambridge, Mass.

Wagner, A.R. and Rescorla, R.A. (1972) Inhibition in Pavlovian conditioning: application of a theory. In R.A. Boakes and M.S. Halliday (Eds), Inhibition and learning. Academic Press, London.
Wagstaff, G. (1983) Hypnosis: compliance and belief. Harvester Press, Brighton.
Wallace, A.F.C. (1959) Cultural determinants of response to hallucinatory experience. Archives of General Psychiatry, 1, 58–69.
Warner, R. (1985) Recovery from schizophrenia: psychiatry and political economy. Routledge & Kegan Paul, London.
Warren, R.M. (1968) Verbal transformation effect and auditory perceptual mechanisms. Psychological Bulletin, 70, 261–270.
Warren, R.M. and Gregory, R.L. (1958) An auditory analogue of the visual reversible figure. American Journal of Psychology, 71, 612–613.
Watson, J.B. (1913) Psychology as the behavourist views it. Psychological Review, 20, 158–177.
Watson, J.B. (1924) The unverbalised in human behaviour. Psychological Review, 31, 273–280.
Watson, S.J., Berger, P.A., Akil, H., Mills, M.J. and Barchas, J.D. (1978) Effects of naloxone on schizophrenia: reduction in hallucinations in a subpopulation of subjects. Science, 21, (4350), 73–76.

259

REFERENCES

Watts, F. and Clements, J. (1971) The modification of schizophrenic hallucinations and associated delusions: a case report. Unpublished paper.
Weingaertner, A.H. (1971) Self-administered aversive stimulation with hallucinating hospitalised schizophrenics. *Journal of Consulting and Clinical Psychology, 36*, 422–429.
Wells, L.A. (1980) Hallucinations associated with pathologic grief reaction. *Journal of Psychiatric Treatment and Evaluation, 5*, 259–261.
West, D.J. (1948) A mass observation questionnaire on hallucinations. *Journal of the Society for Psychical Research, 34*, 187–196.
West, L.J. (1962) A general theory of hallucinations and dreams. In L.J. West (Ed.) *Hallucinations.* Grune & Stratton, New York.
West, L.J. (1975) A clinical and theoretical overview of hallucinatory phenomena. In R.K. Siegel and L.J. West (Eds) *Hallucinations: behaviour, experience and theory.* Wiley, New York.
White, K., Sheehan, P.W. and Ashton, R. (1977) Imagery assessment: a survey of self-report measures. *Journal of Mental Imagery, 1*, 145–170.
White, N.J. (1980) Complex visual hallucinations in partial blindness due to eye disease. *British Journal of Psychiatry, 136*, 284–286.
Wilding, J.M. (1982) *Perception: from sense to object.* Hutchinson, London.
Williams, B. (1971) *Descartes.* Penguin, Harmondsworth.
Wilson, G.D. (1968) Reversal of differential GSR conditioning by instructions. *Journal of Experimental Psychology, 76*, 491–493.
Winters, W.D. (1975) The continuum of CNS excitatory states and hallucinosis. In R.K. Siegel and L.J. West (Eds), *Hallucinations: behavior, experience and theory,* Wiley, New York.
Wing, J.K. (1978) *Reasoning about madness.* Oxford University Press, Oxford.
Wing, J.K., Cooper, J.E. and Sartorius, N. (1974) *Measurement and classification of psychiatric symptoms.* Cambridge University Press, Cambridge.
Wise, G.N., Dollery, C.T. and Henkind, P. (1971) *The retinal circulation.* Harper & Row, New York.
Wittgenstein, L. (1953) *Philosophical investigations.* Blackwell, London.
Wolpe, J. (1973) *The practice of behaviour therapy.* Pergamon Press, New York.
Wong, D.F., Wagner, H.N., Tune, L.E., Dannals, R.F., Pearlson, G.D., Links, J.M., Tamminga, C.A., Broussolle, E.P,, Ravert, H.T., Wilson, J.K., Toung, J.K.T., Malat, J., Williams, J.A., O'Tuama, L.A., Snyder, S.H., Kuhar, M.J. and Gjedde, A. (1986) Positron emission tomography reveals elevated D2 dopamine receptors in drug-naive schizophrenics. *Science, 234*, 1558–1563.
World Health Organization (1975) *Schizophrenia: a multinational study.* WHO, Geneva.
Wozniak, R.H. (1972) Verbal regulation of motor behaviour: Soviet research and non-Soviet replications. *Human Development, 15*, 13–57.

Young, H.F., Bentall, R.P., Slade, P.D. and Dewey, M.E. (1986) Disposition towards hallucination, gender and IQ scores. *Personality and Individual Differences, 7,* 247–249.

Young, H.F., Bentall, R.P., Slade, P.D. and Dewey, M.E. (1987) The role of brief instructions and suggestibility in the elicitation of auditory and visual hallucinations in normal and psychiatric subjects. *Journal of Nervous and Mental Disease, 175,* 41–48.

Zangwill, O. (1969) Intellectual status in aphasics. In P.J. Vinken and G.W. Bruyn (Eds), *Handbook of clinical neurology, Vol. 4.* North Holland Press, Amsterdam.

Zarroug, E.A. (1975) The frequency of visual hallucinations in schizophrenic patients in Saudi Arabia. *British Journal of Psychiatry, 127,* 553–555.

Zigler, E. and Phillips, L. (1961) Psychiatric diagnosis and symptomatology. *Journal of Abnormal and Social Psychology, 63,* 69–75.

Zilboorg, G. and Henry, G.W. (1941) *A history of medical psychology.* Norton, New York.

Zivin, F. (1986) Image or neural coding of inner speech and agency? *Behavioral and Brain sciences, 9,* 534–535.

Zivin, G. (Ed.) (1979) *The development of self-regulation through private speech.* Wiley, New York.

Zubin, J., Magaziner, J. and Steinhauer, S.R. (1983) The metamorphosis of schizophrenia: from chronicity to vulnerability. *Psychological Medicine, 13,* 551–572.

Zuckerman, M. (1969) Variables affecting deprivation results. In J.P. Zubek (Ed.) *Sensory deprivation.* Appleton-Century-Crofts, New York.

Zuckerman, M. and Cohen, N. (1964) Sources of reports of visual and auditory sensations in perceptual isolation experiments. *Psychological Bulletin, 62,* 1–20.

Author Index

265

271

Subject Index